Brian Simon and the Struggle for Education

Brian Simon and the Struggle for Education

Gary McCulloch, Antonio F. Canales
and Hsiao-Yuh Ku

First published in 2023 by
UCL Press
University College London
Gower Street
London WC1E 6BT

Available to download free: www.uclpress.co.uk

Text © Authors, 2023
Images © Copyright holders named in captions, 2023

The authors have asserted their rights under the Copyright, Designs and Patents Act 1988 to be identified as the authors of this work.

A CIP catalogue record for this book is available from The British Library.

Any third-party material in this book is not covered by the book's Creative Commons licence. Details of the copyright ownership and permitted use of third-party material is given in the image (or extract) credit lines. If you would like to reuse any third-party material not covered by the book's Creative Commons licence, you will need to obtain permission directly from the copyright owner.

This book is published under a Creative Commons 4.0 International licence (CC BY 4.0). This licence allows you to share, copy, distribute and transmit the work; to adapt the work and to make commercial use of the work providing attribution is made to the authors (but not in any way that suggests that they endorse you or your use of the work). Attribution should include the following information:

McCulloch, G., Canales, A. F. and K, H-Y, HS. 2023. *Brian Simon and the Struggle for Education*. London: UCL Press. https://doi.org/10.14324/111.9781787359819

Further details about Creative Commons licences are available at https://creativecommons.org/licenses/

ISBN: 978-1-78735-983-3 (Hbk.)
ISBN: 978-1-78735-982-6 (Pbk.)
ISBN: 978-1-78735-981-9 (PDF)
ISBN: 978-1-78735-984-0 (epub)
DOI: https://doi.org/10.14324/111.9781787359819

Contents

List of figures	vii
Abbreviations	ix
Acknowledgements	xi

1	Brian Simon: an introduction	1
2	The making of a Marxist intellectual	7
3	Soldier and schoolteacher in the 1940s	29
4	Marxism, psychology and pedagogy	51
5	An emerging public figure	71
6	Chairman of the National Cultural Committee of the Communist Party	91
7	Campaign for comprehensive education: 1951–79	121
8	Defending comprehensive education: 1979–90	151
9	Afterthoughts and last words	173

Bibliography	179
Index	187

List of figures

Plate section 1

1	Brian as a boy, age about 10, c.1925.	47
2	Brian mountaineering, Dolomite Alps, 1935.	47
3	Brian swimming, Dolomite Alps, 1937.	48
4	The Army soldier, c.1939–1940.	48
5	Young Joan Simon, c.mid–late1930s.	49
6	Joan Simon in the country, c.1940.	49

Plate section 2

7	Brian Simon in girls' class, USSR, 1955.	147
8	Staff of Abbott Street school, 1946.	147
9	Brian Simon with Form 1L, Salford Grammar School 1948.	148
10	Salford Grammar School cricket 2nd XI, 1948.	148
11	Salford Grammar School staff photo, c.1947–1950.	149
12	Brian Simon in the USSR, 1955.	149
13	Brian Simon in the USSR, 1955.	150
14	Reflecting in old age (same photo as on front cover) Brian Simon in the Sears Tower, Chicago, 1975.	150

Abbreviations

ABCA	Army Bureau of Current Affairs
BERA	British Educational Research Association
BSC	British Student Congress
CC	Cultural Committee
CP	Communist Party of Great Britain
CPSU	Communist Party of the Soviet Union
CSC	Comprehensive Schools Committee
CSE	Certificate of Secondary Education
CTC	City Technology College
CUL	Communist University of London
CUP	Cambridge University Press
DES	Department of Education and Science
EC	Executive Committee
ERA	Education Reform Act 1988
ESO	Education and the Social Order
GCE	General Certificate of Education
GHQ	General Head Quarters
HES	UK History of Education Society
IOE	Institute of Education London
IEA	Institute of Economic Affairs
IQ	intelligence quotient
ISCHE	International Standing Conference for the History of Education
LAPP	Lower Achieving Pupils Project
LEA	local education authority
MP	Member of Parliament
MSC	Manpower Services Commission
NUS	National Union of Students
NUT	National Union of Teachers
PC	Political Committee
SCR	Society for Cultural Relations

SHE	Studies in the History of Education
SSEC	Secondary Schools Examinations Council
TVEI	Technical and Vocational Education Initiative
UCL	University College London
USSR	Soviet Union
WEA	Workers Educational Association

Acknowledgements

Many debts have been incurred in the preparation of this work. We should like to thank our colleagues and students who have contributed to our thinking about Brian Simon and his life and career. In particular, these have included the participants in seminars that we have led at the UCL Institute of Education London and at the universities of La Laguna and Complutense de Madrid in Spain, and also at National Chung Cheng University, Taiwan and Minzu University of China, Beijing.

We should also like to take this opportunity to thank the archivists and librarians who have assisted our work, especially those at the Institute of Education Library and Archives in London, the Public Record Office in London, and the People's History Museum archives in Manchester.

We also acknowledge, in helping to form our ideas, the many other published articles and conference papers that we have produced over the years, in particular:

Hsiao-Yuh Ku – 'Ideological Struggle in Education: Brian Simon and Comprehensive Education Movement (1946–1965)'.

Hsiao-Yuh Ku – 'Defending Comprehensive Education: Brian Simon and the Conservative Governments (1979–1990)'.

Hsiao-Yuh Ku – 'The Crisis in Education: Brian Simon's Battle for Comprehensive Education (1970–1979)'.

Gary McCulloch – 'Education, History and Social Change: The Legacy of Brian Simon', (inaugural address of Brian Simon Chair of the History of Education, 21 October 2004).

Gary McCulloch – 'A People's History of Education: Brian Simon, the British Communist Party and *Studies in the History of Education, 1780–1870'.

Gary McCulloch – 'Brian Simon and the Struggle for Education: National Identities and International Ideals', (first Institute of Education Brian Simon Lecture at the University of La Laguna, 2011).

Gary McCulloch – *The Struggle for the History of Education*. (London: Routledge, 2011)

Gary McCulloch - *History of Education*, 39 no. 4 (2010): 437–57

We are pleased to acknowledge also the care and patience of UCL Press in bringing this work to publication in this form, and especially the support of the commissioning editor, Pat Gordon-Smith.

1
Brian Simon: an introduction

Brian Simon (1915–2002) was the foremost British historian of education and a leading public intellectual and educational reformer in Britain in the second half of the twentieth century. His Marxist beliefs were widely known. Yet they constituted in some respects a separate life, in some ways distinct from his public life. He was followed by the security services from the time he became a member of the Communist Party of Great Britain (CP) while a student at the University of Cambridge in 1935, suspected of being a Soviet agent even while he was a soldier in the British Army in the Second World War, becoming a member of the CP executive committee when he was a university lecturer, and an active campaigner against the Education Reform Bill in the late 1980s while in retirement.

Simon's importance as a historian of education is also well known. He produced a very large corpus of published work from the 1950s onwards, continuing through a rapidly changing educational, social and political context into the early twenty-first century. His key work, for which he is most widely renowned, is a four-volume history of education in Britain since 1780, with its first volume published in 1960 when he was 45 years old, and the final one in 1991 at the age of 76.[1] Even if the ensemble as a whole was modestly entitled 'Studies in the History of Education', it came to be regarded as the standard text for the history of education in England. This was one of a number of significant contributions to the history of education. He was an early leader of the History of Education Society (HES) in Britain from its foundation in 1967, its chairman from 1972 to 1975, and also helped to establish the International Standing Conference for the History of Education (ISCHE) in the 1970s. A special conference of the HES dedicated to his memory held in Cambridge in December 2003 led to a special issue of its international journal, *History of Education*, with articles on different aspects of his career.[2]

Nor were Simon's academic contributions confined to the history of education. He produced a wide range of work which has been important for many educators who would not describe themselves as historians. His collected essays in *Does Education Matter?* are particularly strong examples of the diverse character of his scholarship, embracing the relationship between education and society, the theory and practice of education, the roles of the state and of local authorities in education, the nature of pedagogy, intelligence testing, the education of the intellect, secondary education, the crisis in education, and the politics of education.[3] It was fitting that he became President in 1977–1978 of the recently-established British Educational Research Association (BERA). After his retirement as professor of education at the University of Leicester in 1980, a *Festschrift* of essays in his honour, *Rethinking Radical Education*, was published in 1993 with contributions by a wide range of educationists.[4]

And yet, more than twenty years after his death in 2002, there is still no full-length study that attempts to bring together the different facets of Simon's life and career and his contribution to education. Certainly, this is a challenging task, in view of both the exceptional range of his work and the different views held about his role. As Peter Cunningham and Jane Martin have put it: 'Responses vary to the public intellectual who joined the Communist Party in the 1930s, moved to historical analysis from a passion for education, disrupted the traditional bias of the history of education in favour of "acts and facts" with a concern for democratization, analysis and synthesis, and devoted his life to the cause of social justice in education.'[5] This book sets out to explore for the first time the full range of Brian Simon's life as a student, soldier and school teacher; as a CP activist; and as an educational academic, campaigner and reformer.

There are several key themes. First, Simon's Marxism did not lead him into a fully divided or secret life. Such was the case with some other Marxist intellectuals of the twentieth century who, like Simon himself, were attracted to Marxism while they were students at the University of Cambridge, and, unlike him, became spies for the Soviet Union. Simon knew some of these well. Donald Maclean, for example, went to the same public (independent) school as Simon – Gresham's School in Holt, Norfolk – and to the same college at Cambridge, Trinity. At Trinity, it was Maclean who urged Simon to join the CP, which he did in January 1935. Maclean was appointed to the Foreign Office that year, secretly spied for the Soviet Union, and then defected to Moscow in 1951. As Robert Cecil has suggested, his was a true 'divided life'.[6] While at Cambridge Simon also knew figures such as Anthony Blunt, later Surveyor of the Queen's Pictures and exposed as a Soviet spy.[7] Barrie Penrose and Simon Freeman entitled their work on Blunt *Conspiracy of Silence: The secret life of Anthony Blunt*.[8] Another, James Klugmann, also went to Gresham's School and Trinity College, Cambridge, and also persuaded Simon to join the CP. Indeed, Simon was 'inducted after nights and nights of conversation with James Klugmann', according to Blunt's biographer Miranda Carter.[9] Klugmann became a close confidant of Simon before going on to spy for the Soviet Union during the Second World War. Geoff Andrews's biography of Klugmann depicts him as the 'shadow man'.[10]

There is thus a common image of the Cambridge spies for the Soviet Union as living a divided, secret or shadow life. On the other hand, Carter's volume on Blunt merely refers in its subtitle to 'his lives', and she points out that 'While the other Cambridge spies subordinated their lives and careers to espionage, Blunt had a separate life as an art historian quite as, if not more, important to him than his work for the Soviets.'[11] This was also true of Simon's significance as a historian of education alongside his work for the CP. Moreover, although he became a leading figure in the CP, Simon was not a spy. Rather, thanks to the sterling efforts of the British security services, he was, after he joined the CP, consistently spied upon as he moved around. It seems fair to discuss him in terms of his different lives while not attaching the tag of secrecy, and still less that of espionage.

In some respects more similar to the lifetime experience of Brian Simon was that of the historian Eric Hobsbawm (1917–2012). Like Simon, Hobsbawm was committed to historical scholarship, for which he was recognised more widely than Simon partly due to the breadth of his interests in social history. Similarly to Simon, Hobsbawm was drawn into the CP while a student at Cambridge in the 1930s, and also maintained his loyalty to the CP after the Second World War. Unlike Simon, Hobsbawm was a refugee from Europe rather than an upper-class English intellectual, and also unlike Simon he allowed his differences with CP policy in the 1950s and 1960s to become public knowledge and part of the thinking of the New Left.[12]

Furthermore, while to some extent distinct, Simon's involvement in the world of Marxism and the CP also had an impact on his more prominent and public life as a historian of education. His Marxism and his political activism influenced his approach to history, and indeed also to education. So the current work, in addressing the full range of Simon's life, has three principal objectives. The first is to understand Simon's contribution to Marxism and the CP, a contribution that was eventually to be significant in its own right, politically, intellectually and also economically. The second is to explore the influence of Simon's Marxism, and his affiliation to the CP, on his work as a historian of education. The third is to trace the significance of his Marxist beliefs, political associations and historical approach to the cause of educational reform. While we make use of biographical methods and sources, the book is not a conventional biography and focuses on some aspects more than others, not always in strict chronological order. Although broadly sympathetic, it is not a hagiography and seeks to retain some critical distance from its principal subject.

In all of these aims and objectives, the significance of Simon's family, and especially his relationship with his wife, Joan, is to the fore. Joan and Brian were married in February 1941, and went on to forge a formidable partnership in history, the CP, and politics more generally that lasted for over sixty years until Brian's death in January 2002.[13]

There is no shortage of material. A large amount of written evidence is available (published and unpublished) including from the archive of Simon himself at the UCL Institute of Education, the papers of the CP in Manchester, and the security files on Simon and his family, released at the National Archives. These reveal another dimension to Simon's life besides his distinguished scholarly contributions, and are fascinating in their own right. Yet it is no less important to highlight other aspects of Simon's distinct lives which suggest complexities and nuances rather than a straightforward dualism.

The current work appropriately draws on a diverse range of sources that shed light on different aspects of Simon's life and times. His many publications attest to his academic development, and also include a number of less-noticed essays in the Marxist press that reveal his commitment to Marxist theory. He published a short volume of memoirs in 1997, *A Life in Education*, which although a useful source is generally rather guarded and limited in its recall of the range of his experiences.[14] His own personal archive, carefully amassed by himself and Joan and donated to the Institute of Education London archive by Joan after his death, is a substantial record of these experiences over the full extent of his life. It includes an unpublished autobiography, much longer, more wide-ranging and more revealing than the published version. The archive of the CP, opened and fully catalogued, based in Manchester, is a significant source on his CP activities. Even more valuable in many ways are the surveillance files on Brian Simon and his family by the security services, open to researchers at the National Archives at Kew in south-west London.

Chapter 2 explores Brian Simon's early life and upbringing, including as a pupil at an independent ('public') school, and Trinity College,

Cambridge, and at the Institute of Education London. Chapter 3 follows his development during the Second World War and immediately after, first as a soldier in the British Army, and then as a school teacher in Manchester. In chapter 4 we investigate the wellsprings of his approach to Marxist theory and his relationship to the CP. Chapter 5 traces Simon's emergence as a national public figure, both in the CP and in his academic domain. Chapter 6 discusses his significant contribution to reviving the CP's political and intellectual position in the 1960s. Chapter 7 goes on to examine Simon's approach to educational reform, in particular on behalf of comprehensive secondary education. In chapter 8 we highlight his role in educational debates leading to the Education Reform Act (ERA) of 1988. The final chapter reviews the significance of Brian Simon's work in helping to understand his contribution to British public life in the twentieth century, including his role as a public intellectual, his commitment to political ideas, and his support for educational reform.

Notes

1 B. Simon, *Studies in the History of Education, 1780–1870* (later retitled *The Two Nations and the Educational Structure, 1780–1870*), Lawrence & Wishart, London, 1960; *Education and the Labour Movement, 1870–1920*, Lawrence & Wishart, London, 1965; *The Politics of Educational Reform, 1920–1940*, Lawrence & Wishart, London, 1974; *Education and the Social Order, 1940–1990*, Lawrence & Wishart, London, 1991.

2 *History of Education*, 33/5 (2004), 'Brian Simon'; see also P. Cunningham, J. Martin, 'Education and the social order: Re-visioning the legacy of Brian Simon', *History of Education*, 33/5 (2004), 497–504.

3 B. Simon, *Does Education Matter?*, Lawrence & Wishart, London, 1985.

4 A. Rattansi, D. Reeder (eds), *Rethinking Radical Education*, Lawrence & Wishart, London, 1993.

5 Cunningham and Martin 'Education and the social order', 499.

6 R. Cecil, *A Divided Life: A biography of Donald Maclean*, Bodley Head, London, 1988.

7 M. Carter, *Anthony Blunt: His lives*, Picador, London, 2003.

8 B. Penrose, S. Freeman, *Conspiracy of Silence: The secret life of Anthony Blunt*, Farrar, Straus and Giroux, New York, 1987.

9 Carter, *Anthony Blunt*, 112.

10 G. Andrews, *The Shadow Man: At the heart of the Cambridge spy circle*, I.B. Tauris, London, 2015.

11 Carter, *Anthony Blunt*, xviii.

12 See E. Hobsbawm, *Interesting Times: A twentieth-century life*, Allen Lane, London, 2002; R.J. Evans, *Eric Hobsbawm: A life in history*, Little Brown, London, 2019.

13 R. Watts, 'Obituary: Joan Simon (1915–2005)', *History of Education*, 35/1 (2006), 5–9; J. Martin, 'Neglected women historians: The case of Joan Simon', *Forum*, 56/3 (2014), 541–66.

14 B. Simon, *A Life in Education*, Lawrence & Wishart, London, 1997.

2
The making of a Marxist intellectual

Brian Simon was brought up in an upper-class family with parents, Ernest and Shena Simon, who were leading members of the liberal intelligentsia. His early development including his relations with his parents, his education at a progressive public school, Gresham's, and then at Trinity College, Cambridge, and the context of society and the wider politics of the 1930s led him to join the Communist Party while a student in 1935. Both at school and at university he made close links with future and actual CP members, and his brother Roger was also a student at Cambridge and also joined the CP. Brian developed a strong sympathy for the Communist cause in the Spanish Civil War of 1936–1939. He then became prominent in student politics more broadly when training to be a teacher at the Institute of Education in London (IOE), in close association with his CP connections.

'A thoroughly sound fellow, universally admired'

Simon's own upbringing was to all appearances quintessentially English in its nature, or more precisely upper class, or aristocratic English. His family home was a country estate, Broom Croft, a large farmhouse built in the 1820s near Manchester in the north of England, with central heating, a large staff, outbuildings, a gardener's cottage, room inside the house for entertaining guests, and space enough outside for tennis and archery, as well as for a lawn, kitchen garden, and flowers and plants to occupy two gardeners.[1] According to the national census held in June 1921, in residence at Broom Croft together with the Simon family were Jane Clark, a nurse; Alice Fletcher, a servant; Rhoda Fletcher, a cook; Ivy Ullock, a nurse maid; and Mary Hetherington, a fifteen-year-old maid.[2] In the way of the English upper class, the young Simon became used to governesses and servants. This was the typical background of the English gentleman, and Simon himself carried the polite and gentle bearing of an English gentleman throughout his life. According to Mary Stocks's account, 'the young Simons were brought up in comfort without splendour, with all the opportunities that money could provide for the promotion of physical and mental fitness, but with the perpetual reminder, by perpetual example and precept, that these gifts were to be regarded as instruments to be used for the benefit of mankind', the outcome being that they were 'not likely to become spoiled children, nor indeed did they'.[3] Brian himself later recalled that 'growing up at Broom Croft could be counted a liberal education', with no personal taboos.[4]

Yet this English elite scene is far from being the whole picture. Simon's grandfather, Henry Simon, was German, and experienced at first hand the European revolutions of 1848 before moving to Zurich in Switzerland and then settling in Manchester in 1860. Henry Simon established a successful business in England using a Swiss flour-milling plant and a French coke oven.[5] It was the wealth produced by these devices that was to pay for Brian Simon's comfortable childhood and expensive education. Henry Simon's second wife, born Emily Stoehr, was also German. She bore seven children, the eldest of whom, Ernest, was Brian Simon's father. Ernest was sent to a leading public school, Rugby, in 1893, where he studied science before going on to take a degree in engineering at Pembroke College Cambridge, gaining first-class honours.[6] After Henry's death in 1899, Ernest took over the family business.

Shena, Brian's mother, was born in October 1883, in an upper middle-class family, and read economics at Newnham College, Cambridge. Ernest and Shena married in November 1912, the beginning of a long partnership as social reformers that was to last until Ernest's death in 1960.[7] The First World War affected both Ernest Simon and his family as a whole. Prevalent anti-German prejudice led him to anglicise his name from its previous pronunciation of 'Seaman', while all three of his younger brothers were killed fighting for the British Army, during the war.[8] He was international in his experiences, travelling to many different countries around the world on matters of business, although he was less interested in international politics than in home affairs.[9] He became closely involved in Liberal politics and went on to be Lord Mayor of Manchester and a Liberal Member of Parliament. He was knighted in 1932, joined the Labour Party after the Second World War, and accepted a peerage in 1947, becoming the first Lord Simon of Wythenshawe. Shena became involved in the campaign for female suffrage and then particularly in education, advocating the raising of the school leaving age and the introduction of comprehensive secondary education.[10] Ernest Simon himself was committed to ideals of education for public service and citizenship, and in 1934 he established the Association for Education in Citizenship. He preached 'evolutionary progress' in a 'slow and complex world'. Despite what he recognised to have been grave social injustices, he was convinced that through its '700 year fight for freedom', England had 'produced a sensible independent people, who have on the whole set the world an example of civilised development'.[11]

Ernest and Shena had three children – Roger in 1913, then Brian, and then Antonia. From the beginning, they were prepared for public life through liberal values and active citizenship, according to prevailing ideas about child development to encourage mental faculties and character. Ernest provided a commentary on Brian's early progress as an infant, drawing on knowledge of an eclectic mix of international progressive ideas. These included phrenology, or the measurement of bumps on the skull, the open-air movement to ward off illnesses such as tuberculosis, and the work of Truby King and the Plunket Society in New Zealand, which linked child development to the health of the family, nation and Empire.[12] He observed that Brian was born at 2.10 am on 26 March 1915, 'A thoroughly sound fellow, universally admired.' At first he seemed to resemble his father, then appeared more like the mother, 'distinctly Potterish'. The Victorian pseudoscience of phrenology seemed still to influence him, as he commented: 'His head is of excellent shape, lacking Roger's early bumps, he sleeps and eats well, and is altogether making a good beginning of life.' So far as his initial development was concerned, he added, 'He had his first open air on the 8th day, and has from the start had 3-hourly feeds: one step more towards the Truby King theory than Roger. Hence perhaps his more rapid gain after the first week.'[13] Ernest's observations after thirteen months also showed awareness of the Italian progressive educator Maria Montessori: 'His constructive powers develop rapidly. Has just succeeded in building up six bricks on the top of one another, and crowning the tower with a wooden bowl. And is very proud of it! He plays alone most happily, bricks seem as good as any Montessori toy.'[14] At the age of six he was reading Lewis Carroll's *Alice's Adventures in Wonderland* to himself; at eight he enjoyed dancing and playing the piano.[15] When he was eleven-and-a-half years old, too, his father recorded on his steady progress in his diary: 'Has a real talent for drawing, which is pleasant as the only bit of artistic talent in the family. Also developing definite taste and initiative.'[16]

Governesses provided the main early childcaring, supporting the children's access to their parents partly through writing letters, and so encouraging a form of communication that would become familiar and necessary. These letters often expressed affection and love although, as the children grew, such personal feelings were articulated less, especially as the father preferred to emphasise self-control and rationality rather than displays of emotion. These were put to the ultimate test as Antonia (known as Tony) died in September 1929, aged 12, after years of treatment including spells at a Swiss sanatorium, supported by her despairing father, for a form of cancer behind the eye.

Antonia was an exceptionally talented and promising child, and her loss was keenly felt by the family as a whole, including Brian in later years. In 1940, when she would have been 23 years old, he wrote to his parents to recall Antonia's qualities, lamenting that in a time of war 'she would have been a real friend and comrade, giving one the strength that sometimes is lacking', and thinking of her 'actually <u>doing</u> things in the world, and respected and loved by all who worked with her'. Indeed, he urged, 'our efforts must be directed in the end to producing people like Tony… who can work together and live together harmoniously and for common ideals and common ends', and giving rise to 'all sorts of possibilities of human development which we can only guess at now'.[17]

He did not mention Antonia in his published memoir, but in his unpublished autobiography he noted that he still retained vivid memories of her and of 'the extraordinary abilities she developed, mental, moral and social, at so very early an age'. His father had been 'sold' on the notion of individual intelligence in the mid-1920s, he recalled, and had tested Antonia, Roger and Brian for this; Antonia came top, Roger second and himself 'a trailing third'. This seems to have been the Terman Intelligence Test, administered in 1923 when Brian was six years old, with Antonia securing 145 points, Roger 130 and Brian 115.[18] Looking back, he suggested that his sister's unfulfilled promise had helped to create in him a profound belief in human potential, and strongly influenced his thinking about education.[19] These were indeed the early beginnings of Simon's later faith in the possibilities of education, both for the benefit of any individual pupil, and for its limitless potential for humanity in general.

Living in a fascist state

Formal education complemented the Simons' informal social learning. For Brian this included a child-centred progressive kindergarten and a preparatory boarding school where he was apparently often bullied by other children. He then went to Gresham's school in Holt, Norfolk, a school that was popular with the liberal intelligentsia for its progressive views. At the end of his time at Gresham's he ventured to Salem school in Germany, to gain wider experience, in 1933, at the same time that it was taken over by the new Nazi regime.

Brian's first formal educational experience was at a Froebelian kindergarten, Oakdene, near to his home in Didsbury, Manchester, at the age of four. These institutions were first established by the early nineteenth-century German educator Friedrich Froebel, based on ideals of educating the whole child, emphasising the importance of play and learning through nature.[20] Manchester had long been a centre for Froebelian activities, supported by German immigrants such as his grandfather Henry from the 1860s, and they appealed especially to the liberal-minded section of the middle classes.[21] His school reports were positive; according to his head teacher, M.F. Percy, 'Brian has worked well and made good progress. He is greatly interested in his school work and all his teachers are pleased with him.'[22] Brian's father noted that he was 'a bit unreliable', but that 'He makes remarks about the clothes other children wear: more observant in these things than his Father'.[23]

After three years at Oakdene, Brian was sent to a preparatory day-school for boys, Moor Allerton School, also in Manchester. In his unpublished autobiography, he described this as 'an ordinary, dull, average, suburban private school such as could then be found up and down the country'.[24] Then aged 11 he went to a preparatory boarding school, Stratton Park in the village of Great Brickhill in Buckinghamshire, following his brother Roger who had gone there a few years before. This he found an even more difficult experience, despite its progressive reputation, recalling many years later that the head kept order with a stick, and the school was terrified of him.[25] However, he 'survived' this without serious damage, as he put it. He was prepared to concede that his earlier recollection of the school as being 'sadistic' and a 'criminal establishment' may have been 'over harsh'. Moreover, he suggested, 'The worst periods were probably fairly short – a term or two when I was in a particularly brutal dormitory dominated by the headmaster's son.'[26] It was at this time that what was deemed to be his indistinct speech was corrected through elocution lessons at home, which overcame this perceived disability, so that, as he recognised, 'public speaking lecturing etc presented no problem later on'.[27]

Subsequent to this, the main experience of schooling for both Roger and Brian was at Gresham's school in Holt, Norfolk. Gresham's was originally founded in 1555 by Sir John Gresham, as a local endowed grammar school and was re-established as a public school from 1900. It was distinct from the traditional public schools such as Eton and Rugby in having a reputation for taking a liberal approach in its ethos, and was much favoured by the liberal intelligentsia. The Simons were quite a catch for the school and were much courted by its headmaster, J.R. Eccles. Gresham's aspired to encourage an emerging social conscience and a sense of justice on the part of its boys, together with a nascent political and class awareness. The school also nurtured a sense of self-control through its self-styled 'honour' system. Pupils were expected to promise the headmaster and their housemaster to avoid indecency, bad language and smoking, to confess when they broke any of these rules, and to inform on other pupils who failed to confess.

The headmaster, Eccles, saw this as an innovative means of promoting self-discipline and inculcating trust among the pupils. Eccles later produced a detailed account of his life as a public-school master, outlining what he had tried to achieve. He had started as an assistant master at Gresham's in 1900, having been invited by the first headmaster under its new constitution, George Howson. He stayed at the school, becoming its headmaster after Howson's retirement in 1919, until he himself retired in 1935. Howson had established the honour system, which Eccles saw as a bold and original solution to a 'moral problem' that affected boys' public schools, enabling Gresham's to promote a form of inner discipline or self-discipline.[28] Unlike at other schools, he pointed out, it was not necessary to add bars to the windows and locks to the doors, giving Gresham's an unusual amount of freedom. As headmaster, he interviewed all new boys to explain its ideals and emphasise the promises they were to make. The ultimate aim, he concluded, was to 'turn out good citizens', giving the boys 'a sense of public spirit and public service, for him to think first of the community and secondly of himself'.[29] Indeed, he averred, 'In our schools we must turn boys out idealists and optimists, full of faith and hope, with many castles in the air.'[30]

Some pupils who became well known as adults would remember this experience with much less sympathy. The poets W.H. Auden and Stephen Spender, both educated at Gresham's, were fiercely critical of the suppression of emotion and the betrayal that this system fostered, and compared it to living in a fascist state.[31] Comparing their experiences many years later, his brother Roger reminisced: 'My impression is that there was also a promise not to break the school rules, for example, never to touch anyone in the dormitory, I remember Eccles used to burst unexpectedly into the dormitory from time to time.'[32] Brian himself often had a difficult relationship with his headmaster. His brother recalled that Eccles had a 'strange hostility' to Brian.[33] This seemed to be due to Eccles's suspicion that Brian did not conform to the behaviour that was expected of him and harboured radical views. An issue of Gresham's school magazine in December 1931, reporting on a meeting of the school's debating society, noted that 'B. Simon proved himself a champion of the unemployed, and bitterly attacked the suggestion that they should be deprived of a vote.'[34] At one point, Brian even wrote to his parents to confess that 'He's given me a talk and says I'm self-opinionated and I've got a bad side to my character, and I'm awkward…. He's got some idea into his head about me somehow, and perhaps you don't know what he's like when that happens. It takes him ages to get rid of it.'[35]

One indication of Brian's frustrated independence of mind that may have contributed to the headmaster's apparent irritation was a history essay that he produced, entitled 'My point of view', in Michaelmas term of 1932. In this essay, the young Simon asserted that the world was going through a critical period, with great changes and experiments taking place amid an economic breakdown that was leading towards disaster and war. Only education could save the world from this disaster: 'People must be made to realise their danger, and must cooperate and help to save the world, if only to save their own skins. The fault, then, seems to lie in education in not making them realise this, and the cure is to educate them in such a manner so that they realise their duty, first, as inhabitants of the world as a unity, and secondly, as good citizens.'[36] Yet, he continued, modern education for the 'poorer classes' was inadequate for such a task, while the public schools must strive to develop greater international cooperation. A different kind of 'self-education' was needed in order to save the world in this situation, encouraging 'an intelligent and controlled interest in public affairs'.[37] In some ways this argument echoed his father's faith in education for citizenship. At the same time, it suggested a yearning that had yet to be satisfied for a radical alternative. The essay received a grading of a rather grudging B-plus-plus.

Despite his incipient radical and independent leanings, Simon had thus far been personally sheltered from the worsening economic climate and the beginnings of international conflict. A stock-market crash in the United States in 1929 had led to a widespread economic crisis which brought down the minority Labour government in Britain, and resulted, towards the end of 1931, in a National Government dominated by the Conservative Party.[38] In Italy, Benito Mussolini had secured power as the first fascist dictator of a one-party state on the continent of Europe, while in Germany Adolf Hitler's Nazi Party was making a rapid rise to power. Brian's father was a leading light in an initiative by the Liberal Party to update its social and economic programme, and he supported the veteran Liberal leader Lloyd George in this endeavour, although ultimately with disappointing electoral results. At the start of 1933, Simon received an invitation to witness international events at first hand, with a visit to Salem School in Germany. His brother had visited Salem the previous year, and was full of praise. According to Roger, it had some similarities to Gresham's, being based on a form of the honours system. He explained that the school building was a large monastery that, during the Napoleonic wars, had been given as a 'castle' by Napoleon to an ancestor of Prince Max von Baden, who founded the school there after the end of the First World War. He also recommended the accommodation, the food and the social life at Salem, and noted that there were no compulsory Sunday services at Salem, unlike at Gresham's (where there were two).[39] Above all, he extolled the headmaster, Kurt Hahn, 'a most exceptional man, very clever and much admired by everybody', and 'he naturally hates Hitler'.[40]

Brian's father supported the plan, and was able to use his contacts to make the necessary arrangements. So Brian set off, travelling third class, and arrived at Salem in mid-January 1933. At the end of that month, Hitler was appointed chancellor of Germany, and the Nazi Party soon gained power. Salem was surrounded, and Hahn arrested and jailed, with a Nazi official installed in his place. Brian stayed to witness these events, and was able to enjoy the summer term, left largely on his own. In retrospect, he recalled that the experience of actually living in a fascist regime, helped his further development, in that, as he suggested in his unpublished autobiography, it 'encouraged a certain independence of mind after the rather suffocating and certainly highly controlled life at Gresham's'. This early and first-hand experience of the nature and impact of Nazi ideology and practice also shaped his general political awareness. Meanwhile, Hahn escaped to England in July 1933 and then was able to establish a school for boys at Gordonstoun in Scotland, the following year. A close friend of the Simons subsequently, Hahn was to become a leading international educator.[41]

Ernest continued to guide his sons' development, and his further monitoring of Brian led to a detailed report on his intelligence and prospects, aged 18 years and one month, by the National Institute of Industrial Psychology. According to the accompanying intelligence test conducted on Brian, he scored 160 and a half marks, 'a very good result indeed, the average for secondary school boys of his age being 125'. Overall, 'His effort shows fluency and considerably more than average originality. He is able to express himself in a very pleasing lucid manner.' An interview suggested that he was sociable, cooperative, and also active and energetic, capable of reaching the higher grades of the Home Civil Service which would be through competitive examination. The administrative side of educational work might be suitable, but teaching was unlikely to be congenial: 'He would probably find it too "narrowing" and offering insufficient scope for independent effort and initiative.' The profession of a solicitor, or business management, or publishing, might also offer alternatives, it was suggested.[42]

Brian was now ready to enter the University of Cambridge, and also began to assert himself against his father's plans for his public life. Ernest had hoped that Brian could take a degree to prepare himself for public service and was disappointed that Brian chose to begin a degree in English. For his part, Brian, although interested in History was less than enthused with the history teaching at Gresham's and found the classes in English more stimulating. As he told his brother, 'I am having great fun with Denys Thompson and English. I think I shall probably do it at Cambridge, as it is frightfully interesting, much more than History!' Indeed, he added, the History tutor, Kelly, had few new specialist pupils, and 'it is of course entirely his fault for making history so dull – please don't tell Father I said this when it obviously could be made such an inspiring subject'.[43] Thompson was a former pupil of F.R. Leavis, and cowrote with Leavis the school textbook *Culture and Environment: The training of critical awareness* in 1932, also editing the modernist English journal *Scrutiny* for some years.[44] Thompson's innovative teaching clearly appealed to Simon, who added: 'I am spending most of my time on English, and D. Thompson takes a lot of trouble over me, and the 70 minutes a week I have with him (8.00 to 9.10) simply flies by.'[45] Characteristically, Ernest checked on the Cambridge English syllabus, suggested that 'possibly economics, law or History' might be 'rather more solid', and asked Brian to write an essay for him on why he wished to study English.[46] In the end, Brian got his way, and went up to Cambridge in October 1933 to study for an English degree. Eccles' final comment on his student, in Brian's last school report, was: 'With his ability, upright character, and high ideals, he should do very well. I wish him all success.'[47]

Nursery of revolution?

Simon's chosen college at Cambridge was Trinity College, historic and well respected. It was also a key site for Communist Party (CP) members. In his first year, he was approached by Donald Maclean, also the son of a Liberal MP, and who had also been educated at Gresham's school, and in the same house, although three years in advance. He was now a member of the CP at Cambridge University and invited Simon to join also, but Simon declined.[48] Nevertheless, the CP was to form a key part of Simon's life at Cambridge.

After the Russian Revolution of 1917 and the forming of the Soviet Union (USSR), the Communist Party of the USSR established the Comintern, an international organisation to support its interests and ideals. A Communist Party of Great Britain was set up in 1920 and attempted to affiliate to the Labour Party, which after the First World War had become the main opposition to the Conservative Party and the main party of the organised working class, including the trade union movement. However, the Labour Party, committed to a peaceful path through parliament and the democratic process towards an independent socialist society, refused to countenance any dealings with the CP, which remained a separate fringe organisation.[49] It took a militant position in industrial disputes including the General Strike of 1926. The CP's militancy combined with its sympathy for the USSR led to it being suspected of undermining the interests of the UK. This was reflected in the infamous episode of the Zinoviev letter of 1924, just before a tightly-contested general election between the Conservatives and Labour, when the newspaper the *Daily Mail* published a letter purporting to be from Grigory Zinoviev, the head of the Comintern in Moscow, ordering the CP in Britain to engage in seditious activities. The letter was later shown to be a forgery.[50] More generally, members and sympathisers of the CP were regarded by the authorities as being potential security risks, and increasingly in the 1920s and 1930s the security services of MI5 took to tracing and monitoring the movements of individuals implicated in their activities.[51]

When Hitler came to power in Germany, the Comintern decided that national CPs should seek to cooperate with other anti-fascist parties in a 'popular front'. In May 1935, this policy was formally endorsed by the Comintern. A popular front government was elected in Spain in February 1936, and also in France under Léon Blum in May 1936, but in Spain there was a civil war between supporters of the government and right-wing supporters of General Francisco Franco. In Britain, the Labour Party continued to avoid cooperation with the CP, but a number of left-wing groups such as the Left Book Club, launched in 1936, favoured this approach.[52]

In October 1934, at the start of his second year, Simon moved into Whewell's Court, later described by his contemporary, the historian Eric Hobsbawm, as 'the most obvious nursery of revolution ... the set of rooms, bursting with posters and leaflets, in Whewell's Court, Trinity, just below Ludwig Wittgenstein, shared by the American Whitney Straight and the biochemist Hugh Gordon'.[53] Straight later became a Soviet spy and helped to expose Anthony Blunt's spying activities; Simon knew them both while he was at Cambridge. Hobsbawm also worked in Paris with James Klugmann, who like Simon had been educated at Gresham's School,[54] so it is evident that there were many personal as well as institutional connections. Hobsbawm does not mention Simon in his memoir, but his account of life in Cambridge helps us to shed light on Simon's involvements also. As Hobsbawm points out, 'For us it was a time when the good cause confronted its enemies. We enjoyed it, even when, as for most of radical Cambridge, it did not occupy the bulk of our time, and we did a certain amount of world-saving as a matter of course, because it was the thing to do.'[55] Trinity College itself was described by Simon in his unpublished autobiography as the crucible of the movement in Cambridge, with the CP leaders, John Cornford and James Klugmann, also at the college. Klugmann, who had known Simon slightly at Gresham's, was now a research student, also based in Whewell's Court, and was one of a number of CP members who became friends with him.[56]

In such company it was not long before Simon gave way to further persuasion, and in January 1935 he made the decision to join the CP himself. His father was greatly alarmed at this, only too aware of its potential implications for Brian's career prospects and of how it might restrict his ability to provide public service. He suggested delaying a decision until after he had seen the USSR for himself, for two reasons. First, he pointed out that communism would damage or even destroy almost any career prospect, except as a propagandist. Secondly, he argued that an educated man should 'keep an open mind on these great questions till he has enough experience and studied enough to form a sound and reliable judgement'. Poverty and privilege, he insisted, could be swept away through democratic means: 'I am an optimist about all this – I think it is our duty to have faith and to work for peaceful development – and unless one is *convinced* it is impossible.'[57] He recommended a reading of John Stuart Mill's work *On Liberty* to see the opposing case.[58] But Brian was obdurate. He observed that he was reading a great deal about dialectical materialism, 'and the more I read, the more I am convinced, and as it points to the inevitability of the Communist state, and as I am convinced intellectually that it is inevitable, what am I to do?'[59] He also explained that he was doing a lot of work for the anti-war movement, and researching how the university had been used for the purposes of war: 'The main point of the campaign is to get a mass movement in Cambridge Univ. against war, which is lacking at present. The most active movement is the Anti-War movement, which is regarded with suspicion by others, as it is supported in the main by Communists (as admittedly it is).'[60] He was also working with members of the League of Nations Union, New Poems Society, Democratic Front and Labour Club in the interests of forging a Cambridge version of the popular front against fascism. It also meant spending long days selling Marxist tracts and newspapers in the street, as he did on Jubilee Day on 6 May 1935 rather than celebrating the long reign of King George V.[61]

Brian's reading on dialectical materialism was under new tutelage. After his first year he moved from English to study Economics for the second part of his degree, supervised by American economist Maurice Dobb, also of Trinity College, who was an authority on the political economy of Marxism. He also took Politics as a subsidiary subject, tutored by Ernest Barker assisted by Michael Oakeshott.[62] Dobb's approach emphasised a historical perspective to the understanding of Marx's political economy, in particular on changes in the mode of production in the transition between different forms of society.[63] This gave Simon a strongly classical Marxist theory, based squarely on economic change. It also meant that, although he had not specialised in the study of history, he could apply a historical framework to the understanding of contemporary issues. At the same time, he also learned quickly how to hide or obscure the underlying basis of his ideas. He explained to his parents: 'I have been advised to leave out words like "Marxism" and "Dialectical Materialism" from my thesis, because then they won't realise all it implies! The worst of most of my lecturers is that they are nearly all (except for F.L. Lucas!) one-quarter or one-half Marxist, and that they won't follow it to its logical conclusion.'[64] There is little evidence of profound philosophical or critical thinking in Simon's understanding of Marxist theory. On the other hand, he continued to be frustrated by the conventional syllabus as a whole in his economics course: 'Except in the course on Politics, and two or three lectures on Industrial Relations, the word "Socialism" never sullied the lips of any lecturer, while the word "Russia" was equally taboo.' Indeed, he complained: 'The proverbial visitor from Mars, attending a week's lectures at Mill Lane, would have received no hint that any alternative system was even conceivable, and he would have been astounded to hear that the relative merits of the system he would have heard described and commented on, and those of another system, were the subject of disputes among millions of men in every part of the world.'[65]

Ernest tried as best he could to come to terms with his son's new position. He and Shena visited Moscow, the capital city of the USSR, with Brian and a group of experts in 1936, and Ernest acknowledged that Brian had helped him to take a more sympathetic interest in both the USSR and in Marx himself. Yet Brian's relationship with his father had now changed. Ernest pointed out in a fatherly letter to mark Brian's 21st birthday in February 1936: 'You have inevitably the attributes of youth – with a faith and too much certainty of the rightness of your side and too much certainty of the wrongness of the other – lack of tolerance and the power of seeing the other side of the case.' He added: 'I do tend to be rather irritated by your assumption that British politics is always inspired by wicked motives; feeling sure that on the whole it is fairly decent as things go in this complex, extraordinarily difficult world.' Nevertheless, he praised his son for having 'the necessary qualities of body, mind and character to do a good job in the world', and suggested that 'what England most needs is independent competent keen people, who really want to get something done, and it is a great pleasure to see you going so well in that direction'.[66]

Yet Brian was now set on a different path. To an extent it seemed that he had gained freedom from fealty to his family and social class, in exchange for accepting the authority of Marxism and conformity to the expectations of the CP. He had found a new hope for the future in the USSR, a faith to believe in with Marxism, and natural enemies in the form of European fascism. He soon found a cause that seemed worth fighting for, in Spain.

The Spanish syndrome

Brian Simon graduated from Cambridge in 1937 with lower-second honours, hardly among the most distinguished of his generation, even if, as his father wrote to console him, Brian had gained far more from his experience of Cambridge than he had himself.[67] By now, he had been accepted to study at the Institute of Education in London, recently confirmed as part of the University of London, for a one-year diploma course to study to be a teacher.[68] This was a further stage in his intellectual development, as it helped to shape in more substantial detail not only his approach to education, but also his commitment to the CP and educational reform.

Simon recalled in his published memoir that the IOE had emerged during the interwar years to become, in his words, 'the leading university-based centre in the Commonwealth for the study of education and the training of teachers', and that when he became a student there in 1937 it seemed 'a forward-looking, innovative organisation at odds with the stagnation imposed on the nation's schools in the bleak inter-war years'.[69] He found the Institute overall 'interesting, even exciting, as a way towards a job in the "real world"'. This was an intensive course of study that challenged his thinking not only about education, but also a wide range of related areas about life and society. As he noted in his memoir, 'In the 1930s psychology, history, philosophy and other core subjects, such as health education, were taught – usually – by mass lectures delivered consecutively on Friday mornings in the newly built Senate House of the university in Russell Square.'[70] It was this that established his professional ideals as well as his moral and social outlook.

During his time at the IOE, Simon lived in Woburn Square, close to the institute and in spacious accommodation. He was soon invited to act as National Union of Students (NUS) Secretary and became closely involved in educational issues, both local and international.[71] In his views about the relationship between education and society, Simon was deeply influenced by the ideas of the director of the institute, Fred Clarke. The main themes in Clarke's approach were set out in a short book that he published in 1940, soon after the outbreak of the Second World War, entitled *Education and Social Change: An English interpretation*.[72] Clarke argued that the problems of English education should be understood in relation to its socio-economic history. Education was itself, he argued, 'a process conducted and conditioned by social forces, all of which have a history'. Educational institutions were to be examined in the light of their determination by historical forces'.[73] And yet, as he maintained elsewhere, no such history of education had yet been published, and this should be one of the key priorities for the new educational studies.[74]

Clarke was not a Marxist; indeed, he was a liberal thinker, with Anglican religious views.[75] Nevertheless, his ideas on education had a strong influence on Simon's thinking. They gave strong hints as to how to apply a historical perspective to current educational problems, just as Maurice Dobb's approach in his Economics course at Cambridge showed the importance of history in an understanding of economics. This was evident in a student essay produced by Simon while at the IOE, entitled 'The function of the school in society'. In this he suggested that 'the school is always a function of society, it cannot differentiate itself radically from society for any long period of time, it is a part of society'.[76] Britain was undergoing a rapid change in its economic structure and in ideas and society, he argued. Therefore, there were implications for the function of the school in the changing society of the time. This function would be 'to develop all the qualities of the individual to the greatest possible extent, so that he will be given every opportunity to live as full a life as possible'. At the same time, there would be a need for the individual to live in harmony with others in society. Overall, he concluded, the function of the school should be to educate for adaptability and change, to educate for the future rather than the present, through the use of reason: 'Only in this way can we free ourselves from the bondage of the past, and give our children an education which will be truly honest and free.'[77]

In this respect, Simon was clearly aware of his debt to Clarke, and he was later frank in his praise for Clarke's role in sketching out what was, in Simon's view, 'a new function for the educational historian, that of unravelling the social and historical influences which have played so potent a part in shaping both the schools and what is taught inside them; and, most important, of distinguishing the genuine educational theory from the rationalisation which seeks to explain away rather than elucidate'. According to Simon, writing in the 1960s, it was precisely this that enabled the history of education to take on a new aspect, 'as a vital contribution to social history – rather than a flat record of acts and ordinances, punctuated by accounts of the theories of great educators who entertained ideas "in advance of their time"'.[78]

Simon's commitment to Marxism was sharpened at the same time through the international events of the late 1930s. Franco's opposition to the Spanish Popular Front government led to civil war which soon drew in rival forces from across Europe, taking sides for and against the government. In his published memoir, Simon referred to the emotional and political impact of the Spanish civil war as the 'Spanish syndrome'. He mentions briefly that John Cornford, a leader of the CP who was an 'exact contemporary' of Simon's at Trinity College, was one of the first to join the International Brigades in Spain, only to be 'tragically killed on the Cordoba front … in December 1936 – a death which had a profound and lasting impact on many of his contemporaries'.[79]

Some of Simon's contemporaries discussed these issues in greater detail, and much more eloquently. Eric Hobsbawm, for example, evocatively recalled the conflicts and emotions of the time. Spain was the focal point for these, even if Hobsbawm hardly experienced the civil war himself, having been expelled from Spain after wandering without papers around the town of Puigcerdà, near the border with France.[80] Another contemporary, the poet W.H. Auden, described the connection with Spain even more poignantly. Auden had also been educated at Gresham's School, although well before Simon, and he went on to Christ Church, Oxford, to study English. His was the generation that experienced the General Strike of 1926 as students, rather than European fascism and war, but after beginning as an English teacher in independent schools, he too became embroiled in the Spanish Civil War.[81] He went to Spain with a medical unit organised by the Spanish Medical Aid Committee in

January 1937, and arrived in Barcelona before travelling south to Valencia. He then reached the front at Sarinena before returning home to London.[82] Such an experience might not have been exceptional in itself, but it produced the extraordinary poem 'Spain', written after Auden returned to England. This poem has an underlying ambivalence about the conflict, and a distaste that borders on disillusionment towards the end, with its bleak conclusion:

> The stars are dead. The animals will not look.
> We are left alone with our day and the time is short, and
> History to the defeated
> May say Alas but cannot help or pardon.[83]

Here, Auden is already retreating into the desolation he was to express in his later poem, 'September 1, 1939': 'Uncertain and afraid / As the clever hopes expire / Of a low dishonest decade...'.[84] Auden is significant in relation to Simon because he expresses the ideals of the time as a fleeting and fraudulent illusion. Simon meanwhile is certain rather than uncertain, hopeful rather than disillusioned, refreshed rather than disappointed by 'the flat ephemeral pamphlet and the boring meeting', (as in Auden's poem 'Spain').

Another case was the author George Orwell, a product of Eton College but not of Oxford or Cambridge, who also ventured to Spain and left a classic record of his experiences in *Homage to Catalonia*. Orwell supported the Trotskyist group POUM rather than the CP which followed Moscow's political line, and so was in a position to see at close hand the compromises and betrayals among the opposition left-wing groups, or as he put it 'the cruelty, squalor, and futility of war and in this particular case of the intrigues, the persecutions, the lies and the misunderstandings'.[85] His early idealism was rapidly shed, and his life almost lost in the process.

Simon's experience and its legacy proved to be different from all of these. It was Spain above all else that seemed to inspire him, and to harden his resolve and commitment. His brother Roger, who had also joined the CP and was working in Chester, was also highly committed to working for Spain, setting up a Spanish aid committee and supporting fundraising.[86] Brian himself wrote to his parents in the early months of 1937, complaining bitterly that Malaga had just fallen to the nationalist forces, which were made up, as he pointed out, of twelve-thousand Italians, ten-thousand Germans and five-thousand foreign legionnaires. He lamented: 'It looks as though Spain will certainly fall unless England does something. No generation has been brought up on the edge of a volcano like this one has.' The National Government had been inactive, while the Labour Party, he argued, had done little except criticise the CP. 'How can they say this,' he asked, 'when 14 members of the CP have already been killed in Spain fighting for democracy I don't know, it passes my comprehension.' He concluded sadly: 'The outlook is bleaker than it has ever been.'[87] According to Hugh Thomas's magisterial study of the Spanish Civil War, the fall of Malaga in February 1937 was 'a skirmish only'.[88] Yet it had an emotional impact on Simon and other sympathisers following events as closely as they could.

A key difference perhaps between Simon's experience of the Spanish Civil War and that of many of his contemporaries was that Simon did not witness it at first hand but only vicariously through the reports of the liberal newspapers, the *Manchester Guardian* and the *News Chronicle*. Thus the emotions and betrayals of the front line were obscured as he watched from afar, without even the television coverage of the postwar era, and the ideals came across unrefined, impinging on the daily life of this student and confirming his awareness of the world around him.

The IOE's base at that time was in Southampton Row, 'a far cry from the Great Court at Trinity' as Simon later remembered, but 'a friendly place, full of bustling activity, with staff and students merging most effectively'. Intriguingly, he also related this familiar, comforting scene to the international conflicts of the time, and specifically to the war in Spain. As he recalled it, 'In the event of civil commotion, we used to feel, it would be good to hold the Institute since, set at a slight angle near the High Holborn Road crossing, it commanded the whole of Southampton Row to Aldwych to the south, and up to Euston Road north.' This notion he described as the 'Spanish syndrome', which he averred with some nostalgia 'was much on our minds in those days!'[89]

Moreover, the enduring significance of this distant international episode may have been not only the effect of nostalgia. One of his few attempts to explain his enduring commitment to the CP in the 1950s and 1960s, when most of the intellectuals of the 1930s had left it or wavered in their loyalty, was in his unpublished autobiography. There, he recalled his involvement in the CP with greater depth and candour than in his published memoir. He also acknowledged the errors of the CP and its failure to take an independent line after the USSR invaded Hungary in 1956. Nevertheless, overall he was unapologetic, quoting the French singer Edith Piaf: 'Je ne regrette rien, as Piaf sang.' Indeed, he insisted, 'If I had to choose again, I would have taken the same road, only perhaps with detours now and again.'[90] In 1935, when he had joined the CP,

THE MAKING OF A MARXIST INTELLECTUAL

this had been the only serious and decent option in his view, and, 'Having joined, I found myself increasingly bound in, a connection reinforced by very many personal ties, with the living and the dead.'[91] This lasting commitment and political idealism certainly marks him out by comparison with the rapidly sourced Auden and Orwell, and even with Hobsbawm, who stayed with the CP in the 1950s but was publicly critical of it.

Another aspect of Simon's activities at this time that was to have lasting resonance was his contribution to education reform activities in Britain. Thanks to the political connections of his parents, and still concealing his membership of the CP, at the age of 23 he was made the assistant secretary of the Labour Party's education advisory committee. This committee was seeking to respond to the recommendations of the Spens report on secondary education, which was published at the end of 1938.[92] The Spens report had favoured the development of a system of secondary schools in which there would be different types of school with 'parity of esteem'. The Labour Party committee, after some debate, found that such an approach would not meet its objective of secondary education for all, and instead proposed that multilateral schools for pupils of all abilities should be considered further. A paper by a leading member of the London County Council education committee, Barbara Drake, argued strongly that local education authorities (LEAs) should be 'required to plan a systematic development of "multilateral" schools as *an immediate practical policy*' [emphasis in the original]. This would establish between children from different backgrounds 'that common social and cultural background which is the basis of all true democracy', while breaking down the social distinctions between them.[93] Simon's ringside seat to this debate put him in a strong position to make the case for multilateral schools in the years after the war.

Conclusions

Simon passed his diploma examination at the IOE, as he recalled in his unpublished autobiography, 'in spite of my faineant attitude', and was now a trained, recognised '"professional" teacher, though it was to be nearly another seven years before I tried my hand on a class of actual schoolchildren'.[94] His father retained high hopes for him, and 'The perspective was that, after spending some time teaching, I should move into administration through a local authority and finally, with education as an area of expertise, into parliament (presumably as a Labour MP).'[95] Nevertheless, by 1939, on the eve of the Second World War, Simon's intellectual and political development was far advanced. This showed the combined effects of his early learning experiences and schooling. For all his privileges, these had left a negative mark, and his search for alternatives had led him to the CP, an idealised view of history and the potential of humanity, and hopes for educational reform.

His own verdict on these experiences was expressed in a letter baring his soul to his then fiancée, Joan Peel, who he married a few months later. First, he outlined his own ambitions, which were akin to the Soviet ideal of 'changing man': 'I would like to plan new Universities for new needs, and discuss it with all sorts of people in all kinds of jobs with different experiences. I would like to play a part in developing new men with new qualities – which will be possible.' This prospect, he continued, contrasted with his own learning experiences:

> The waste of people is appalling…. When I was at Greshams I was a very simple lad not particularly intelligent. But like most people most of the really creative instincts and emotions had been driven out of me, or deep underground. [I] had been repressed perhaps by the constant care of father and mother who kept me tightly in hand, partly by the bullying hectoring and intellectual hammering of a horrible bourgeois prep school.

Moreover, he complained:

> I had always lived at home with servants and not known many people, or been immersed in great schools in the middle of the country. Absolutely cut off and isolated from anything. There was nothing for me to write about, nothing for me to put my energies to which would satisfy that feeling…. And if that happened to me it happens to scores and scores of other people in various forms. And when we can find a way of giving scope to that latent energy – what people there will be!

He had taken advantage of the opportunities offered by his elite upbringing, schooling and university education, while also reacting intellectually against his own social background and in favour of a utopian political ideal. Still in his early twenties, as war approached, he was the very image of a Marxist intellectual.

Notes

1 M. Stocks, *Ernest Simon of Manchester*, Manchester University Press, Manchester, 1963, 79.
2 1921 national census, entry for Brian Simon.
3 Stocks, *Ernest Simon*, 1963, 80.
4 B. Simon, unpublished autobiography, 1990s, chapter 2.
5 Stocks, *Ernest Simon*, 1963, 4–5.
6 B. Simon, *In Search of a Grandfather: Henry Simon of Manchester, 1835–1899*, Pendene Press, Leicester, 1997, chapter 5.
7 B. Jones, 'Simon, Ernest Emil Darwin', in *Oxford Dictionary of National Biography*, vol. 50, 653–56, Oxford University Press, Oxford, 1960; B. Jones, 'Simon, Shena Dorothy', in *Oxford DNB*, vol. 50, 669–70.
8 Stocks, *Ernest Simon*, 1963, 49.
9 Stocks, *Ernest Simon*, 1963, 14–15, 54–5.
10 J. Martin, 'Shena D. Simon and English education: Inside/out?', *History of Education*, 32/5 (2003), 477–94; H.Y. Ku, 'In pursuit of social democracy: Shena Simon and the reform of secondary education in England, 1908–1948', *History of Education*, 47/1 (2018), 54–72.
11 E. Simon, letter to B. Simon, 1935 (Brian Simon papers, IOE, SIM/4/5/10). See also H.Y. Ku, 'Education for democratic citizenship: Ernest Simon's ideals of liberal democracy and citizenship education in England, 1934–1944', *Historia y Memoria de la Educación*, 7, 2018, 499–532.
12 See S. Tomlinson, 'Phrenology, education and the politics of human nature: The thought and influence of George Combe', *History of Education*, 26/1 (1997), 1–22; M. Cruickshank, 'The open-air movement in English education', *Paedagogica Historica*, 17/1 (1977), 61–74; E. Olssen, 'Truby King and the Plunket Society: An analysis of a prescriptive ideology', *New Zealand Journal of History*, 14/2 (1981), 3–23.
13 E. Simon, Notes on Brian's progress as an infant (Brian Simon papers, IOE archive). See G. McCulloch, T. Woodin, 'Learning and liberal education: The case of the Simon family, 1912–1939', *Oxford Review of Education*, 36/2 (2010), 187–201.
14 E. Simon, Notes on Brian's progress.
15 E. Simon, Notes on Brian's progress.
16 E. Simon, diary, May 1927 (Brian Simon papers, IOE, SIM/4/5/1/4).
17 B. Simon to E. and S. Simon, 20 August 1940 (Brian Simon papers, IOE).
18 B. Simon, note, 'Antonia Simon (Tony), 1917–1929', 28 August 1997 (Brian Simon papers, IOE).
19 B. Simon, unpublished autobiography, 1990s (Brian Simon papers, IOE).
20 See e.g. H. May, K. Nawrotski, L. Prochner (eds), *Kindergarten Narratives on Froebelian Education: Transnational investigations*, Bloomsbury, London, 2017; H. Wasmuth, *Froebel's Pedagogy of Kindergarten Play: Modifications in Germany and the United States*, Routledge, London, 2020.
21 B. Simon, unpublished autobiography (Brian Simon papers, IOE).
22 Oakdene, school report on Brian Simon, Michaelmas term 1921, comment by M.F. Percy (Brian Simon papers, IOE).
23 E. Simon, Notes on Brian's progress (Brian Simon papers, IOE).
24 B. Simon, unpublished autobiography, chapter 2 (Brian Simon papers, IOE).
25 B. Simon, unpublished autobiography, chapter 2 (Brian Simon papers, IOE).
26 B. Simon, notebook on early development (Brian Simon papers, IOE).
27 B. Simon, notebook on early development (Brian Simon papers, IOE).
28 J.R. Eccles, *My Life as a Public School Master*, Blackburn, 1948.
29 J.R. Eccles, *My Life as a Public School Master*, 38–9.
30 J.R. Eccles, *My Life as a Public School Master*, 39.
31 See G. Greene (ed), *The Old School*, Oxford, OUP, 1934/1984; S. Spender, *The Autobiography of Stephen Spender*, 1951.
32 R. Simon, 'Gresham's School – Comments', 8 December 1997 (Brian Simon papers, SIM/4/5/1/7, IOE).
33 R. Simon, letter to B. Simon, 8 December 1997 (Brian Simon papers, SIM/4/3/1/7, IOE).
34 *The Gresham* school magazine, 12 December 1931.

35 B. Simon, letter to E. Simon, S. Simon, n.d. [September 1930?] (Brian Simon papers, SIM/4/5/1/4, IOE).
36 B. Simon, essay, 'My point of view', 1932 (Brian Simon papers, IOE).
37 B. Simon, essay, 'My point of view', 1932 (Brian Simon papers, IOE).
38 See R. Skidelsky, *Politicians and the Slump: The Labour government of 1929–1931*, Macmillan, London, 1967.
39 R. Simon to B. Simon, 11 May 1932 (Brian Simon papers, IOE).
40 R. Simon to B. Simon, 11 May 1932 (Brian Simon papers, IOE).
41 B. Simon, unpublished autobiography (Brian Simon papers, IOE).
42 National Institute of Industrial Psychology, Report on Brian Simon, 2 May 1933 (Brian Simon papers, IOE).
43 B. Simon, letter to R. Simon, 19 November 1932 (Brian Simon papers, IOE).
44 See S. Matthews, '"Say not the struggle naught availeth": *Scrutiny* (1932–53)', in P. Brooker, A. Thacker (eds), *The Oxford Critical and Cultural History of Modernist Magazines*, vol. 1, Britain and Ireland 1880–1955, Oxford University Press, Oxford, 2009, 844 (article 833–56).
45 B. Simon to R. Simon, 19 November 1932 (Brian Simon papers, IOE).
46 E. Simon, letter to B. Simon, 13 June 1933 (Brian Simon papers, IOE).
47 B. Simon, Gresham's school report, Michaelmas term 1932 (Brian Simon papers, IOE).
48 B. Simon, unpublished autobiography, chapter 3 (Brian Simon papers, IOE).
49 See e.g. H. Pelling, *The British Communist Party: A historical profile*, Macmillan, London, 1958.
50 S. Crowe, 'The Zinoviev letter: A reappraisal', *Journal of Contemporary History*, 10/3 (1975), 407–32; G. Bennett, *The Zinoviev Letter: The conspiracy that never dies*, OUP, Oxford, 2018.
51 See C. Andrew, *The Defence of the Realm: The authorised history of MI5*, Penguin, London, 2010.
52 See e.g. G. McCulloch, '"Teachers and missionaries": The Left Book Club as an educational agency', *History of Education*, 14/2, 1985; B. Pimlott, *Labour and the Left in the 1930s*, CUP, Cambridge, 1977.
53 E. Hobsbawm, *Interesting Times: A twentieth-century life*, Allen Lane, London, 2002, 111.
54 E. Hobsbawm, *Interesting Times*, 123.
55 E. Hobsbawm, *Interesting Times*, 119.
56 B. Simon, unpublished autobiography, chapter 3 (Brian Simon papers, IOE).
57 E. Simon to B. Simon, 9 January 1935 (Brian Simon papers, IOE, DC/SIM/4/5).
58 E. Simon to B. Simon, 15 January 1935 (Brian Simon papers, IOE, DC/SIM/4/5).
59 B. Simon to E. Simon, 31 January 1935 (Brian Simon papers, IOE, DC/SIM/4/5).
60 B. Simon to E. Simon, 31 January 1935 (Brian Simon papers, IOE, DC/SIM/4/5).
61 B. Simon to E. and S. Simon, n.d. (1935) (Brian Simon papers, DC/SIM/4/5).
62 B. Simon, unpublished autobiography, chapter 3 (Brian Simon papers, IOE).
63 See M. Dobb, *The Collected Works of Maurice Dobb*, 7 vols, London, Routledge, 2012; Hans S. Despain, 'The political economy of Maurice Dobb: history, theory and the economics of reproduction, crisis, and transformation' (PhD thesis, University of Utah, 2011).
64 B. Simon, letter to E. and S. Simon, 31 January 1935 (Brian Simon papers, DC/SIM/4/5). Lucas was a classical English scholar, an anti-fascist campaigner but not a Marxist.
65 B. Simon, letter to [check], (Brian Simon papers, IOE, DC/SIM/4/5/1/26).
66 E. Simon to B. Simon, 2 February 1936 (Brian Simon papers, IOE).
67 E. Simon to B. Simon, June 1937 (Brian Simon papers, IOE).
68 See R. Aldrich, T. Woodin, *The Institute of Education: From training college to global institution*, 2nd edition, UCL Press, London, 2021, ch. 5.
69 B. Simon, *A Life in Education*, 15, 16, 19.
70 B. Simon, *A Life in Education*, 19.
71 B. Simon, unpublished autobiography (Brian Simon papers, IOE).
72 F. Clarke, *Education and Social Change: An English interpretation*, Sheldon Press, London, 1940.
73 F. Clarke, *Education and Social Change*, 66–7.
74 See also G. McCulloch, S. Cowan, *A Social History of Educational Studies and Research*, London, Routledge, 2018, esp. ch 3.
75 See e.g. F.W. Mitchell, *Sir Fred Clarke: Master-Builder, 1880–1952*, New Jersey, Prentice-Hall, 1967.
76 B. Simon, 'The function of the school in society' (Brian Simon papers, SIM/5/2/5, IOE).
77 B. Simon, 'The function of the school in society' (Brian Simon papers, SIM/5/2/5, IOE).
78 B. Simon, 'The history of education', in J.W. Tibble, *The Study of Education*, Routledge, London, 1966, 95.

79 Simon, *A Life in Education*, 4.
80 Hobsbawm, *Interesting Times*, 339–40.
81 H. Carpenter, *W.H. Auden: A biography*, George Allen and Unwin, London, 1981.
82 H. Carpenter, *W.H. Auden*, 214–15.
83 Auden, *Spain*, 1937.
84 Auden, *September 1, 1939*, 1939.
85 G. Orwell, *Homage to Catalonia*, Penguin, London, 1938 / 1977, 240.
86 R. Simon, letter to E. and S. Simon, 2 May 1936 (Brian Simon papers, IOE, SIM/4/5/1/17); Letter to B. Simon, 5 January 1937 (Brian Simon papers, IOE, SIM/4/5/1/17).
87 B. Simon, letter to E. and S. Simon, n.d. [1937] (Brian Simon papers, IOE).
88 H. Thomas, *The Spanish Civil War*, 3rd edition, Penguin, London, 1961 / 1977, 582. Yet it had an emotional impact on Simon and other sympathisers following events as closely as they could.
89 B. Simon, *A Life in Education*, 16.
90 B. Simon, unpublished autobiography (Brian Simon papers, IOE).
91 B. Simon, unpublished autobiography (Brian Simon papers, IOE).
92 Board of Education, *Secondary Education*, HMSO, London, 1938.
93 B. Drake, paper LG109, 'Memorandum on the Report of the Consultative Committee on Secondary Education', February 1939 (Brian Simon papers, IOE, DC/SIM/4/5/1/23).
94 B. Simon, unpublished autobiography (Brian Simon papers, IOE).
95 B. Simon, unpublished autobiography (Brian Simon papers, IOE).

3
Soldier and schoolteacher in the 1940s

Brian Simon signed up to join the British Army in 1940, was commissioned in October 1941 and posted to London District Signals. However, he continued to be under suspicion, and was followed by the security services. His brother Roger, also a soldier in the British Army, had his application for a commission turned down due to his political associations. After the war, Brian became a teacher in different Manchester schools, including an unreorganised (post 1944 Education Act) all-age school, Abbott Street School, that took children from seven to fourteen years of age, Yew Tree Central School, and Salford Grammar School, where he taught English and Economics. He agitated for reforms both within these schools and in the school system, through his local position in the CP. He was frustrated in his hopes for reform in his own schools and increasingly looked towards reforms at a national level, including the development of comprehensive education.

'A feisty, strong-minded woman'

Brian and Joan were a perfect match for each other. Their upbringing and education were of a kind, upper-class and English, leading to public school. Joan, whose family name Peel could be traced back to Sir Robert Peel, was born in 1915 to Captain Home Peel and Gwen (née Emmott). Her father was killed in action in the First World War, near Longueval in March 1918. Her maternal grandfather was Alfred Emmott, Liberal member of parliament for the northern city of Oldham from 1899 to 1911 and then raised to the peerage as Baron Emmott. Brian's mother, Shena, knew Joan's mother, Gwen, through their shared Liberal Party connections.[1] Brian could remind his parents that they knew Joan's family: 'Her mother is a bit queer but very nice – she knows Granny.'[2]

Their political beliefs were also of the same kind, and clearly they both had an independent streak. Joan was sent to Roedean, the leading girls' public school, in 1925, but left in 1932 without going on to university, working in a Montessori nursery school in the East End of London.[3] Brian explained to his parents that Joan 'broke away from Roedean etc and that sort of life at a moment's notice'. They had first met at an international conference held in Paris in spring 1939.[4] On 12 February 1941, they married, appropriately enough in a registry office in Manchester, with few people present and little fuss, neither of Brian's parents able to attend.[5] Brian described his new bride as being 'smallish with a charming face and brown hair, and with a considerable amount of energy and vitality'.[6] They were married for 61 years, until Brian's death in January 2002, and formed an exceptionally strong partnership in support of their shared commitment to education, Marxism, and the history of education. After Joan's death at the age of 90, in August 2005, the historian Ruth Watts, who knew her well, recalled in an obituary that she was 'a feisty, strong-minded woman whose sharp intelligence made her appear formidable to some', although, as Watts added, 'Those closer to her loved her for her warm-heartedness, humanity and passionate support of people and causes she believed in.'[7]

Brian and Joan were also both, and separately, under continued surveillance from the British security services, due to their Marxist sympathies and connections. Brian had been aware that such monitoring was likely once he had joined the CP in 1935, even though he made efforts to conceal his membership and his direct links with the CP's leaders. His brother Roger had also joined the CP in Manchester after graduating from Cambridge, even though he became a civil servant, and Brian had advised caution in his movements. As he wrote to him while still at Cambridge, 'Re CP I am keeping quiet. I asked James Klugmann about you, and he said it would be best if you were in contact direct with the Centre in Manchester.' This would mean that no one would know Roger in Chester, and only William Rust, a local party organiser, would know that he was in the party. Brian continued his letter to Roger: 'The point is that it is dangerous to write to the Headquarters in Manchester direct, as the letter will probably be opened, and Rust will have some cover address. I expect I have wrecked my chances by writing and telephoning to him!'[8] Roger later confirmed that after three years in the University Socialist Society, and under the influence of Keynesian economics, he had joined the CP in 1936 but was advised not to go public with this. His party education, he affirmed, was mainly from self-study and various classes at branch level which he attended from time to time, and also as a tutor on subjects such as political economy, trade unionism and the state.[9]

In fact, by this time Brian had already come to the attention of the security services. In April 1935, he was observed as being one of what was described as 'a party of 6 students and 2 girls' who came to the Ferndale district of Glamorgan in south Wales to canvas and distribute literature supporting Communist candidates in the local elections. Simon was driving a Morris Minor car to help convey communists to vote in the elections.[10] Within a few days, no less a figure than Colonel Sir Vernon Kell, the director of the security services (otherwise known as MI5) was sounding the alarm with an enquiry to the Chief Constable of the Manchester police force. Was this person, he asked, a member of the CP? 'I need hardly add that it is essential that this person should not become aware that he is the subject of interest.'[11] Simon was soon being followed routinely, and his possessions checked when returning from travelling overseas, for example at Dover in September 1937 on his return from Calais, when it was noted that 'A discreet search of his baggage by H.M. Customs revealed nothing of interest to Special Branch.'[12]

Quite separately, Joan's activities also came to the notice of the authorities at this time, in episodes later recounted by the then director-general of MI5, Brigadier Sir David Petrie. He recalled (for her security file, together with a photograph of her, described as 'five foot five inches in height, with grey eyes and fair hair') in 1944 that she had first come to his attention in 1937 when she paid a visit to Leningrad in the USSR. She had then supported the international secretariat of the world student movement as a personal secretary of Elizabeth Shields-Collins, the CP's agent for the World Youth Congress Movement (WYCM). Recent research has called attention to the importance of student activists for an international popular front movement embracing liberals and communists; the WYCM being both a means for the CP to broaden its appeal but also a vessel to support the shared interests of student liberals and communists to resist fascism and war.[13] According to Kevin P. Lavery, the involvement of several 'covert communists' such a Shield-Collins and Joan Peel on the WYCM national committee ensured that the Council was firmly under communist control.[14] Petrie also observed that Joan Peel had attended a meeting of the National Youth Campaign Committee of the Young Communist League in January 1939, and was the secretary of another organisation called 'Youth News for Intellectual Liberty' in 1941, as well as continuing to support the work of Elizabeth Shield-Collins.[15] Her work as a journalist at the well-respected *Times Educational Supplement* during the war received less attention.[16]

Brian Simon had also been active in these international youth movements. In 1939, he discussed plans for further international conferences with James Klugmann, his old school friend and his communist mentor at Cambridge. Klugmann was now the secretary of the 'Rassemblement Mondiale des Étudiants' (RME; World Student Association) and was arranging to hold an international conference of this association in Paris in August 1939. Brian explained to his parents: 'It is run by a sort of genius called James Klugmann, who I think I have told you about. He is a great friend of mine, and was at Greshams and Trinity.' Brian assured his parents: 'The organisation has a definite progressive type of policy: that is, it takes its stand again on what might be called the defence and extension of democracy.'[17] Apparently, he was now short of money for his activities. He had visited India and China the previous year to meet key political leaders, so a shortage of money was perhaps not surprising, but it is not clear whether Brian was aware of this background.[18] Brian therefore wrote to his father to ask whether he could speak at the conference, and also to seek financial support for this organisation.[19]

Ernest was always generous in supporting his son financially, but drew the line at giving money to the CP. He had already provided for Brian's financial security, giving to him and his brother Roger 5,000 ordinary shares in his company, Henry Simon Ltd. This would save on taxation and potentially on death duties; also, by giving him a stake in the current system, Ernest added, tongue in cheek, that it might turn Brian into a capitalist. However, Ernest insisted that Brian should keep the shares while Ernest himself was still alive, and that he should not sell or give any away without his permission, 'nor leave them during my life to the Communist Party'.[20] In any case, the approach of a European and soon a world war was about to reduce the scope for this kind of international collaboration, in the short term at least.

Thus, the marriage of Brian and Joan was of two kindred spirits, both independently minded but committed to Marxism, and now set on a common path in an uncertain world that was hastening into conflict and war.

Soldier

The ideal of an anti-fascist 'popular front' had drawn progressives, liberals and communists together during the 1930s, and these efforts gained urgency with the military advances made by Germany in 1938–1939. By the summer of 1939 war seemed inevitable, but it was at this moment that Germany and the USSR signed a non-aggression pact. Germany then launched an invasion of Poland, and Britain and France declared war on Germany, while the USSR remained neutral. These events served to divide erstwhile proponents of a progressive alliance against fascism. What many had anticipated as being an international war against fascism was now recast by sympathisers of the USSR as an imperialist war. The British CP soon changed its line, to oppose the war and support the stance of the USSR. Marxist intellectuals such as Brian Simon were left in a dilemma, not for the last time, about how to direct their efforts and energies.[21] Simon himself claimed privately that although he was often accused of being against the war, 'I am not against the war, although I admit freely to being rather worried about some aspects of it', and moreover was 'anti-Government and rather apt to be pro-Russia'.[22] Doubts and divisions were to continue until June 1941, when Hitler turned on his erstwhile partner and attempted to invade the USSR. Britain, holding out against Germany in the west, quickly agreed to support its new eastern ally, and the British CP once again changed its political line to support the war effort. By this time, Brian and Joan had also joined forces on a personal level to begin their own formidable partnership.

In 1940, despite the doubts of many Marxists about the nature of the war, Simon demonstrated his own support for the war effort by joining the British Army as an ordinary soldier. In the summer, posted to an infantry training depot with the Dorset Regiment in Dorchester, he confided to his parents that 'it is rather like being back at school!' – a strong statement given his experience at Gresham's. Indeed, he complained: 'Any independent thought or initiative will be frowned upon, and it is difficult for someone with fairly strong views and used to discussion and argument to listen quietly to hair-raisingly jingoistic morale upraising speeches of one of our officers. However, it is easy to get used to.'[23] Perhaps for the first time, he was now in close and regular contact with working-class people of his own age, and he found that he engaged well with them. They had little interest in politics, he reported, and nearly all read the main newspaper aimed at working-class readers, the *Daily Mirror*. 'I have revised my opinion of this journal, in some ways it seems quite good.'[24]

Simon's strict army regime contrasted with the life that he continued to lead as the elected president of NUS, with meetings continuing to take place around the country. His ambitions for the NUS were high, as he explained to his father: 'As you have realised, it has been my purpose to divert the NUS and the students into really constructive channels of activity, activity which all types of people, whatever their opinions – political and otherwise – can realise as constructive and worthwhile.'[25] An interview with him in *Student News* in February 1940 depicted him as the 'blue-eyed wonder boy of the student movement'. This noted that he gave his long family connection with education as the reason why he never learned anything at school. He had travelled extensively in Europe: 'Only in Europe, I'm afraid,' he says apologetically, 'Yugo-slavia, Sweden, and the usual countries.' He observed that he had no habits but was fond of climbing mountains, and that his nonconformist conscience always made him think twice before doing anything.[26] More seriously, he argued that the war was endangering the universities, and that their grant should be increased, with military training postponed to the end of the university course.[27] He later recalled that he had received strong support in his stance from his former director at the Institute of Education (IOE), Fred Clarke, who had invited Brian to visit him, to express his agreement and encouragement for what the NUS was trying to say.[28]

The highlight of Simon's NUS presidency was perhaps the British Student Congress held in Leeds in April 1940. The BSC had been organised by Simon himself as an initiative to represent student opinion about universities and the war, raising the possibility to discuss a range of social, political and economic problems.[29] It would be as he put it, 'an experiment in education for democracy', led by the students themselves.[30] In his speech, he attacked social inequality and the aloofness of the older universities, and called for the idea of service to society to be the basis of university work rather than knowledge for its own sake.[31] The idea of a charter of students' rights and responsibilities was also raised at the congress.[32] Overall, Simon was judged to have been highly successful both in his address and in his handling of the 500 delegates at the congress. According to the report of the event in the *Journal of Education*: 'It will be gathered that the Conference was very much alive, very earnest in its desire to remedy abuses, and sincere in expressing even unorthodox opinions with moderation and respect for opposing views.'[33] Ernest Simon would have been impressed by such a verdict. Indeed, Brian stressed the importance of tolerance of different opinions in his subsequent contributions, combined with an idealistic vision of the future which had become a hallmark of his ideas, in which universities might be converted into 'centres of culture connected with the needs of the people, into institutions which can help humanity forward into a just and peaceful world, a world in which we can take our examinations with different feelings to those we have today'.[34]

Simon's work with the NUS eventually led to his first published book, *A Student's View of the Universities*. Slight in appearance, this made a powerful case for radical reform of universities and their curriculum. It began with a historical overview of their growth and development and an analysis of their present position in the social process. It argued that universities were key points not only in the education system but also in the social structure. Their social function should be 'to help to make a reality of the social potentialities of the present time, and to discover how the development of science and technology can be devoted to the needs of man'.[35] An essential part of this activity was to make their students understand the prospects facing modern society. The curriculum should not be about study for its own sake, but to understand and address social changes, as 'centres of a vital and creative culture, shedding their light over thousands and millions of people in their locality, closely linked with daily activities and problems, and essentially, therefore, at the disposal of the people'.[36] Due to wartime conditions and with Simon himself now back in active army service, it was his father who ensured the publication of the book, delayed though it was until November 1943. No less a figure than R.H. Tawney, revered in the Labour Party for his strong support for secondary education for all and radical educational reform, lent his approval to the young man's contribution in a review of this work in the *Manchester Guardian*: 'Mr Simon has rendered a genuine service to university education by explaining the reforms which are believed to be necessary by a considerable body of opinion among those who have received it.'[37]

Back at his army camp, having been moved to larger barracks at Catterick, near Richmond in north Yorkshire, in 1941 Simon applied for a commission. To all appearances he was the perfect candidate, with his height, impeccable speech and public-school background. His military training at Gresham's had confirmed that he was officer material. Simon also made a favourable impression on his commanding officer, Lt.Col. J.R. Pinsent, who reported that his military character was very good, and his general character was 'a good type, promising well as an officer'. According to Pinsent, moreover, Simon had character and his influence appeared to be entirely in the right direction; there was no indication of any subversive tendencies or propaganda. Overall, he concluded, 'A very promising cadet. Doing quite well technically and has a good report as regards leadership.'[38] Yet there was a problem. A communist cell was identified at the Catterick garrison which involved among others Peter Astbury, a contemporary at Gresham's, and Simon was reported to be associated with this. Major W.A. Alexander of MI5 soon raised concerns: there was a record of Simon in connection with his communist activities, and 'There can, therefore, be no possible question of his being allowed to receive a Commission, until such a time as we are completely satisfied with regard to his loyalty.'[39] However, Simon's commanding officer seems to have been firm in his support, and he made a point of remarking in his report: 'If he has in the past taken interest in Communist activities I should be inclined to put it down to the influence of Cambridge university. Many undergraduates do so without of any necessity accepting their doctrines and subsequently indulging any propaganda.'[40] Simon was commissioned in October 1941 and posted to London District Signals.

Simon's travails in the army were not over. He joined GHQ Liaison Regiment, a special unit with the code name of 'Phantom', as a signals officer with a role in reconnaissance, and rose to the temporary rank of captain. The headquarters of the Phantom regiment were in the Richmond Hill Hotel in Richmond, Surrey, and its officers' mess at Pembroke Lodge, a Georgian house in Richmond Park. His movements continued to be monitored, and it was found to be odd and rather suspicious that his movements in New York, Africa and Sicily were difficult to trace. It was suspected that he maintained contacts with the CP through his wife and friends, although there was no firm evidence.[41]

His brother Roger was not as fortunate in his attempt to be commissioned after he enlisted in May 1942. A special-branch note recalled that on leaving Cambridge, Roger had become articled to the Town Clerk of Chester and qualified as a solicitor in 1939. The record seemed somewhat mixed in terms of his political sympathies. He had 'dabbled' in Fabianism and Communism at Cambridge and was the son of 'politically-minded' parents. As a soldier, it was observed that he was 'not exactly a barrack-room lawyer but a somewhat critical person', and was 'popular and will make a leader'. His commanding officer was also sympathetic but hesitated. On the one hand, 'He was in civil life a practising solicitor and a better educated town clerk than most in the ranks.' On the other, Roger had reported to him that lectures of the Army Bureau of Current Affairs were being neglected; the ABCA had largely left-wing tendencies, so this apparently counted against him. He was 'tall and good at games', and his CO would have considered recommending him for a commission 'if this report did not hang over him'.[42] Continued monitoring could not identify any activities of a subversive nature, nor attempts to influence his fellow soldiers to his way of thinking, but it was recommended to keep him under surveillance for a further eighteen months.[43] A further note recognised that no positive evidence could be found, but insisted: 'I do not like him.' His articles to the newspaper 'although NOT subversive have a strong Leftish Tendency'. Overall, 'My impression is that he is being very careful to keep at the right sight side of the law whilst he is quietly keeping controversial subjects to the fore. It is fair to state that the above is my <u>impression</u>.'[44]

Another report on Roger Simon was still unable to produce any clear evidence of disloyal activities, but this time it was asserted that 'there appears to be little doubt that his activities are calculated to undermine loyalty and morale in the unit'. An interview to consider him as an officer was cancelled, and despite his father attempting to intercede on his behalf at the highest levels, his application was turned down in a special case ruling. Brigadier A.D. Buchanan-Smith, the Director of the Selection of Personnel at the War Office in London, sent instructions that 'If he desires a reason, will you please say that you have been informed that he was lacking in drive and qualities of leadership in comparison with the others who have been selected. He should be discouraged from making any further applications for a commission.'[45] Roger did indeed make further applications, but these were consistently rejected, and he was also not accepted for the Army Education Corps after the War Office objected.[46] In an autobiographical note several years later, he recalled that he had worked as an instrument mechanic in England and then France and Belgium, becoming lance-corporal and then sergeant, but was never able to secure a commission.[47]

Thus, Brian Simon and his wife and brother continued to live under suspicion of communist sympathies and subversive activities during the Second World War, despite Brian's and Roger's work in the British Army and Joan's efforts at the *Times Educational Supplement*.

Schoolteacher

After the end of the Second World War in the summer of 1945, a general election returned the Labour Party for the first time as the party with a large majority of MPs, and Clement Attlee became prime minister. The new Labour government was responsible for introducing a wide range of social reforms, including the implementation of the Education Act of 1944. While the Act itself had not mentioned different types of secondary school in the new framework of secondary education for all children up to the age of fourteen (soon to become fifteen), there was strong pressure within the new Ministry of Education and in many LEAs for a 'tripartite' system of selective grammar schools and secondary technical schools, with the majority of pupils going at the age of eleven going into non-selective secondary modern schools on the basis of failure to pass an '11-plus' examination. Only a few LEAs favoured the alternative approach of a multilateral or comprehensive school for pupils of all abilities and aptitudes, which Simon had supported since before the war, and to which he argued Labour had already committed itself.[48] As the Labour government showed its willingness to accept differentiation between schools Simon became fully engaged in a debate over the future of secondary education.

Simon left the army in December 1945, and within a fortnight after demobilisation, but over seven years after completing his training, he was teaching in a school in Manchester. He spent the next five years as a schoolteacher in Manchester and Salford. He commented later that, in retrospect, these five years were 'crucial and formative in terms of my own educational outlook'.[49]

Testimonials provided for Simon while he was a student at the IOE served him well in securing a teaching position, highlighting his character and his commitment. For example, Professor Ernest Barker, chairman of the University Board of History and vice-president of the University Education Society at the University of Cambridge, noted that Simon had guided and inspired a movement among undergraduates of different faculties in his final year at Cambridge to discuss curriculum, teaching and examinations in their various subjects, including history, economics, languages, mathematics and natural sciences. Barker concluded that this activity reflected well on Simon, and in particular demonstrated his interest in the problems of education, his ability to get things done, and his capacity to enable committees to work effectively.[50] Maurice Dobb, his economics tutor at Cambridge, observed that Simon had worked under his supervision during part of his course, for part two of the Economics Tripos. Dobb pointed out that Simon had a high level of intelligence, was well educated, and possessed a well-rounded, pleasing personality, with interests in education and social problems.[51]

At the IOE, his tutor, D. Gurrey, and the deputy director, H.R. Hamley, attested that he had spent most of his teaching practice for his diploma course at the City of London School (an independent school), where he taught English and Economics. They commented that he was 'a man of integrity, with high ideals, a sense of humour and engaging personality'. Moreover, they continued, he was a clear-minded and effective teacher. Indeed, they added:

> He brings a critical and well stocked mind to his work, and the handling of his subject has variety, dignity, courtesy and thoroughness. He handles his classes with dignity, courtesy and firmness. He will undoubtedly be a much-valued member of a

school staff. His prowess at rugby football, cricket, hockey, and swimming, and his musical gifts, enable him to play a useful part in the general life of a school.[52]

Clearly, Simon had strong potential as a teacher. W.T. Stevenson, the chief inspector of schools in Manchester, interviewed him and arranged for him to go initially to Yew Tree Central, which was to be designated as a multilateral school in a difficult part of the city.[53] According to Stevenson, Simon was keenly interested in educational research: 'Problems of classification and grouping of pupils, of social studies and social education of pupils' interests, and of teacher-pupil relationships, are among the problems to which he has given thought.'[54] Despite his strongly held educational and social convictions, however, Simon found it difficult and often frustrating to try to make headway with them as a teacher in the schools.

At Yew Tree Central School, in the Lent Term of 1946, he noted that the intake of about 120 children per year were organised into three classes, 1A, 1 Alpha and 1 Beta, mainly in accordance with their marks in the eleven-plus examination, and were tested again towards the end of the first year with the Simpler Junior Tests. The teachers he found to be mainly professional and collegial. However, school subjects were in 'water-tight compartments taught by "specialist" teachers', with the teachers tending to turn into instructors. Classes were too large at about 35–40 pupils in each, and the latest equipment was lacking. It was not possible to give individual attention to children, while every class in all subjects had 'bright, medium and backward' pupils and it was the 'bright children' who suffered most in his view. He was critical of many aspects of the school, but saw it as a good school in general. There was, he concluded, good potential for the future: 'The opportunity exists for a really good young head with ideas to make the multilateral school into something quite unique in the county, providing he gets the necessary facilities (equipment, teachers etc) and support that he will undoubtedly need.'[55] Yet this was hardly the account of a teacher who had made a strong impression on the ideas and practices of the school, and he appears to have been rather isolated in his thinking.

The same was true of his experience at Abbott Street School in the summer of 1946. This was an unreorganised all-age school that took children from seven to fourteen years of age. The environment, he noted, 'could not have been much worse'. It was located in a derelict slum area of the city: 'The lights have to be used in summer in some of the classrooms because of the closeness of the nearby buildings and the smoke and dirt which settles daily on the windows.' The school building had been erected in 1875, and the playground was very small, and surrounded by a high brick wall. On the other hand, he found the teachers to be keen, devoted and professional, and mainly traditional in their methods of teaching. He was impressed with provision for school meals, now made compulsory under the 1944 Education Act. Sixty per cent of children took the midday meal, and, he reflected, 'There is no doubt what a tremendously important reform this is. The head master ran the meals extraordinarily well, all children always finished the meals and liked them (in contrast to Yew Tree where they scarcely ever finished their meals and definitely disliked them). The food was well cooked and normally attractive.' In his own teaching, he concentrated on class management, but was conscious of his own inadequacy, and more broadly the 'lack of a clear and concrete lead from the educational world generally on the whole question of basic educational theory and its concrete application in the schools'.[56] Again, though, there is evidence here that even in these depressed conditions, he was something of a lone voice as a teacher in challenging the underlying approach of the school.

E.G. Simm, the headmaster of Salford Grammar School, where Simon was a member of staff from September 1947, confirmed that Simon taught English to all forms throughout the school, including the fifth form and both upper- and lower-sixth divisions of the school. He had broken new ground by starting Economics as a Higher School Certificate in the sixth form, his teaching of English was viewed as being satisfactory for younger and older pupils alike, and he had worked out an impressive scheme for a social-study project to be undertaken with the fourth form involving a study of the life and work of people in Salford. Apparently he was also prominent in the general life of the school. He was a fine cricketer who coached the first eleven. He had helped to build up the junior drama group. He gave advice and counsel, was a splendid colleague, and appeared fitted to a position of greater responsibility.[57]

Yet frustration persisted in his experience at Salford Grammar School, reflected in his surviving diary notes from July 1948. He was frustrated first of all by the emphasis on examinations: 'Here we rely on marks, marks, marks to keep them going. Frighten them with School Certificate and Higher School Certificate. The modern school lacks objectives, ours are the wrong ones.'[58] He complained bitterly about the 'obtuseness of the traditional teacher'. One of these, he notes, 'exults (almost) over the fact that 3S gets an average of 16% in German. "They're hopeless."' When Simon suggests that the subject is too difficult, meaning that it us not taught in the right way, the other teacher 'erupts'. Simon concludes: '"Backwardness" is a problem of the grammar school as much as in the modern school (relatively). Hence the necessity for new methods.'[59]

A few days later, Simon finds himself finishing off the 'clerical work' at the school following the examinations and marking. With reports and comments to be completed on all of the pupils: 'All this rush happens at the end of each term, but particularly at the end of this one. Most of it could, of course, be done by clerical labour. Our teaching tends to suffer.'[60]

An incident in a staff meeting held later the same day further exposes Simon's isolation as a teacher: 'In the evening, a staff meeting, which, like most others, scarcely touches on "education", but is concerned with arrangements about next year's exams etc. and included a diatribe by Simon against the SSEC proposals.' He continues: 'It does not occur to these people that it may be them that is wrong, or rather the whole colossal system of which they are small cogs.' Indeed, he laments:

> It is surely clear enough 1) that they are failing to teach these boys because they teach in the wrong way i.e. too didactically and solely verbally, 2) that a totally different approach to learning is necessary in the case of the C stream and even some of the B stream as a necessity. Probably better results would be achieved if there were a different approach to the A stream as well.[61]

Simon was particularly concerned about pupils in the C-stream who were destined for failure in this system:

> But really there can be no doubt that as far as the grammar school is concerned, it is ruining the C stream boys and more by the excessive concentration on abstract narrative methods which neither focuses their interest nor develops their abilities ... They get little opportunities to use their abilities socially or in any other direction. These boys are considered 'backward' in this school, in a modern school they would be the leading and the most intelligent children.

These arguments reflected Simon's underlying belief that all children should be considered educable with innate potential. At the same time, he suggested that they might benefit if examinations were delayed to the age of 16 so that those who did not stay for so long might receive an educational certificate from the school rather than sitting for an external examination:

This does provide an opportunity to those schools prepared to experiment in that it would be possible for these boys not staying till 16 to take a course entirely free from University authority and control. A more realistic and active form of education could be developed for these children along the lines of project and activity work etc.

Simon's arguments however appear to have been little heeded at the school.[62]

While working as a teacher, Simon was also formulating radical ideas about educational change, especially in promoting the concept of the comprehensive school for all abilities. Following the typology of the Norwood Report of 1943, grammar schools were selective academic schools for about 15 per cent of pupils, modern schools were nonselective schools for the majority of children, and technical schools were intended to prepare pupils for commercial and industrial occupations.[63] Simon continued to strongly prefer the comprehensive-school model, and produced articles in the communist press to support this.

Simon had resumed his membership of the CP when he demobilised from the army, and soon became secretary of the Didsbury branch of the party. His branch was awarded a prize in 1947 for its high level of recruitment, and he also became a member of the district committee covering Lancashire and Cheshire. He also convened a Manchester group of the New Education Fellowship at this time. His educational interests merged with his political sympathies, as he later recalled in his unpublished autobiography: 'Educational issues were taken seriously by the Communist Party both nationally and locally, so political involvement also furthered educational involvement of a different level than the individual school and classroom, though these furthered each other.'[64]

In a CP circular for the Lancashire and Cheshire district, circulated in 1946 under the title 'The education campaign', Simon located the problems of education in a historical context and linked them to the demands of a capitalist society, an early example of the approach he would later develop in detail as a historian of education. Although the education system often seemed part of the natural order of things, he argued, 'The Marxist ... is equipped to analyse and understand the true function of these institutions, maintained and dominated by the ruling class for their own purpose.' Thus, he affirmed:

The chief lesson that history has to show with regard to education is that the ruling class has always without exception used education (the social power inherent in the instructing set up) for its own purposes as a buttress to support and perpetuate its dominating position, and have always opposed the extension of education to other classes except to that limited extent which, at certain periods, may have been necessary for its more effective domination.[65]

The education system had maintained a rigid class structure since the Elementary Education Act of 1870, with working-class schools providing 'education on the cheap for the masses'. Moreover, the 1944 Education Act 'reflected the weakened position of the ruling class and the increased strength of the working class'. This, he claimed, was based on a broad campaign led by the labour movement which should be taken forward to make further gains including common schools, an increased school-leaving age, county colleges, improved school buildings and more trained teachers.[66] At a CP teachers conference organised in March 1947, moreover, Simon insisted that the CP should take the lead in a movement for the development of 'new forms of education in the school'.[67]

Simon's historical analysis sparked a debate among CP activists. In particular his contemporary, Max Morris, also a graduate with a teaching diploma from the IOE in the 1930s, had published a tract entitled *The People's Schools* in 1939 which argued that the working class had benefited from state schooling.[68] Morris protested that Simon's historical argument was 'too mechanical', and was therefore 'in my opinion not a satisfactory Marxist account of the historical development you outline'. Indeed, he complained:

> You do not tackle at all the whole struggle for education in the 19th century nor the divisions within the bourgeoisie on the issue. It is not properly linked within the growth of the working-class movement. The result seems to be a general defeatist picture of the education system as a bourgeois institution with the counter assertion that education is nevertheless vital for the workers. You may not have intended this and it may be the result of over-condensation but that is the impression I received.[69]

Morris's view that Simon was overstating the dominance of the middle class in working-class education was potentially a significant corrective to Simon's historical analysis. Thus began Simon's reflections on the nature of the contestation of the working class and middle classes over the development of the education system.

In endorsing comprehensive schools, Simon made a close link with the labour movement and with a wider public. For example, Radcliffe Open Forum in October 1947 invited speakers from the different parties, including the CP, to give their views on education, to a large audience. The Conservative Party was not represented and the Labour Party speaker did not attend, but still Simon made a strong case on behalf of the CP.[70] He insisted that comprehensive schools would widen educational opportunity, and for this reason were 'strongly opposed by the forces of reaction, ably assisted by the State machine in the form of the Ministry of Education'. Nevertheless, he pointed out: 'it must not be forgotten that such schools cannot themselves bring about equal educational opportunity in a class society, where the "public" schools and ancient universities remain the preserves of the ruling class'. They were 'no short cut to Utopia', but 'Their success will depend on the speed with which our society moves towards Utopia.'[71] Simon was also able at this time to develop a closer analysis of psychometry, intelligence testing and psychology in general, benefiting from taking an MEd course at Manchester University which emphasised educational psychology. His stance again involved a debate with other CP activists, who had defended the use of intelligence testing. He pointed out that Soviet psychology emphasised the educability of human beings, while the use of IQ testing was 'highly reactionary in content'.[72]

Overall, he commented many years later, his articles in the communist press, written while he was teaching at Salford Grammar School, expressed the basic approach to problems of education and culture that was to underlie most of his work over the following forty years. Both Joan and Brian were increasingly interested in 'the whole field of education as a social function in its historical development', influenced by Clarke's *Education and Social Change*.[73] The prospect of extending these ideas will surely have influenced his decision in 1950 to leave school teaching behind and to move into higher education. Yet it is difficult also to resist the conclusion that he was disillusioned with teaching in schools, which had been a frustrating experience in that he had not been able to bring about the change he sought. Perhaps the universities would offer a better opportunity to exercise the power of ideas.

Notes

1   Brian Simon, unpublished autobiography, chapter 6 (Brian Simon papers, IOE).
2   Brian Simon to Ernest and Shena Simon, 3 February 1941 (Brian Simon papers, IOE).

3 For Joan Simon's life and contribution, see also R. Watts, 'Obituary: Joan Simon (1915–2005)', *History of Education*, 35/1 (2006), 5–9; and J. Martin, 'Neglected women historians: The case of Joan Simon', *Forum*, 56/3 (2014), 541–65.

4 Brian Simon, unpublished autobiography, chapter 6 (Brian Simon papers, IOE).

5 Brian Simon to Ernest and Shena Simon, 3 February 1941 (Brian Simon papers, IOE).

6 Brian Simon to Ernest and Shena Simon, 3 February 1941 (Brian Simon papers, IOE).

7 Watts, 'Obituary', 9.

8 Brian Simon, letter to Roger Simon, n.d. [October 1935?] (Brian Simon papers, IOE).

9 R. Simon, 'Autobiography' (n.d.; 1949?) (National Archives security files, KV.2/3927).

10 'Subject: B. SIMON', 10 April 1935 (Security files, National Archives, KV2/4175).

11 Col. Sir Vernon Kell, letter to Mr. J. Maxwell, 15 April 1935 (Security files, National Archives, KV2/4175).

12 Metropolitan Police, note, 1 September 1937 (Security files, National Archives, KV2/4175).

13 See K.P. Lavery, '"Youth of the world, unite so that you may live": Youth, internationalism, and the Popular Front in the World Youth Congress Movement, 1936–1939', *Peace and Change*, 46 (2021), 269–85.

14 See K.P. Lavery, 'Youth of the world, unite so that you may live', 283.

15 Brigadier Sir David Petrie, letter to Joseph Bell (Chief Constable, City Constabulary, Manchester, 4 August 1944 (security service files, Brian Simon, 1935–52, KV2/4175, National Archives).

16 See J. Simon, 'Promoting educational reform on the home front: *The TES* and *The Times* 1940–1944', *History of Education*, 18/2 (1989), 195–211.

17 Brian Simon to Ernest and Shena Simon, 1939 (Easter) (Brian Simon papers, IOE).

18 See Andrew, *The Shadow Man*.

19 Brian Simon to Ernest Simon, n.d. [spring 1939] (Brian Simon papers, IOE).

20 Ernest Simon to Brian Simon, 7 February 1937 (Brian Simon papers, IOE).

21 See e.g. G. McCulloch, 'The politics of the Popular Front, 1935–45' (University of Cambridge History PhD thesis, 1980, chapter 5) for further details of these divisions.

22 B. Simon to E. and S. Simon, 28 April 1940 (Brian Simon papers, IOE).

23 B. Simon to E. and S. Simon, 23 July 1940 (Brian Simon papers, IOE).

24 B. Simon to E. and S. Simon, 23 July 1940 (Brian Simon papers, IOE).

25 B. Simon to E. Simon, 1 February 1940 (Brian Simon papers, IOE).

26 *Student News*, 15 February 1940, 'Brian Simon'.

27 B. Simon, 'The universities must live', *Student News*, 15 February 1940.

28 B. Simon, unpublished autobiography, chapter 6 (Brian Simon papers, IOE).

29 B. Simon to E. and S. Simon, 4 November [1939] (Brian Simon papers, IOE).

30 B. Simon, 'British Student Congress: The Leeds meetings', 18 March 1940.

31 *Manchester Guardian*, report, 1 April 1940.

32 *Manchester Guardian*, report, '"Cluster of students' rights and responsibilities": Possible outcome of Leeds Congress', 2 April 1940.

33 *Journal of Education*, report, 'The National Union of Students', May 1940.

34 B. Simon, 'The past and the future: Face the past with pride, the future with confidence', *Student News,* 23 May 1940.

35 B. Simon, *A Student's View of the Universities* (Longmans, London, 1943), 13.

36 B. Simon, *A Student's View of the Universities*, 142.

37 R.H. Tawney, 'The universities', *Manchester Guardian*, 16 December 1943.

38 Lt-Col J.R. Pinsent, report on Brian Simon, 4 July 1941 (National Archives security files, KV.2/4175).

39 W.A. Alexander, note to Major Lord George Cholmondeley, Northern Command, 26 June 1941 (National Archives security files, KV.2/4175).

40 Pinsent, report on Simon, 4 July 1941 (National Archives security files, KV.2/4175).

41 Note, 'BRIAN SIMON', 2 March 1944 (National Archives security files, KV.2/4175).

42 Special observation report form, note on Roger Simon, 3 June 1942 (National Archives security files, KV.2/3925).

43 Captain E. Johnstone, note to Major Lord George Cholmondeley, n.d. (National Archives security file, KV.2/3925).

44 Special observation report form, August 1942 (National Archives security file, August 1942, KV.2/3925).

45 Brigadier L.D. Buchannan-Smith, note, personal and confidential, March 1943 (National Archives security file, KV.2/3925).
46 Applications in September 1943 and June 1944 (National Archives security file, KV.2/3925).
47 Roger Simon, 'Autobiography' (n.d.; age 36–1949?) (National Archives security file, KV.2/3927).
48 See e.g. G. McCulloch, *Educational Reconstruction: The 1944 Education Act and the 21st century* (London, Routledge, 1994), esp. chapter 5; G. McCulloch, *Failing the Ordinary Child? The theory and practice of working-class secondary education* (London, Open University Press, 1998); G. McCulloch, 'Local education authorities and the organisation of secondary education, 1943–1950', *Oxford Review of Education*, 28/2–3 (2002), 235–46.
49 B. Simon, unpublished autobiography, chapter 8 (Simon papers, IOE).
50 E. Barker, reference for Brian Simon, 1937 (Brian Simon papers, IOE).
51 M. Dobb, reference for Brian Simon, 1937 (Brian Simon papers, IOE).
52 Gurrey and Hamley 1938, reference for Brian Simon (Brian Simon papers, IOE).
53 B. Simon, unpublished autobiography, chapter 8 (Brian Simon papers, IOE).
54 W.T. Stevenson, reference for Brian Simon, 29 April 1948 (Brian Simon papers, IOE).
55 B. Simon, note, 'Yew Tree Central School (Lent Term 1946)' (Brian Simon papers, IOE).
56 B. Simon, note, 'Abbott Street School (summer term 1946)' (Brian Simon papers, IOE).
57 E.G. Simm, reference for Brian Simon, 1950 (Brian Simon papers, IOE).
58 B. Simon, note, 'Aspects of schoolmastering', 10 July 1948 (Brian Simon papers, IOE).
59 B. Simon, note, 'Aspects of schoolmastering', 10 July 1948 (Brian Simon papers, IOE).
60 B. Simon, note, 'Aspects of schoolmastering', 15 July 1948 (Brian Simon papers, IOE).
61 B. Simon, note, 'Aspects of schoolmastering', 15 July 1948 (Brian Simon papers, IOE).
62 B. Simon, note, 'Aspects of schoolmastering', 15 July 1948 (Brian Simon papers, IOE).
63 Board of Education, *Curriculum and Examinations in Secondary Schools* (Norwood Report), HMSO, London, 1943.
64 B. Simon, unpublished autobiography, chapter 8 (Brian Simon papers, IOE).
65 B. Simon, 'The education campaign', 1946 (Brian Simon papers, IOE).
66 B. Simon, 'The education campaign', 1946 (Brian Simon papers, IOE).
67 CP Teachers' Conference 1947 (Brian Simon papers, IOE).
68 M. Morris, *The People's Schools* (London, Gollancz, 1939). See also M. Cavanagh, '"Against fascism, war and economies": The Communist Party of Great Britain's schoolteachers during the Popular Front, 1935–1939', *History of Education*, 43/2 (2014), 208–31.
69 M. Morris, letter to B. Simon, 7 October 1946 (Brian Simon papers, IOE).
70 *Radcliffe Times*, report, 'Open forum holds its inaugural meeting. Political speakers give their views on the crisis'.
71 B. Simon, 'The comprehensive school', *Communist Review*, April 1949, 486–91.
72 B. Simon, 'The theory and practice of intelligence testing', *Communist Review*, October 1949, 687–95.
73 B. Simon, unpublished autobiography, chapter 8 (Brian Simon papers, IOE).

1   Brian as a boy, aged about 10, c.1925.
    Courtesy of UCL IOE Archives, SIM/5/4/1b.

2   Brian mountaineering, Dolomite Alps, 1935.
    Courtesy of UCL IOE Archives, SIM/5/4/1.

3   Brian swimming, Dolomite Alps, 1937.
Courtesy of UCL IOE Archives, SIM/5/4/1.

4   The army soldier, c.1939–1940.
Courtesy of UCL IOE Archives, SIM/4/5/1/37.

5   Young Joan Simon, mid–late1930s.
© Simon family. SIM/5/4/2, UCL IOE Archives.

6   Joan Simon in the country, c.1940.
© Simon family. SIM/5/4/3, UCL IOE Archives.

SOLDIER AND SCHOOLTEACHER IN THE 1940s   49

4
Marxism, psychology and pedagogy

Brian Simon's solid ties to Marxist thought over the course of his life ran parallel to his commitment to improvements in education. He was without question a prominent figure, first in his support for comprehensive education and, second, in his opposition to conservatism. Beyond his academic production as an historian of education, it is his advocacy of the comprehensive school that constitutes the best-known aspect of his legacy in education. But the comprehensive school itself, though inextricably linked to numerous other educational issues, far from exhausts his reflection on education. This gives rise to the question of just what a Marxist approximation to education meant to an activist communist such as Brian Simon. What could classic Marxism contribute to the pedagogical concerns that thinkers had been grappling with over the previous two centuries, and especially in the twentieth century? This is the question that this chapter will tackle, through the analysis of the published articles and conference presentations by Simon during the decade of the 1950s.

In these bleak years of the Cold War, prior to the Khrushchev thaw and the renovation of the 1960s, Simon focused his Marxist perspective towards education on two aspects. The first of these was his frontal opposition to intelligence tests and, by extension, psychometrics. This matter was intimately connected not only to the defence of the comprehensive school, but also to Soviet psychology, which provided Simon with a scientific base for such a rejection. Another area of reflection of specifically Marxist education was polytechnic education, a cardinal principle of Marxist educational thought which Simon approached from the experiences taking place in the USSR. In both of these realms, Simon's view was linked unconditionally to Communism. We could even go so far as to affirm that his Marxist concept of education was thoroughly subordinated to Soviet orthodoxy. He allowed himself no deviation whatsoever from the official discourse of the USSR, rejecting any critical analysis and showing a zealous loyalty to the Soviet regime.

The decidedly partisan nature of Simon's writings in the 1950s destined them to remain situated outside of the academic circuit. The texts that are analysed in this chapter were in fact published in the journals *Communist Review*, *The Educational Bulletin*, *Education Today*, *Education Today and Tomorrow* and *Marxism Today* and with the publishing house of the CP, Lawrence & Wishart, the only exceptions being the two compilations of Soviet psychology that the academic publisher Routledge & Kegan Paul deemed worthy of publication. The correspondence between Simon and Boris Ford, the editor of the *Journal of Education*, gives us an idea of how hard a time he had fitting into the academic sphere. Ford, who had coincided with Simon at Gresham's School and then again in the Educational Society in Cambridge,[1] rejected the article sent by Simon to the journal after his visit to the USSR in 1955, justifying the rejection on the weak foundations of the article's arguments ('unsubstantiated statements'), especially regarding academic standards, and on its scant analytical rigour. Ford anticipated the predictable reaction that the rejection was no more than political censorship: 'There is no doubt that there is much to be learned from the experience of Soviet education, but quite honestly I do not feel it is to be learned from this account of it', concluded the editor. For his part, Simon gave as an argument his first-hand experience in the USSR (on an official visit and without knowing the language), even invoking in his favour the criteria of his mother, Shena Simon.[2] Similarly, in a book published by the party, the authority used by Simon as the basis for his assertion that most young Soviet students had a comparable level at the age of 17 as their British counterparts in grammar schools, was indeed a grammar school director;[3] what he fails to mention is that this director was an enthusiastic CP member who had published articles praising Stalin's humanity.[4] The officialism and propagandistic nature of Simon's writings on education in the USSR appears all the more obvious when we see how they extol the wonders of a ten-year-old comprehensive school that was never actually established in practice. Simon's perspective on Soviet education constitutes an excellent example of the suppression of any critical – or even analytical – sense whatsoever, that affected numerous communist academics who in other areas were perfectly competent. Such loyalty constituted a profession of faith, of sorts, and it is not easy to determine if this was born of cynicism or naivete. In any case, the axiom of Simon's thought during this time can be summed up in the idea that the Marxist position was neatly embodied in that of the CP of the USSR, which was its most faithful advocate.

Simon has generally been considered as an 'educationalist', even though his approach to education came from outside of the discipline, given that his training was not in this specific field. This was due at least in part to the weakness of the discipline in England, something he would denounce much later. He was not a 'pedagogue', at least not in the continental sense that he would have wished, but rather someone who approached the field from outside; a politician always, his approximation was initially that of a practitioner and, later, a social scientist. Nevertheless, his perspective skipped over nothing less than the crucial area of educational methods, the pillars upon which New Education and Progressive Education had been constructed. Given his fundamentally political priorities, it is not surprising that he scarcely explored this area. But it is well worth paying attention in the final section of this chapter to the few lines that he dedicated to these issues. As we will see, these display some insights that are of surprising resonance even today, and whose relevance outweighs many of the other questions to which he dedicated so much of his energy.

Critique of intelligence tests and Soviet psychology

Over the course of the 1950s Brian Simon took a belligerent stand against intelligence tests, as well as psychometrics, in many articles and a book. As Deborah Thom has pointed out, while he was not the first to do so, he was one of their most outspoken critics.[5] Simon saw these tests as a mechanism for legitimising the tripartite system of secondary education that followed the eleven-plus examination established after the Education Act of 1944. The IQ test served to convert a selection that was social into a *fair* assignation of itineraries based on supposedly natural endowments. From his earliest writings in the late 1940s Simon identified intelligence tests with mechanisms for perpetuating a class-based organisation of education.[6]

The technical basis for his critique lay in the inability of these tests to measure what they were supposed to measure, and he went to great lengths to show that such tests in no way assessed any natural capacity, but rather skills that were acquired through education. Their use resulted in a tautology that confirmed a favourable development in those who had benefitted from an adequate prior education.[7] But even worse than this sterile, circular logic was the fact that these tests constituted a powerful method for naturalising social differences and certifying scientifically the inferior intelligence of the working class.[8] One way out of this conundrum could have been an improvement in the design of such tests and a search for tools that eliminated cultural influence and isolated innate mental processes.[9] But the path chosen by Brian Simon was altogether different: the radical negation of any type of innate intellectual attributes in children.

As a disciplinary foundation for this negation, Simon turned to Soviet psychology, of which he was an active advocate throughout the 1950s and early 60s. Soviet psychology was one of the main arguments he used in 1949 against Monte Shapiro and Mary Flanders, psychologists from the CP who defended the use of intelligence tests.[10] Simon was convinced that the authority of Soviet psychology should not be limited to party members but should spread its refutation of such methods throughout the West.

Three years later, in a lecture at the Institute of Education sponsored by the Society for Cultural Relations with the USSR (SCR), Simon sketched out the evolution of educational psychology in the Soviet Union. He explained how, in their striving for scientific efficiency and modernity, the USSR had also resorted to the use of intelligence tests.[11] According to Simon, these methods were used on a large scale during a first stage of experimentation in the first Soviet decade, the result of this new science being that thousands of children – most of them from proletarian origins – were sent to special schools. Paradoxically, the revolutionary dream of applying science to education resulted in the creation of a new aristocracy of the children of professional workers of the old regime and the functionaries of the new government.[12] This outcome gave rise to harsh criticism, leading the party's Central Committee to issue a decree in 1936 prohibiting the tests, developing a new psychology and establishing the *reeducation* of the psychometrists.[13] This 1936 prohibition becomes a central reference in Simon's accounts and is reiterated in all of his writings on the topic (although some authors question its actual effects and contend that the psychometrists continued to dominate the Soviet school system).[14] His constant, approving reference to this decree is quite revealing of Simon's conception of the academic debate at the time, ratifying the idea that the authority on psychology was to be found in the political domain – the Central Committee of the Communist Party of the Soviet Union – rather than in the scientific community. Even more revealing is his applause for the way that such a political decision affected professionals in the form of firings, contempt and reeducation. Likewise, the economic and military achievements of the USSR came to represent for Simon living proof of the validity of Soviet psychological theories. In this way, at the start of the 1950s, the Soviet Union in and of itself constituted the definitive argument in matters of scientific and academic authority.

In the middle years of the decade Simon made a notable contribution to the dissemination of Soviet psychology in the West. In 1957, two years after his trip to the USSR, arranged through an invitation by the Academy of Educational Sciences, Simon edited the book *Psychology in the Soviet Union,* which brought together ten works selected by Smirnov and Menchinskaya, director and subdirector respectively of the Institute of Psychology of the Academy. Given the official nature of his contact, Simon could not avoid reproducing in his discussions the hierarchies of power in Soviet psychology at the time, along with their official narrative. Although in his autobiography Simon claims to place this book in the wake of Vygotsky,[15] in fact, in accordance with the official Soviet genealogy, it *erased* Vygotsky, who, in addition to reintroducing the concept of conscience (used repeatedly by Simon), had developed some of the most interesting theories in Marxist psychology. Although the book included some of Vygotsky's closest collaborators, such as Luria and Leontiev, along with other members of his circle,[16] only Luria dared to offer praise for his colleague, who he had worked with to great advantage since an early age. In keeping with Soviet orthodoxy, Simon completed this erasure of Vygotsky by vindicating the role of Pavlov, despite the fact that the latter had never accepted Marxist positions and did not really even have a place in the research being undertaken. Similarly, Pavlov was the only reference to Soviet psychology in Simon's notes for a lecture in Glasgow in 1957.[17] Simon thus echoed the Pavlovisation of Soviet psychology under Stalinism and the nationalist (and anti-Semitic) principles underlying it.[18]

The thaw of the early 60s brought with it changes in the Soviet community of psychologists. Then, a rehabilitated Vygotsky suddenly found himself occupying a privileged position in a new book by Simon and his wife Joan.[19] Published in 1963 after another trip to the USSR, the volume featured a selection made this time by Vygotsky's direct disciple, Menchinskaya.[20]

In the mid-1950s, however, any deviation from the official Stalinist version would have been quite hard to imagine, for several reasons, considering that Simon was a disciplined member of the CPGB, carrying out his role in the service of the CPSU. Additionally, although he had completed a Master's degree in educational psychology at Manchester University in the late 1940s, he was mainly a teaching practitioner. It follows that Simon's approach to Soviet psychology in the 1950s was, in a doubly instrumental sense, as an orthodox communist intent on extolling the virtues of Soviet science on the one hand, but also as an educator committed to social change who, out of an entire theoretical construct, was appropriating one fundamental principle that aligned with his position towards education: a refusal to accept the existence of innate intellectual endowment. This idea constitutes the pillar of all of his psychological considerations from his very first writings: 'The concept of "intelligence" as an innate, more or less immutable human "ability" which can be isolated as quantitatively measured is one which Marxists cannot accept.'[21] On the contrary, mental capacities develop as a result of social practices.

This basic principle fitted within a broader conception of Marxist psychology, based on dialectical materialism and opposed to the mechanism used by bourgeois psychology to study the relationship between humans and their surroundings,[22] which Simon believed derived from an idealism that negated the original materialism.[23] This dialectical conception provides him with a way out of the reductionism of the human mind to the social structure, since the principle that all mental faculties derive from the objective conditions of life[24] should not be taken to imply a passive, mechanical receptions of one's surroundings, but rather that the conscience is constructed actively through its dialectical relationship with social activity.[25] In other words, intellectual capacities emerge from the opportunities that human beings are offered socially.[26] This idea of the dialectical emergence of mental faculties from social activity[27] is central to Simon's approach to psychology, even if he himself never used the term.

At the beginning of the 1950s this conception of active interaction with the environment steered Simon towards the metaphysical Lamarckism which Lysenko succeeded in imposing as official doctrine in the USSR and which would have disastrous consequences for Soviet science. Simon lauded Lysenkoism for how it had supposedly shown that an organism actively selects from its environment the specific conditions that it needs for its own evolution. He sought to justify the application of this approach to psychology by citing Leontiev,[28] who in all likelihood was simply reproducing those 'nomadic quotes'[29] asserting survival in Stalinist science. At this point Simon displayed his blind, naive faith in a profound identification of the Soviet order with the natural order of the world. Obviously, Simon was not a geneticist, and in his defence we should point out that his scientific colleagues in the party, who he would have relied on, were not likely to have been able to do much in the face of Lysenko's doctrines.

In any case, all of these philosophical-theoretical ruminations were aligned with the central idea of Marxist psychology, which for Simon was always embodied in the rejection of the existence of innate intellectual endowment. In its most radical formulations, this refutation led him to reject any biological base to human psychology. Assertions such as negating the existence of a natural limit to the development of children's minds[30] cannot simply be attributed to the heated pitch of a polemic. Even in a more systematic exposition such as that appearing in the introduction to his academic book on Soviet psychology, Simon resorted to formulations that can be understood in this radical sense. The reintroduction by Vygotsky of the term 'conscience' in the realm of psychology allowed Simon to connect with the Marxist tradition and reaffirm – without great fanfare – the materialist vision that conscience is a reflection of the objective world, that it acquires form through practical activity, and that it is revealed in the course of activity. This formulation is no more than a psychologisation of a Marxist locus, which claims for Soviet psychology the legacy of the empiricist-associationist tradition of Hobbes and Locke to Priestley:[31] all that is in the brain is a reflection of the external world, whose organisation and relationships the brain must apprehend. But Simon does not stop there; he goes on to affirm the subordination of neuro-mental activity to the conditions of existence. The brain itself should be seen as having evolved in a dialectical relationship with the human activity of procuring the needs for our survival, going back to the development of our hands and the elaboration of tools. We therefore need to do away with the false dualism that claims a nervous system on one hand and conscience on the other; all is material.[32] Although this might seem to imply a biological conception of psychology, for Simon it was quite the contrary. Soviet psychology saw itself as a social science, not as a biological science,[33] given that social activity – as opposed to physiology – was the determining element of human psychology.

Simon seems to have been aware to some degree of the weak points in his radical negation of the biological base, which would explain the fact that in his more controversial writings (but not in the more academic ones) he resorts to substituting – albeit speciously – the adjectives 'by birth' or 'innate' with 'hereditary', a term with clear, negative eugenicist connotations. As late as 1981 he did not hesitate to label defenders of intelligence tests as heirs to Darwin and eugenics.[34] But these protective strategies, in a Lakatosian sense, could not save him from having to acknowledge, in 1954, the existence of a psychological make-up at birth,[35] which, he accepted in 1962, 'conditioned development', though never decisively.[36]

This radical rejection of innate capacities could, in Simon's case, stem from his two facets, as a communist and as a pedagogue. It is not too difficult to see how for a communist the dependence of the human mind on social conditions was of utmost transcendence, this being the idea on which the dream of creating a new man was based. If intellectual ability depended on one's living conditions, then the establishment of new social-production conditions opened up not only the possibility of a man freed of the false, mystifying conscience of the previous existing relationship, in line with the Marxist concept of alienation, it also opened the door to the possibility of a man capable of developing new mental abilities, once freed of the constrictions placed by capitalism on his own mental development. That is to say, this would be someone capable of thinking without bourgeois prejudices, but also able to think in a way superior to anything known before. The idea of the constriction of potential resulting from capitalist production relations, which was always present in all aspects of communist analysis, was applied by Simon to intellectual development itself. Socialism would also serve to free man from human cerebral limitations, allowing him, quoting the Soviet philosopher Mikhail Kammari, to 'develop within himself to a still greater extent the finest, loftiest and noblest moral qualities, his most conspicuous faculties, talents and gifts, and will become an all-sided, harmoniously developed being'.[37] For as much as Simon couched it in terms of conditions of existence, it clearly amounts to a conception that goes beyond utopian, denoting a radical idealism far removed from any materialism, dialectical or not.

But beyond this utopian dimension that so seduced the communist, for the pedagogue the important thing was its implications for education, in practical terms. In the absence of innate intellectual abilities, all intellectual differences are reduced to a simple question of education. As he summarised in a lecture at the Marx Memorial Library in 1968: 'Whatever may be the child's original endowment, in terms, for instance, of the structure of his higher nervous system, the child's particular abilities, his capacity for carrying through specific mental operations of various kinds, are formed in the process of his education, and of his life generally. Such is the conclusion of psychologists orientated by Marxism as well as through scientific investigation.'[38] Education, it follows, plays a pivotal role in human development.

A determinist, mechanistic interpretation of the link between mental capacity and social conditions would certainly be coherent with the Marxist legacy, although education would likely be relegated to a secondary position. Yet this was not the interpretation sought by Simon, who identified the educational system with those objective conditions with which the mind interacted dialectically to produce emerging properties. In other words, the development of mental faculties depended dialectically on the education that was offered. His belligerent stance against intelligence tests, including affirmations that any detectable differences were the result of social education and that a low IQ simply denoted the lack of a proper education,[39] not only refuted the notion of natural intelligence but served as a vindication of the school. Formal education was the determining factor for human development,[40] not just any type of general social activity leading to learning, in the way of informal education. This belief in the central role played by the school offered him the platform to respond to his critics with 'all children are *educatable*, not "*equal*" (whatever that may mean)'.[41]

The centrality of the school also provides us with another derivation of Simon's writings: the recognition of the role of the teacher. For Simon, the direct consequence of the acceptance of innate intelligence implies the negation of the teacher's role; after all, what could be done with the poorly endowed student?[42] This pedagogical fatalism would be revisited by Simon in 1957.[43] On the contrary, from his developmental vision the teacher's role became central. Notwithstanding his belief in the possibility of a didactical science that had yet to be fashioned,[44] Simon defended the practical know-how of the teacher, as opposed to external psychologists intent on imposing their set criteria on the educational process. As he would continue to assert much later, in 1968, education 'is what teachers do in the schools, not what philosophers do in studies'.[45] In sum, Simon, quoting Makarenko, believed 'in the unlimited power of educational work',[46] and this was something that could ultimately only be done by teachers.

Simon's entire psychological trajectory ultimately led to his firm belief in the possibilities for development offered by education. And as an active teacher until 1950, he shared this belief with thousands of colleagues who like him fought against the application of segregationist measures promoted by advocates of the scientific management of educational systems, although they were frustrated by the system. Ultimately, as well, and notwithstanding Soviet orthodoxy, beneath his condition as a communist lay his unshakeable faith in the possibility of a future with justice for humanity.

The polytechnic principle

The polytechnic principle is the second pillar of Simon's Marxist conception of education. Overcoming the division between manual and intellectual work was one of the objectives of the working-class movement's thought regarding education, as this division was seen as a way of reproducing and justifying social classes, a theme that was extensively developed in the sociology of education. Simon even referred to Marx in pointing at this division as the origin of private property.[47]

The Socialist school had to find a way to overcome this dichotomy and fuse the development of cultural and intellectual abilities with labour – a key concept of Marxism. The problem, as was soon recognised by Krupskaya, Lenin's wife and one of the figures in charge of education in the early years of the USSR, was that this theoretical perspective was not easy to put into practice. In the midst of the Russian civil war, there was a real danger that this principle could lead to teams of child workers, a derivation that Marx's defence of combining work and education in the factory did not necessarily exclude. However, this option was discarded early on. The ensuing debate pitted advocates of reconverting the entire educational system into a vocational school that would supply the specialised, qualified personnel that socialism required against those, like Krupskaya herself, who believed in an education structured on the principle of labour, but that avoided any early specialisation that might determine the social fate of the children.[48] Both sides sought a formula that prioritised the centrality of labour in society and that linked children to their communities' production processes by facilitating their comprehension of their underlying principles.[49]

Simon's reflections found their place in a new stage of this debate. In the mid-1950s the Soviet Union planned the establishment of a common ten-year school without internal specialisation that postponed vocational education until after the age of seventeen. In this context of the definitive defeat of vocationalism, renewed attention was paid to those who had always defended the idea that the polytechnic consisted basically of a scientific-technological curriculum. It is in this framework that we should situate Simon's writings on the polytechnic principle. More than any solid reflection on the actual aspects of the debate, his was basically a laudatory exposition of the precarious equilibrium achieved in the USSR, which, as in psychology, was automatically ratified by spectacular results.

In a first text from 1951 on education in the USSR Simon provides an account of the end of educational experimentation in the 1920s. He explains the recovery of the system of subjects, exams, grades and the general disciplinarisation process of the decentralised experiences. But far from criticising or second-guessing this move, he praises the change,[50] justifying it as part of a polytechnisation. Significantly, he does not identify this with any mode of introducing labour, but rather with the establishment of a comprehensive school until the age 18 in the city and 14 in rural areas.[51] Simon then succumbs to what could almost be described as a religious ecstasy in his description of the paradise created in the USSR. He resorts to the Stakhanov parable, applauding the subordination of the educational system to the economic needs of the Soviet Union's development. He concludes that this subordination to the economy somehow marks the end of all prior contradictions between school and society and frees education of all constrictions. In the Soviet Union, pride in one's work progressively obliterated the division between intellectual and manual labour, between those who produced and those who enjoyed, between those who had the opportunity to develop their personal aptitudes and those tied to a job that did not allow for such things. But above all, any contradiction between school and society had disappeared for good:

> School and society were now welded together, the function of the school changing and developing in tune with the constantly raised requirements of socialist economy but also contributing in its turn to raising the technical and cultural level. There is no dichotomy between school and society; each school is bound to the community by many threads. It becomes clear that the basis of the Soviet school is Soviet society itself; its aim is the aim evolved by and accepted by the whole people; the transition from socialism to communism.[52]

Having overcome all contradictions and constrictions, the time was ripe for educating the whole man, as an individual and a citizen, as a worker and a 'cultured man'.

This idealised, propagandistic vision of Simon's can be seen as another iteration of the axiom of the party mentioned above: the overcoming – in any field – of all contradictions once the prior constrictions imposed by capitalism had been eliminated. This applied to science, mental processes and to education itself. However, in this text we get no inkling of how Simon faced the real possibility that this entire idea could be reduced to nothing more than a rhetorical exaltation of workers, akin to the approach to maternity in natalist regimes; in other words, that it was little more than a slogan, one declaring that work in the USSR was no longer alienating, by definition. His affirmations about the new honour of labour or about the fact that now men were judged and gratified in accordance with their contribution to the social good – as opposed to their clothes, their accent or their material wealth – were little more than a smokescreen allowing him to skirt the fundamental question of how to achieve the education of this new, complete man.[53] In the quasi-religious rhetoric imbued in this text, the axiom becomes an article of faith.

MARXISM, PSYCHOLOGY AND PEDAGOGY

Ultimately, what remains of his discourse is the construction of socialism as an educational end in itself from which personal educational developments were derived.[54] This concept, while undoubtedly revolutionary in political terms, was of scant pedagogical worth.

In an article from 1954 Simon abandons this propagandistic rhetoric to return to the domain of education and address the issue of extending compulsory schooling to the age of 17, an objective that three years earlier he claimed had been achieved in 1937.[55] He starts with the notion that the 'basic human aim' of communism, that is, the eradication of the distinction between mental and physical work, lies not in any early vocational specialisation,[56] but rather in the understanding of the processes of production. This was an important assertion, not only because it was made in a journal specialised in vocational education, but because such a conception implied a refutation of Marx's ideas. In truth, it was a position shared by Lenin, who seemed to carry greater weight at the time.[57] In a sense, and as indicated above, Simon was simply giving a faithful account of the precarious equilibrium achieved in the USSR. In another article he would insist that this attempt to avoid early specialisation also applied to the polytechnisation of the educational system in Poland.[58] However, against the third group participating in the debate, the polytechnic principle in no way implied the hegemonisation of scientific-technical contents, a trivialisation that was spread widely by the western press to which he was opposed; the objective of the ten-year school continued to be general education. In Simon's view it did not make sense to add an isolated subject of technology. Rather, the traditional science subjects needed to be reformulated so as to understand the theoretical principles underlying their practical applications.[59] At this point, it seems that according to Simon polytechnisation took the form of a transversal application that comprised a part of an integral education, and was never meant to be separated from the theory.

Following his 1955 visit to the USSR Simon wrote a text, presumably for a lecture, where he gave a more detailed account of the polytechnic organisation of the curriculum. The existing version of this text is somewhat confusing, as we do not always know if he is talking about a project, a line of research or actual schools,[60] an ambivalence not uncommon in his writings. In any case, the approach evidences several variations with regard to the posture defended previously. Here he refers to an intersection with labour by means of the three new subjects of agriculture, engineering and electronics, which would serve to develop the practical implications of physics, chemistry and biology.[61] However one looks at it, the solution contradicts his earlier refusal to separate theory from practice and also seems to fly in the face of his defence of a curriculum that was broader than science and technology.

Much later, in 1965, Simon used texts by Marx to try to systematise these complex equilibriums. The synthesis he proposes in this case recovers the principles of Krupskaya to defend a broad understanding of science and technology that was in opposition to a narrow vocational formation, but it did not exclude training in the handling of basic tools of production. This implied a fusion of theory and practice that would prepare each student to carry out a number of activities; it was a way of achieving what Marx called 'fully developed human beings'.[62]

Simon and the New Education

From what we have seen so far, Brian Simon's conception of Marxist education seems composed of two elements: a constructivist psychology that negates the measurement of intelligence and an educational policy based on the polytechnic principle, both of these aspects perfectly congruent with his advocacy of the comprehensive school. One could get the impression that for Simon, Marxism in education could completely sidestep the question of taking a stance regarding the fundamental movement of the first half of the twentieth century: the New Education. However, a small, practically unknown text proves most revealing of his position on the question. The reflection, published in the spring of 1951 in *The Educational Bulletin* – an educational journal of the British Communist Party – lays out what should be the communist position regarding the active methods.[63]

Simon begins with the necessary denunciation of these methods from a Marxist perspective. The core of his critique is directed against the idealist conception of the individual child as a being disconnected from his or her social surrounding. Simon believed that this individualist perspective hindered psychology from being able to provide a rational account for something so key as the concept of motivation, which, with this conception, could only have its origin in the internal conscience of the child. In opposition to this conception, Simon defends the social nature of the child postulated by Makarenko and, consequently, the exterior nature of motivation and its dependence on problems that need to be resolved. He saw the active response of the child as being a result of the community's demands. The teacher, therefore, was not a passive guide to spontaneous learning but rather a crucial, active agent who posed problems and elicited responses. With this formulation of motivation, Brian Simon clearly evokes the pragmatism of Dewey while anticipating to a certain degree the conception of significant learning, all the while positioning himself radically against the methods traditionally associated with these conceptions from a class position.

Simon held a hard materialist conception of the resolution of problems, which he viewed from the Marxist perspective of the struggle of the human being against nature, in an effort to survive. In such a clearly Darwinian framework, education fulfilled the mission of offering children the 'weapon of knowledge', in the words of Krupskaya, 'to be master of life'. With this approach, there could be no doubt that the priority was the content, not the method. This leads to his refutation, from a Marxist stance, of the 'free activities', which become an end unto themselves, and of the implicit separation between practical activity and theoretical learning. Similarly, there is no sense in subordinating the school to the interests of the child, whose 'divine manifestation' then determines his own education. On the contrary, the school's mission should be to organise the child's experiences in such a way as to favour the development of interests that are of value to his or her social and cultural development. All of this should be done in a way that facilitates children's access to knowledge systematised by humans over the course of history. Simon completes this defence of the contents of education with an appeal to the years of accumulated educational experience.

This vindication of contents and pedagogical tradition clearly pits Simon against the New Education, leaving him in a position that could easily be seen as traditionalist or conservative. Yet unlike most educationalists, through to today, he did not take part in the fear of such an anathema, owing to the fact that he had surpassed educational progressivism on the left, from a solidly established ideological position. Socialism demanded that all children enjoy equal access to systematised knowledge through education. With this criterion in mind, any educational proposal getting in the way of this objective could only be reactionary because it deprived children of the tools necessary for dominating life, placing those who were deprived in a situation of inequality and subordination. Simon went as far as to openly accuse progressive education of acting in practice in defence of the most reactionary interests, by hampering access to knowledge by the working classes, precisely when these underprivileged classes had finally achieved access to schooling after a long, historic struggle. This constituted a harsh political accusation, one that changed the habitual terms of the pedagogical debate. The article's opposition to progressive education concluded with his demand for 'the right of the children to a real education which will equip them with the knowledge which is their birth-right'.[64]

It is worth examining the implications contained in the two basic ideas of this conclusion. On the one hand, the reference to a 'real education' carries implicit the accusation, mentioned previously, that progressive education was offering a pseudo-education to workers, a watered-down version meant to satisfy their ambition to receive education, but lacking in the empowerment that comes with knowledge. On the other hand, the demand for a 'right to knowledge' implies an important qualitative leap in pedagogical discourse when seen against the preference of activist pedagogy for the child's right to happiness. Simon's formulation adds a degree of radicalness in claiming that this is an absolute birthright, akin to the foundational naturalism of human rights. It is striking that an educator situated so clearly on the left would end up appealing to content, traditionally associated with educational traditionalism, as a fundamental right for a child. However, it is perhaps even more surprising that he was not the only one to do so. In summing up a third-of-a-century of progressive education in an essential book on North American educational thought, Boyd H. Bode used literally the same expression in concluding that: 'If we start with the needs and insist on following their lead, things of central importance never get into the picture and youth is robbed of its birthright.'[65]

This brief text is especially transcendent historically in the way that it allows us to see just where one of the principal advocates of the comprehensive school in England stood pedagogically, as well as throwing new light on the perspectives of his initial defenders. The school-for-all to an advanced age that Simon dreamed of was not the school focused on happily addressing the interests of the child and adolescent that the progressive tradition embraced. Rather, it was a school designed to guarantee access for everyone to the systematised knowledge of humanity, understood as a weapon in the struggle for social emancipation. In this conveyance of knowledge, the teacher was meant to play an active role in their relationship with the child as well as in their relationship with educationalists, owing to the fact that they were the carrier of accumulated educational experience. This conception of the teacher was perfectly coherent with that described above in relation to educational psychology.

Simon continued to maintain this position in the face of new challenges in the 1960s posed by advocates of a curriculum based on workers' culture, to which he opposed Lenin himself in defending accumulated human knowledge.[66] Twenty years later, in the early 1980s, Simon incorporated developments in the 'new' sociology of education to point out the danger of basing education on children's limited and distorted concepts and again emphasised the centrality of goals and structures external to the child.[67]

This was Simon's major point of disagreement with the 1967 Plowden Report, *Children and their Primary Schools*. While appreciating its advocacy of mixed-ability groups and rejecting the criticism it received from the Black Papers,[68] Simon considered the report to be the pinnacle of pedagogical romanticism and child-centred methods. For Simon, the complete individualisation advocated by the report, as well as being unrealisable in practice ('this is not a practical possibility in any realistic sense'), was an erroneous starting point, since it was impossible to derive any effective pedagogy from individual cases.[69] For Simon, education was not an individual process, but basically and primarily a social one.

Formal schooling was thus a key tool in the struggle for social change. 'Formal education in school, therefore, can play a vitally important part in human development.'[70] Indeed, as mentioned, Simon saw it as one of those objective conditions with which the mind interacted dialectically in its development of mental abilities not predetermined by birth. However, it is questionable whether one can apply to the 1950s context Kevin J. Brehony's claim that Simon gave education an autonomous role in the production of social change.[71] Simon was certainly not a vulgar, mechanistic Marxist, but even less was he a leftist romantic of the kind abounding in the progressive pedagogical field. His dialectical conception of social change made it impossible for him to separate school from society. Thus, in 1949, he did not hesitate to express his distrust of the American high school, because he understood that the comprehensive school was solidly linked to the road to socialism and not to the spread of the American way of life.[72] Similarly, in 1951, he stressed that in the USSR the school was not a laboratory of socialism, but that it accompanied society in its construction.[73] Years later, in 1965, he continued to express a radical rejection of social experimentalism in schools: 'Any analysis which elevates education into a kind of *primum mobile* – as *the* factor changing society – would clearly be rejected by Marx.'[74]

Conclusions

It has been more than five decades since Simon published his writings, and the issues being debated today in education are not those that concerned him in the mid-1950s. In fact, the regime that he served so faithfully, and in which he placed all of his hopes for the emancipation of humankind, collapsed, making plain for all to see the enormous contradictions between its luminous ideals and its obscure practices and showing just how vacuous many of its arguments were. Nonetheless, many of the solid principles that Simon defended steadfastly are as relevant as ever today. The notion that beyond our psychological differences we are all equally educable continues to be a cardinal principle that we must not lose sight of. Likewise, belief in the unlimited power of educational work should constitute, if not a dogma of faith, at the very least a beacon for every educator. We would also do well to not confuse the battlefields and remember that the school accompanies social change, but does not produce it. Similarly, in these times of multiple empowerments, the conception of humankind's accumulated knowledge as a weapon for confronting power has lost none of its relevance. And on the heels of this idea, belief in the comprehensive school as the true school for all – and not a light version meant to entertain the working class – has lost none of its validity. Finally, how could we not consider perfectly applicable to our day Simon's prophetic warning from 1949 that comprehensive schools were not a 'short-cut to Utopia'?[75]

Notes

1. Brian Simon, *A Life in Education* (London: Lawrence & Wishart, 1998), 12.
2. Letters from Boris Ford to Brian Simon, 14/12/1955 and 24/4/1956 and from Brian Simon to Boris Ford, 16/12/1955. SIM/6/1/7, IOE Archives.
3. Brian Simon, *Intelligence Testing and the Comprehensive School* (London: Lawrence & Wishart, 1953), 104.
4. G.C.T. Giles 'The humanity of Joseph Stalin', *Educational Bulletin* June (1953): 3.
5. Deborah Thom, 'Politics and the people: Brian Simon and the campaign against intelligence tests in British schools', *History of education* 33, no. 5 (2004): 515–29, 522.
6. Brian Simon, 'Science and pseudo-science in psychology', *Educational Bulletin* October (1949): 12; Brian Simon, *Intelligence Testing and the Comprehensive School* (London: Lawrence & Wishart, 1953), 26; and Brian Simon, 'Glasgow. Feb 1957. Education and psychology'. SIM/ 1/4, IoE Archives.
7. Brian Simon, 'The theory and practice of intelligence testing', *Communist Review*, October, 1949, 694.
8. Simon, *Intelligence Testing*, 62.
9. Simon, *Intelligence Testing*, 87.
10. Simon, 'The theory and practice', 687.
11. For pedology in the first years of the revolution see Andy Byford, 'Pedology as occupation in the early Soviet Union' in Anton Yasnitsky (ed.) *A History of Marxist Psychology: The golden age of Soviet science* (New York: Routledge, 2020), 109–27.
12. Brian Simon, 'Educational psychology in the USSR' [Lecture delivered under de SCR's auspices at the University of London Institute of Education], February 13, 1952, 2. SIM/1/5, IOE Archives.
13. Brian Simon, 'Educational psychology in the USSR', [Lecture delivered under de SCR's auspices at the University of London Institute of Education], February 13, 1952, 4. SIM/1/5, IOE Archives.
14. Jennifer Fraser and Anton Yasnitsky, 'Deconstructing Vygotsky's victimization narrative: A re-examination of the "Stalinist suppression" of Vygotskian theory', *History of the Human*

Sciences, 28, 2 (2015): 128–53, 143; and Deborah Thom, 'Politics and the people: Brian Simon and the campaign against intelligence tests in British schools', *History of Education*, 33, 5 (2004): 515–29, 520.

15 Simon, *A Life*, 79–81.

16 Anton Yasnitsky, 'Vygotsky circle as a personal network of scholars: Restoring connections between people and ideas', *Integrative Psychological and Behavioral Science* 45, 4 (2011): 422–57.

17 Brian Simon, 'Glasgow. Feb 1957. Education and Psychology'. SIM/1/4, IoE Archives.

18 Anton Yasnitsky, 'The archetype of Soviet psychology: From the Stalinism of the 1930s to the "Stalinist science" of our time'. In Anton Yasnitsky and René van der Veer (eds), *Revisionist Revolution in Vygotsky Studies* (London: Routledge, 2016), 3–26, 11.

19 Simon, Brian and Joan Simon (eds). *Educational Psychology in the USSR* (London: Routledge and Kegan Paul, 1963).

20 Anton Yasnitsky, 'Vygotsky circle as a personal network', 422–57, 448.

21 Simon, 'Science and pseudo-science'.

22 Brian Simon, 'Educational psychology in the USSR' [Lecture delivered under de SCR's auspices at the University of London Institute of Education], February 13, 1952, 1. SIM/1/5, IOE Archives.

23 Brian Simon, 'Introduction' to *Psychology in the Soviet Union* (London: Routledge and Kegan Paul, 1957), 4.

24 Brian Simon, 'Educational psychology in the USSR'.

25 Although he neither cites him nor edits him, Simon's position seems to coincide with that of Peter Zinchenko, who criticised the dualism between biological and psychological functions and attacked the semiotic mediation of culture introduced by Vygotsky. Alex Kozulin, 'Vygotsky in context', foreword to Lev Vygotsky, *Thought and Language* (Cambridge, MA: MIT Press, 1986), xi–lvi, xlvi.

26 Brian Simon, 'Educational psychology in the USSR'.

27 Human beings as 'capable of developing new qualities as a result of social practice'. Simon, 'Science and pseudo-science', 12.

28 Brian Simon, 'Educational psychology in the USSR'.

29 Yasnitsky, 'The archetype', 21.

30 Brian Simon, 'Are children equal,' *Education Today* July (1954): 6.

31 Brian Simon, 'Some aspects of research in educational psychology in the USSR', *SCR Soviet Education Bulletin*, 2, 4, October, 1955, 52, and Simon, 'Introduction', 1.

32 Simon, 'Introduction' 2; Brian Simon and Joan Simon, 'Soviet psychology and the West', *Marxism Today* 6, 3 (1962): 81.

33 Brian Simon, 'Educational psychology in the USSR'.

34 Brian Simon, 'Why no pedagogy in England', in *Education in the Eighties: The central issues*, edited by Brian Simon and William Taylor (London: Batsford, 1981), 124–45, 133.

35 Simon, 'Are children equal', 6.

36 Simon and Simon, 'Soviet psychology', 83.

37 Brian Simon, 'The basis and purpose of education in the Soviet Union', [SCR 1951], 19, SIM/6/1/7, IOE Archives.

38 Brian Simon, 'Marxism and education', *Marxism Today*, 12, no. 9 (1968): 273–83, 279.

39 Brian Simon, 'Intelligence and attainment', *Education Today and Tomorrow*, March/April, no. 4 (1957), 8.

40 Brian Simon, 'Are children equal', *Education Today*, July 1954, no. 6, 12.

41 Brian Simon, 'Are children equal', *Education Today*, July 1954, no. 6, 10.

42 Brian Simon, 'The educational debate: Innate intelligence again', *Education Today*, October–November, 1954, 12.

43 Brian Simon, 'Intelligence and attainment', *Education Today and Tomorrow*, March/April, 4 (1957): 8.

44 Brian Simon, 'The basis and purpose of education in the Soviet Union', [SCR 1951], 16. SIM/6/1/7, IOE Archives.

45 Brian Simon, 'Marxism and education', *Teachers of the World* 3, November (1968): 32–3, 32.

46 Simon, 'The educational debate', 12.

47 Simon, 'Karl Marx and education', 235.

48 Larry E. Homes, *The Kremlin and the Schoolhouse: Reforming education in Soviet Russia, 1917–1931* (Bloomington, IN: Indiana University Press, 1990), esp. 19–24 and 83–92.

49 K.F. Smart, 'The polytechnical principle', in *Communist Education*, edited by E. King (London, Methuen, 1963), 153–76; Sheila Fitzpatrick, *The Commissariat of Enlightenment: Soviet organization of education and the arts under Lunacharsky, October 1917–1921* (Cambridge: Cambridge University Press, 1970), 26–34 and 59–68.

50 Brian Simon, 'The basis and purpose of education in the Soviet Union', [SCR 1951], 16, SIM/6/1/7, IOE Archives.

51 Brian Simon, 'The basis and purpose', [SCR 1951], 5, SIM/6/1/7, IOE Archives.

52 Brian Simon, 'The basis and purpose', [SCR 1951], 9, SIM/6/1/7, IOE Archives.

53 Brian Simon, 'The basis and purpose', [SCR 1951], 10, SIM/6/1/7, IOE Archives.

54 'Only if young people are bought up in this way, to fake a conscious part in the life of the community, to share to the full in its efforts, will they be able to develop their own individual powers and find fulfilment for theses'. Brian Simon, 'The basis and purpose', [SCR 1951], 9, SIM/6/1/7, IOE Archives.

55 Brian Simon, 'The basis and purpose', [SCR 1951], 5, SIM/6/1/7, IOE Archives.

56 Brian Simon, 'Polytechnical education in Soviet schools', *The Vocational Aspect of Secondary and Further Education* 6, no. 12 (1954): 3–13.

57 Simon, 'Polytechnical education', 3.

58 Brian Simon, 'Educational standards in Poland', *Educational Bulletin* October (1952): 9.

59 Simon, 'Polytechnical education', 6.

60 Brian Simon, 'Polytechnical education in the USSR', 1955, SIM/6/1/7, IOE Archives.

61 Brian Simon, 'Polytechnical education in the USSR', 1955, 9, SIM/6/1/7, IOE Archives.

62 Brian Simon, 'Karl Marx and education', 240.

63 Brian Simon, 'Activity Methods', *The Educational Bulletin*, March–April (1951): 10–11.

64 Brian Simon, 'Activity Methods'.

65 Boyd H. Bode, *Progressive Education at the Crossroads* (New York: Newson, 1938), 536. Quoted by Herbert M. Kliebard, *The Struggle for the American Curriculum, 1893–1958* (New York: Routledge Falmer, 2004), 213.

66 Brian Simon, 'Contemporary problems in educational theory', *Marxism Today* 20, no. 6 (1976): 169–77.

67 Brian Simon, 'Why no pedagogy in England', in *Education in the Eighties: The central issues*, edited by Brian Simon and William Taylor (London: Batsford, 1981), 124–45, 143.

68 A series of articles on British education, published in the *Critical Quarterly*.

69 Brian Simon, 'Why no pedagogy in England', 140–1.

70 Brian Simon, 'Are children equal'.

71 Kevin J. Brehony, 'Education as a "social function": Sociology, and social theory in the histories of Brian Simon,' *History of Education* 33, no. 5, (2004): 545–58, 546.

72 Brian Simon, 'The Comprehensive School', *Communist Review* April (1949): 485–91, 490.

73 Brian Simon, 'The basis and purpose of education in the Soviet Union', [SCR 1951], 11, SIM/6/1/7, IOE Archives.

74 Brian Simon, 'Karl Marx and education', 239.

75 Simon, 'The comprehensive school', 490; see also e.g. S. Hart et al., *Learning without Limits* (Maidenhead: Open University Press, 2004), dedicated to Simon who had recently died.

5

An emerging public figure

Brian Simon emerged as a public figure over the course of several years in the 1950s and 1960s, during which he became established nationally both in the CP and professionally as a leading historian of education. MI5 continued to monitor the activities of both Brian and Joan, although a check on letters received by Brian proved to be 'almost totally unproductive'.[1] He was regarded as 'a thoroughly indoctrinated and committed Marxist', on 'intimate terms' with many leading communists,[2] but it was acknowledged that 'the majority of the letters which he receives appear to be devoted almost entirely to educational policy, a subject in which he is known to take an active interest'.[3] As the international 'Cold War' intensified, tensions grew. Joan Simon later recalled how intimidating the political atmosphere of the 1950s had been, 'years when, besides what went on in the open, nameless men in belted mackintoshes called on those responsible for staffing to impart warnings about individuals of left-wing views, so spreading alarm and despondency in a way calculated to quench open protest'.[4] In these circumstances, left-wing criticisms could be denounced for following the CP's current party line and support for Soviet interests. Academic and other educational journals carried clear echoes of the wider ideological struggle, with frequently anonymous reviews and commentaries of hostile intent.

A loyal party man

Behind the scenes, Brian Simon could be highly critical of the USSR's aggressive activities in eastern Europe. Thus, in the case of the Soviet invasion of Hungary which was to become infamous for spurring many intellectuals to leave the CP or criticise it in public, Simon was forthright in his views when directed privately to CP leaders. He wrote to Peter Trent, the secretary of the national university staff committee: 'Yesterday I sent a telegram to the EC – in my own name only – saying they should pass a resolution demanding the Soviet govt accede to the Hungarian govt's request for the withdrawal of all Soviet troops. Then this morning they have moved in. What the hell! I can't possibly support this move by the USSR.'[5] The day before, he had indeed written to the party secretary, John Gollan, in the strongest terms, insisting that Soviet troops must withdraw from Hungary: 'I am well aware that problems of Russian security are involved. But I cannot condone what appears to be the Russian action on these grounds. Their action puts them morally in the wrong, and may well provoke further upheaval in Eastern Europe. I do not think they will gain anything in the long run by this action.'[6] Yet, unlike Eric Hobsbawm and many other intellectuals, he remained publicly silent and loyal to the party line, enhancing his own position in the national party.

Another indication of Simon's emerging national profile was his elevation to the CP's executive committee six months later. No less a sign was the hostile reaction of the national press against Simon personally. At the end of April 1957 he was accosted on his doorstep in Leicester by journalists from the national tabloid newspaper, the *Daily Sketch*. As he related the incident to a party colleague, 'I am still somewhat flabbergasted. The immediate result has been a literal siege by the Daily Sketch – warded off very effectively by Joan, Christ knows what they're cooking up.'[7] To another, he recounted: 'I have been hounded by the Daily Sketch which I gather (from the Daily Express!) is producing a lot of fantastic bloody nonsense about me and Joan and my parents and Christ knows what tomorrow.'[8] The following day's edition of the *Daily Sketch* confirmed his worst fears. Under the headline 'The Hon Brian is Red Party leader', it was announced that Simon was now a member of the CP's executive committee, observing that 'The Hon Brian, tall with fair, tousled hair, and just home from a ski-ing holiday in Norway, is not anxious to talk about his "promotion".'[9] Other newspapers followed up in the next few days with suggestions that Simon might be dismissed from his post at Leicester, while he resorted to not answering the telephone to respond to inquiries for two days.[10]

Simon's financial position was a further source of his growing prominence within the CP. In 1957, it was reported that he was funding the party with £7,500, together with a regular donation of £125 per month, while his brother Roger was supporting the party's publishing house, Lawrence & Wishart, with £5,000.[11] The Simons' financial support for the CP became all the more significant following the death of their father,

Lord Simon, in October 1960. As the elder son, it was Roger who inherited their father's hereditary noble title, Baron Simon of Wythenshawe. The financial implications were also far-reaching. Brian had been funded generously by his father since the war, and was now in a very comfortable financial position.[12] His commitment to Marxism had not affected the personal relationship between his father and himself. He reflected that 'My father was ambivalent about Communism – he thoroughly admired the ability of the Socialist state to "get things done", but the question of freedom was a stumbling block.'[13] His father's death now left him free to dispense his money as he wished. The following year he made a gift of £50,000 to the CP by selling shares from his father's firm. He commented that he did not want this money himself: 'His personal position was quite clear at the moment. It was really by chance that he had received this money – his father had not intended to give him any or only a small amount, and he would like to give most of it away.'[14] At the same time, he preferred to keep this arrangement private.

MI5 was in no doubt as to the significance of this donation to party funds. Simon's contribution would now amount to a very substantial figure. He had already contributed £30,000 to the CP pension fund, he had recently given £2,000 to the party newspaper, the *Daily Worker*, to launch a six-page edition, he was in the middle of a five-year plan to provide £1,500 per year to the party, and in 1958 he had given £4,000 to Lawrence & Wishart. These contributions were in addition to Simon's regular contributions to his District Committee and the Fighting Fund.[15] Further calculations highlighted the extent of the Simons' largesse,[16] and it was concluded that Brian Simon was now 'the most important financial supporter of the CPGB, his contributions running into many thousands of pounds, most of them made secretly'.[17]

Studies in the history of education

It was in this context that Simon also emerged as a prominent intellectual in his own right, with his new historical work greatly outweighing his earlier critiques of intelligence testing. Between 1955 and 1960, Simon concentrated his literary efforts on consolidating his scattered historical ideas into a single work, and this culminated in the publication of *Studies in the History of Education, 1780–1870*. The challenge was to maintain a distinctive Marxist analysis that would support his political ideals, while appealing at the same time to a broad audience in a climate that was increasingly hostile to both the CP and the Soviet Union.

Simon had been interested in historical studies since he was at school, although he had not gone on to take any formal advanced qualifications in the subject. Impressed by Fred Clarke's work, as we have seen, he began to develop his ideas while at Manchester, although he had little opportunity to take them further. He was also little noticed. He later recalled that while in Manchester he had been invited to give a twelve-week course for the Workers' Educational Association on educational change and society since the Reformation. This seemed a useful means of taking his nascent ideas forward, and he worked hard on developing a detailed syllabus. However, unfortunately, 'I remember well going one dusky October evening to an ex-elementary school in the centre of Manchester where the local WEA office told me to find my class. No one was there – neither from the WEA nor as students.'[18]

Joan also developed an interest in the history of education at this time. She had no formal qualifications, having left school without going on to university, but was determined to demonstrate that she could contribute at least as much as the male scholars in the academy. The main focus of her attention was initially the English Revolution of the seventeenth century, which the distinguished Marxist historian Christopher Hill was beginning to reappraise in depth.[19] Joan was especially interested in the new educational theories which had emerged at this time, and their antecedents in the Reformation, arguing that these also had continuing significance: 'And just as the fight of the seventeenth century reformers for a new educational system was inseparably linked with the establishment of the Commonwealth, so is the fight for a new context, method and conduct of education to-day an integral part of the struggle for socialism', she wrote.[20]

Brian's appointment as a lecturer in education at Leicester University College in 1950 gave him much more opportunity to deepen his historical insights and to become established more widely in this area of study. The school of education at Leicester was one of the leading departments of educational studies in the country, with some of the foremost educational academics including the conservative scholar Geoffrey Bantock. The different disciplines of education were offered in a general education course, with Simon teaching the history of education.[21] His initial forays in the history of education were around regional studies of schools, 'focusing attention on developments in a particular area and relating these to their wider social context', as he described these interests, which he recognised as 'a relatively new technique of historical study'.[22] To this end he embarked on a detailed study of seventeenth-century documents of schools in Leicestershire.

Meanwhile, Joan's historical studies were increasingly concentrated on education in the English Reformation of the sixteenth century. In particular, she set out to challenge the findings of A.F. Leach, whose works published several decades earlier had argued that schooling had declined following the dissolution of the chantries under the Chantries Act of 1547 and the educational interventions of King Edward VI.[23] Indeed, Leach became Joan's bete noire, as she published a large number of articles that comprehensively attacked Leach's work. She was highly critical of Leach's 'lack of historical perspective' and dismissed the quality of his research, to take the directly contrary view that it was at the Reformation that the foundations of modern educational organization were laid, to be steadily built upon until the Restoration of 1660.[24] One later article, published four decades later, continued to take Leach to task, denouncing him as 'something of a maverick medievalist, who succeeded in fooling Tudor specialists for half a century'.[25] A final essay published after her death persisted in the destruction of what was left of Leach's reputation.[26] Her vigorous pursuit of Leach reflected her tenacity, which she also used to support and defend Brian's reputation against potential or supposed criticism.

Studies in the History of Education was developed and published during a period of Conservative government in the UK. In 1955, Winston Churchill retired as prime minister and Anthony Eden took over, leading the Conservatives to a substantial victory over the Labour Party. Labour's leader, Clement Attlee, subsequently retired and was replaced by Hugh Gaitskell, a moderate 'revisionist' who sought to reorient the party towards policies that were regarded as realistic in the context of economic recovery and relative social harmony. Eden was forced to resign as prime minister in 1956 due to a disastrous incursion in the Suez Canal, which demonstrated the changed balance of world power, with Britain much diminished since the war and the USA and USSR now dominant, but the Conservatives were able to continue in government under Harold Macmillan who went on to win another general election in 1959. This was therefore a frustrating period for Labour and for radicals and socialists intent on social and political change. Radical educational change also seemed a distant prospect under Sir David Eccles as secretary of state for education. Against this background, Simon sought to question the basis for the education system as a whole.

The usual perspective adopted in histories of education published in the 1950s was to emphasise steady social and economic progress associated with the rise of modern schooling. For example, a collection of papers was published in 1952, edited by A.V. Judges, the professor of the history of education at King's College London, under the title *Pioneers of English Education*.[27] In his editorial introduction, Judges argued that the English education system had benefited from the gradual efforts of English reformers in the nineteenth century, rather than the continental educators who usually were given credit for their experimental and radical initiatives. Sir Philip Morris, Vice-Chancellor of the University of Bristol, suggested that education had made a strong contribution to social improvement over the past century.[28] Another pillar of respectability, Sir John Maud, Permanent Secretary at the Ministry of Education, celebrated how twentieth-century administrators had helped to develop the education system in partnership with LEAs, schools and teachers.[29] These hymns of praise for the history of education did not impress one critic, writing anonymously in the obscure communist journal *Educational Bulletin*, but in Simon's characteristic style and outlook, who asked sternly:

> Is the history of education important? Students are given it at college and university, teachers at refresher courses. Today, more and more books are being written, courses of public lectures organised. Clearly it is considered important. But the question is, *What kind of history?*[30]

The review continued that Judges's volume represented only middle-class efforts on behalf of education, whereas the working-class struggle for education was entirely neglected. Moreover, 'The real causes of educational developments are not revealed in these highly respectable lectures, which, with one or two exceptions, skate on the surface in a superficial manner, as if fearing to probe any deeper.' The real pioneers of English education, it insisted, were the working-class leaders who struggled against the demands of the bourgeoisie.[31] This was a struggle that continued to the present day. It concluded stirringly that the history of education was important for this purpose: 'It clarifies the real issues, strengthens us in our struggle, points the way forward. But it must be *our* history, one that recognizes the part played by the working class, and which assesses the spokesmen of the bourgeoisie in the light of their real motives.'[32]

It was on this basis that Simon sought to produce an alternative version of the history of education, which would be concerned with the social class struggle for social equality. His commitment to history was closely related to his political activism. This was an approach to history that Raphael Samuel has described as 'people's history'. According to Samuel, this tended to be oppositional and offered an alternative to orthodox scholarship. It was also 'shaped in the crucible of politics, and penetrated by the influence of ideology on all sides'.[33]

The CP was already well established in setting agendas in relation to history. The party's Historians' Group had been organised in 1946, with many leading intellectuals being attracted both to the CP and to history. Among its most prominent figures was A.L. Morton, whose *People's History of England*, first published by the Left Book Club in 1938, had total sales of over a hundred thousand by the 1970s.[34] Morton was regarded, according to his fellow CP historian Maurice Cornforth, as 'a model type of Communist intellectual'.[35] In the area of economic history, Simon's former Cambridge tutor Maurice Dobb produced a further influential text with his *Studies in the Development of Capitalism*, published in 1946.[36] This emphasised the nature of history as being generated by class struggle. According to historian Bill Schwartz, Dobb's work showed the potential of stressing the struggle of the common people against the expanding regime of capital on Marxist principles. This made it possible for Dobb to present history in terms of a heroic revolutionary and democratic struggle on the part of the subordinate classes.[37] The rationale for such historical work, as Schwartz suggests, was political and ideological in nature, 'to *repossess* the past in order to make the future: *our* history was the history of the English common people'.[38]

The CP's historians' group suffered a severe setback when the events of 1956 caused many of its members to leave, but it continued its activities.[39] Simon's wife, Joan, became secretary of the group from 1957 until 1962, on her own account its 'secretary, treasurer, editor of *Our History*, production messenger, bibliography distributor and general dogsbody'.[40] Brian Simon himself undoubtedly recognised the significance of such work for the ideological struggle as a whole. As he pointed out in 1962:

> Historical studies are, of course, of particular importance in establishing the correctness and validity of the Marxist approach. This is the only strictly 'ideological' field in which we have a functioning group and, from the point of view of actual production, together with the impact made, this is at present one of the most effective fields of our work, the group producing a considerable number of articles in *Marxism Today* on historical subjects, the quarterly – *Our History* – as well as a number of books, some of which have made a considerable impact.[41]

Through the recovery of the active struggles of working people in the past, it was hoped, Marxist ideals would gain greater resonance and support in the present. Simon's early plans for his book envisaged a set of connected essays that would explain the nineteenth-century background to contemporary educational issues. He began by discussing his preliminary ideas with James Klugmann, who generally approved the plan.[42] The fundamental idea was to demonstrate the diverging interests of the middle class and the working class in the area of education, and the emergence of a struggle between them. A middle-class educational philosophy developed in the early decades of the nineteenth century, and it enlisted working-class support, but from the 1830s onwards the working-class movement established an independent approach. In the 1850s and 1860s, a moment of change occurred, as 'The middle class, finally achieving state power (1846 Corn Laws) and higher forms of organization and concentration of capital, concentrates on remodelling and developing education to suit its needs. Uses state apparatus for this purpose, and sets out deliberately to construct an educational system to buttress its power.' The Elementary Education Act of 1870 thus consolidated 'the firming up of a class system of education'. He also intended to include an epilogue to demonstrate the continuing significance of these social class differences. The 'key', as he saw it, was that 'there are those who labour, and those who rule', and that education would come into its own with the ending of these differences.[43]

A more detailed synopsis served to clarify the working out of the argument. The first essay would examine the rise in the social prestige and political influence of the industrial middle class at the start of the nineteenth century, leading to the growth of the new industrial cities, and its ideological expression ultimately in utilitarianism. These new ideas came into open opposition to the aristocracy and underpinned a struggle for social, political, religious and educational reform. In the area of education, the bourgeoisie attacked the institutions that supported the old aristocratic order, in particular the universities of Oxford and Cambridge and the public and grammar schools, and also sought to establish their own educational institutions under their own control and serving their needs. This culminated with the founding in 1826 of University College London, 'the highest expression in practice of bourgeois educational theory, achieved only in the process of struggle, and breaking the monopoly of University education, i.e. the harbinger of the future'.[44]

In the second essay, Simon set out to examine the form of education that was provided for the working class. First, he noted the wholesale alienation of craftsmen and husbandmen and their transformation into a propertyless proletariat, splitting society into 'exploiters and exploited'. Educational policy reflected these social conflicts. The middle class found working-class allies in its struggle with the aristocracy, but after the passage of the Great Reform Act in 1832 tensions between the middle and working classes became increasingly acute. Utilitarian educational theory in this context struggled to achieve a 'capitalist society comprising exploiter and exploited', and argued in favour of a limited education and religious indoctrination as 'the alternative to the prison house' to counter working-class morality and political objectives. These independent educational aims of the working class were to be emphasised in the third essay. The Chartist movement gave the working class its fullest expression as an independent political force, including the right to a full education: 'The more class conscious sections, therefore, consciously rejected the ideology (i.e. political economy) and the educational ideas of the bourgeoisie, and evolved their own educational theory and practice in opposition to those of the bourgeoisie.' The fourth essay, on the period 1850–1870, was to survey the compromise between the bourgeoisie and the landed interest, based in increased economic prosperity, leading to the Victorian upper-middle class emerging as the ruling class. The bourgeoisie took advantage of its new political influence to use the state apparatus to reinforce its power. A series of Commissions in the 1850s and 1860s on a wide range of educational institutions provided the foundations for 'a clearly stratified class system of education'.[45]

At this stage, Simon was hopeful that he would also be able to include the period after 1870 and into the early twentieth century in this volume. He envisaged a fifth essay that would explore the relationship between education and imperialism. In the 1890s, he suggested, class interests were again sharpened as the British Empire spread while socialism revived, so the state intervened again for the Education Act of 1902 'to complete a reorganization of education in lines with the new needs of the bourgeoisie'. The independent public schools were untouched, but elementary education was restricted to a limited education for the working class, a sharp division was created between elementary and secondary education, and technical education was neglected. The 1902 Act thereby laid the basis for the scope and character of education in the twentieth century. Finally, Simon sought to include a sixth essay on education and labour. This would examine the working-class struggle to shorten the hours of labour and to raise the school leaving age. It would also show how bourgeois ideology stemming from the eighteenth-century economist Adam Smith inculcated bourgeois ideas and morality, while the ideals of such figures as Godwin, Paine, Shelley, Wollstonecraft, Owen, Lovett, Marx, Engels, Ruskin and Morris pointed in the direction of education as a means of full human development in a classless society.[46]

In practice, Simon was unable to find space to include these later developments, and his book culminated in the Elementary Education Act of 1870. However, the general scheme remained intact. The first three chapters explored the development of middle-class educational ideas and the provision of education for the working class. Chapters 4 and 5 considered the working-class movement and education. The final two chapters examined the role of the state in education with the establishing of an educational system and elementary schooling for the working class. However, he did not feel ready to share his work with others until 1958. His mother, Shena, was encouraging, although she found the arrangement in his manuscript confusing as she came across the same people in different sections at different periods of time. She also took issue with the lack of emphasis given in the manuscript to the role of denominational bodies in teaching working-class children: 'I am quite sure that the ordinary historians of education give far too much space to the Voluntary Societies, but do you go to the other extreme?'[47] Joan also commented on a draft in the summer of 1958, and by the end of the year he had completed the work.

It was significant at this stage that Simon looked for advice on his final draft mainly from leading members of the CP. Apart from Joan, these were Maurice Cornforth, James Klugmann and A.L. Morton. He explained to Cornforth, who received it on behalf of Lawrence & Wishart, that the book had developed from three essays 'which got longer and longer and divided into sub-sections'. He remained uncertain about the final presentation, and in particular was anxious that 'at various points the main lessons – conclusions etc., need bringing out more clearly'.[48] At this point he was still considering the addition of an epilogue to cover the period from 1870 up to the present, and so to bring it up to date. However, he had already provided an introductory 'note to the reader', which was intended to explain the longer-term significance of his work. He was conscious that he had 'had to dash it off rather rapidly without time for thought',[49] but this gave a frank appraisal of the education system in the twentieth century. He was emphatic that this remained a class-based system despite the changes of the past century:

> In all its essentials the present system is precisely that laid down so carefully 80 to 100 years ago in order to buttress the rule of the property owners. The reformation and reorganization of the public schools, their establishment, once reorganized, outside any form of parliamentary control – these steps, carried through at that period, have ensured the maintenance of what is a unique system of schools serving the needs of the ruling class – few today attempt to deny that they serve this function today as they did then.[50]

Moreover, he added, contemporary struggles over independent schools, comprehensive schools and the abolition of selection comprised 'the contemporary expressions of this continuing struggle'. This was, in his view, less complex in character than it had been in the nineteenth century, for now it involved only two opposing social classes whereas in the nineteenth century there had been three. The working class had continued to make considerable gains, he acknowledged, yet, he insisted, 'so long as the society is divided into property owners on the one hand and a propertyless working class on the other, the final fruits of this policy – in the form of the fullest equality of opportunity – cannot be enjoyed'. This would require changes outside the schools: 'As the following pages show, it was not until the industrial middle class finally achieved full political and economic power that they were able to carry out their aims in full measure.'[51] The contemporary lesson seemed clear enough.

The advice provided by Cornforth and Klugmann was designed to help the work achieve a broad readership by avoiding Marxist rhetoric as far as possible, while at the same time ensuring that the argument followed a Marxist logic. Cornforth confirmed that the book would be published and proposed that it needed very little further work. He enthused that: 'The theme develops in a natural and logical way, and it is easy to read and absolutely attention-compelling all the way through.' Although he did not know the existing literature in the area, he felt able to affirm that 'this is a book of great importance which will make its way and have an influence, delighting persons of good will and seriously embarrassing others'. His advice was principally to reduce and tone down the material that Simon wished to use to emphasise contemporary implications. An epilogue was not necessary, he proposed. Since it would have to be brief and deal with 'the most frightfully "controversial" questions', it was best to avoid it altogether. An introduction was appropriate, he allowed, but part of the present version 'should be rewritten in a more careful and persuasive way, so as not to antagonize a lot of readers right at the start'.[52]

On the other hand, Klugmann was keen to encourage Simon to depict working-class organisation as independent and active throughout the book, rather than as 'a purely passive mass, that the rulers do as they like with'.[53] Simon agreed with this approach and was relieved at Cornforth's encouraging words: 'I must say I got a bit depressed about the book at one time, but you have cheered me up.'[54] For his part, Klugmann was also impressed, although he had a number of detailed points for Simon to consider. His principal concern appeared to be that Simon defined the working-class movement too broadly. For example, the book included Robert Owen's movement within the working class, whereas Klugmann argued that this was 'not really working class but "for the working class" and is a form of Utopian socialism'. Klugmann was anxious that there should be a clear distinction drawn between the struggle to give education to the working class and the fight of the working class to get education for itself. If this distinction was not fully developed, Klugmann warned, 'part of the spirit of the book gets slurred over'.[55] Meanwhile Morton, the doyen of Marxist historians, also raised a doctrinal issue to help to clarify Simon's argument. He was, overall, highly supportive of the work, noting that: 'I really have nothing but admiration for your book. It is most illuminating to have the history of education dealt with in this systematic political way, and there is practically nothing that I would want changed.' His main suggestion was to be more specific about the use of the term 'middle class':

> I do think that sometimes you use middle class not in a Marxist way, in relation to the productive forces, but in the popular way of their relation to the state apparatus and the way they tended to think about themselves and whether they had the airs and graces. Ought we not to keep the term middle class, at any rate after the early nineteenth century, for the sections that did not live mainly on rent and profit?[56]

The title of the book was still unresolved, and when he submitted the final manuscript Simon proposed 'Education, Class and Politics, 1760–1870'.[57] However, this was not approved, perhaps because it might have appeared too narrow, and the bland *Studies in the History of Education, 1780–1870* was adopted instead. Gone also was the 'Note to the reader' that Simon had originally contemplated, to be replaced by a short introduction addressed to the 'ordinary reader' but emphasising in more modest terms its intention to direct attention to 'neglected aspects of educational history'. [58]

The careful reining in of Simon's usual flourishes paid dividends in terms of helping to achieve a broad audience that was receptive to the book. Reviews of the work were generally appreciative, if cautious. One such was by H.C. Barnard, the author of *A History of English Education from 1760*, very much a book in the old style. Writing in the *British Journal of Educational Studies*, Barnard recognised that Simon had produced 'a solid and scholarly contribution', even though it lacked a bibliography. Despite its title, he acknowledged, it was not just 'a series of detached essays', but presented 'a well-organised and continuous account'. He agreed too that the challenge of the working-class movement and its educational repercussions was a significant theme that had required 'enunciating', although he maintained that it was 'only one aspect', and that 'the emphasis tends to be on one side'. Barnard suggested overall that 'to gain a clear picture of the educational history of the period one would need to supplement (and perhaps modify) Mr Simon's account from other sources'.[59] It would clearly take time to win over many historians of education, but they were at least allowing Simon a respectful hearing.

Professor of education

Simon's growing stature as a leading intellectual in the CP did not go unchallenged, and there remained limits to Simon's influence in the party. This became clear in a dispute within the CP over a manuscript produced by Joan entitled 'Marxism and education'. This was originally commissioned by the party publishers, Lawrence & Wishart, and was refereed by other CP members before Max Morris, now a member of the executive committee, raised objections to its publication. After protracted and difficult negotiations, the manuscript was turned down. Joan, understandably furious, destroyed the manuscript and refused to re-register for membership of the party from 1964. The incident was faithfully recorded by MI5, whose agent noted with some amusement that Joan, 'a notoriously peppery lady', in his hostile view, alleged that she had not been properly briefed on what was wanted.[60] Brian, unable to intercede on Joan's behalf, took out his frustration with a seven-page memorandum pointing out the wider implications for the role of intellectuals in the party, and Joan's own loyalty to the CP over many years:

> Until these events took place, her position was one of absolute loyalty to the Party. At the time of Hungary [1956] she played a particularly useful role among intellectuals, after that she acted as secretary to the historians' group, helping to keep it functioning as an effective group during a most difficult period She has for many years contributed to the party press making useful theoretical contributions.[61]

In spite of such devotion of her 'considerable energy' to 'party and near-party work', Joan was now alienated from the CP.[62] It was a difficult episode that highlighted the essential fragility of the position of intellectuals in the CP, whatever their stature or profile.

On the other hand, Simon's position as a historian of education continued to prosper. The second volume of his historical work included the post-1870 material that had originally been intended for the first book. He intended initially that this sequel would embrace an extended period from 1870 to 1940, although eventually it concluded in 1920. He envisaged that the book would explore a fresh phase in the struggle for education, with the challenge of the working class at a higher level and more active and conscious than previously, due to the emergence of socialism in the mid-1880s. As he noted privately:

> This is the challenge. The working-class movement was becoming increasingly clear as to what they wanted and how they would get it (socialist theory). Whereas previously the working class had made a largely unconscious challenge with clear objectives, backed by political and economic understanding (but deal here with the different groups among the workers – the Reformists, the largely neutral and the Marxist).[63]

He visualised the argument as being that in the late nineteenth century the bourgeoisie attempted to prevent the development of a socialist awareness and political activity among the workers, but that the working class resisted by fighting for free education, secular education, elected school boards, and against child labour. A chapter on the Education Act of 1944 would follow, which he saw as 'crucial' because 'all the contradictions and struggles around education come to a head in the fight around this Act'. The fight for secondary and higher education in the early twentieth century would follow on from this, leading to the 'Labour compromise' in the years after the First World War.[64]

In this volume, Simon emphasised what Fred Clarke's short work had only been able to sketch out briefly: the differing educational routes that developed in England during this period. This was not a unitary education system with a single pathway, but a differentiated system based on elementary schools for the working class, grammar schools for the middle classes and independent 'public' schools for the social elite. This continued to differ from most accounts which argued that the education system supported a growth in equality of educational opportunity: 'No doubt there was, in one sense, a "silent social revolution" at this time, but the changes brought about in the educational system were ultimately the outcome of battles fought out amid much noise and dust.' Thus, he insisted:

> This is not merely a story of philanthropy and growing enlightenment, resulting in a continuous upward curve of development but rather a history of breakthroughs and retreats from which the lesson to emerge for the Labour movement was that nothing is gained (or retained) without persistent and determined pressure.[65]

He acknowledged nevertheless that 'Even this may fail to avert severe setbacks.'[66] Ultimately, while the historical model of continuing social and political antagonism between the middle and working classes was straightforward enough, the more detailed argument around 'breakthroughs and retreats' was a sophisticated one. It was no longer a matter of simple middle-class dominance, such as he had suggested in his early work in the 1940s, but one of a struggle between rival social forces with often unpredictable results.

Cornforth was again highly enthusiastic about Simon's new work: 'It seems to me to be most extremely good and interesting, a most extraordinarily readable, exciting and creative book.'[67] He remained concerned that Simon should retain his Marxist ideological rigour. For example, he detected at the end of chapter 9 'a most flagrant deviation from Marxism-Leninism' in a description that suggested that trade unions were part of the machinery of the state. This, he explained, was an 'essentially Fabian view', which had been corrected as long ago as 1932 at the CP Congress at Battersea Town Hall, which he had attended.[68] Nonetheless, both he and Klugmann remained anxious to restrain Simon's use of Marxist rhetoric, language and argument in order to retain a broad readership. Klugmann suggested that:

> Whereas ... all the other chapters are beautifully unsectarian and will be appreciated by nonMarxists, even if they don't accept it all, the first chapter is rather like a short Marxist syllabus on labour history. Even the language is a bit jargony. This is a pity, as it might put some people off before they really begin it. This should be looked into – and perhaps it should be spelt out a bit more and made less like a syllabus.[69]

They also advised him not to indulge in a 'peroration' at the end of the volume, unless this was 'both brief and restrained'.[70] Nevertheless, this volume retained a clear Marxist message, while one that could be digested without difficulty by a broadly sympathetic audience, a historical popular front, as it were.

Meanwhile, Joan's abilities as a historian of education were also coming to be recognised, rather belatedly, although continuing to be contested in some influential quarters. She enjoyed the approval of a number of established scholars, both in England and the USA, who shared her dislike of Leach's work. This was in itself an achievement for someone without any university qualifications or historical training, although she perhaps resented the refusal of some academics to acknowledge her success. She had brought her research on sixteenth-century education into a single volume, initially entitled *Education and the Social Order, 1500–1600*. This was at first turned down by Cambridge University Press (CUP) following a hostile review which objected to the Marxist perspective underlying the text.[71] It was eventually published by CUP under the title *Education and Society in Tudor England*.[72] This was a gratifying outcome, although the work was still not to all tastes. According to an anonymous review in the *Times Literary Supplement*, Joan's substantial research-based monograph included important information and analysis on the 'purely educational aspects of the period'. However, the book was weaker in its treatment of the relationship between education and society; 'when she comes to discuss the relation between classes, the social forces behind changes in schools and colleges, and the impact of those changes upon the social structure, she too readily asserts conclusions that are vaguely stated and insecurely based'.[73]

By the time that Simon's second historical volume was published, in 1965, the Labour Party was once again in government, with Harold Wilson as prime minister, having narrowly won the general election of 1964. The new government was embarking on a range of reforms in primary, secondary and university education, and this helped to create renewed interest in educational research that might underpin such changes. Simon himself was now established as the leading historian of education in the country, and his burgeoning academic reputation was further enhanced through two further contributions at this stage. The first was an essay produced for a general work, *The Study of Education*, edited by J.W. Tibble, also at the University of Leicester.[74] This was a collection designed to represent the key disciplines in the study of education, and Simon was the natural choice to represent the history of education.

Simon's essay in this collection was a tour de force; not only an elaborate explanation of his own, 'new' approach to the history of education, but a detailed overview of current work and proposals for further study. It includes some of his best-known and most telling aphorisms: 'The historical approach should bring educational developments into perspective, and in so doing open the teacher's eyes to the real nature of his work.... There is, perhaps, no more liberating influence than the knowledge that things have not always been as they are and need not remain so.'[75] It emphasises the potential importance of the history of education in terms of understanding education as a social function, or 'a vital contribution to social history'.[76] Rather than dwelling on the ideas of great educators with ideas supposedly 'in advance of their time', the historian of education should consider the social origins of such ideas, 'the elements in society ready for change at different times... why changes of a particular kind were needed, what assisted or prevented their realisation, what compromises were made, break-throughs achieved, and with what effect'.[77] This was an approach to the study of the history of education that seemed to resonate with contemporary political tensions over the direction of education policies, and above all with controversies around education and social class.

Another key contribution was Simon's professorial inaugural lecture, presented in 1966. Since the success of his first historical volume, he had been aware of the possibility of securing a more senior academic position. In 1962, he was apparently offered the opportunity to move to London as deputy principal of the recently opened Sidney Webb College, a constituent college of the Institute of Education (IOE), London, but he declined the invitation.[78] He was encouraged to apply for a professorship at the University of Birmingham. In the event, he was promoted to a professorship at Leicester on the retirement of J.W. Tibble.

Simon's inaugural lecture, presented on 15 November 1966, was itself a significant occasion.[79] He proposed in this lecture that while the education system developed in the Victorian period had lasted well into the twentieth century, the new task was to reshape the system with an inbuilt capacity for change in the future. This would not be based on the theory of 'intelligence' but would engage with a new understanding of human learning. This would demand new qualities in the teacher, and also in education as a faculty of the university. It would require engagement with the disciplines, but also interdisciplinarity, a conscious cultivation of interrelations at all levels, inspired by the vision of the seventeenth-century educator Comenius.

This was the lecture of an intellectual at the height of his powers on a public platform. So far had Simon emerged from obscurity, preparing his WEA course for a class that was not there, to become a public intellectual redefining his area of study for an attentive national audience.

Yet he was at the same time rehearsing his lines for another audience, the cultural committee of the CP, and it is to this that we now turn.

Notes

1 J.L. Vernon, note, 6 January 1953 (National Archives, KV.2/4176).
2 J.L. Vernon, note, 4 December 1951 (National Archives, KV.2/4175).
3 J.L. Vernon, note, 6 January 1953 (National Archives, KV.2/4176).
4 Joan Simon, *Shena Simon: Feminist and educationist* (Leicester: privately printed, 1986), 18. See also Roger T. Fieldhouse, *Adult Education and the Cold War* (Leeds: University of Leeds, 1985).
5 B. Simon to P. Trent, 4 November 1956 (National Archives, KV.2/4177; intercepted by the security service).
6 B. Simon to J. Gollan, 3 November [1956] (National Archives, KV.2/4177; intercepted).
7 B. Simon to J. Cohen, Monday [29 April] (National Archives, KV.2/4177; intercepted).
8 B. Simon to Mick Jenkins, Monday 29 [April 1957] (National Archives, KV.2/4173; intercepted).
9 *Daily Sketch*, report, 30 April 1957.
10 B. Simon to Syd Abbott, 5 May [1957] (National Archives, KV.2/4173, intercepted).
11 Intelligence report on Brian Simon, 1957 (National Archives, KV.2/4178).
12 Ernest Simon, letter to Brian Simon 14 May 1945 (Brian Simon papers, IOE).
13 Brian Simon, letter to John Gollan, 'Friday' [10 October 1960] (National Archives, KV.2/4181, intercepted).
14 B. Simon, conversation with J. Gollan, 12 June 1961 (National Archives, KV.2/4183, overheard by security services).
15 Note, 'Brian SIMON and CPGB finances', 6 June 1961 (National Archives, KV.2/4183).
16 Memo, 'The contributions of Lord Simon of Wythenshawe (Roger Simon) and the Hon Roger Simon to the finances of the Communist Party', 7 July 1961 (National Archives, KV.2/4183).
17 J. Chenhallis, note, 27 February 1962 (National Archives, KV.2/4184).
18 Simon, unpublished autobiography, chapter 8; WEA draft syllabus (Simon papers IOE).
19 See C. Hill, *The English Revolution 1640: An essay*, London, Lawrence & Wishart, 1940.
20 J. Simon, 'Educational policies and programmes', *Modern Quarterly*, 4/2, 1949, 168.
21 D. Jones, *School of Education 1946–1961*, Leicester, University of Leicester, 2001.
22 B. Simon, 'Leicestershire schools 1625–40', *British Journal of Educational Studies,* 3/1 (1954), 42.
23 See e.g. A.F. Leach, *English Schools at the Reformation*, London, 1896; and *Schools of Mediaeval England*, London, 1915.
24 J. Simon, 'A.F. Leach on the Reformation: I', *British Journal of Educational Studies*, 3/2 (1955), 143; J. Simon, 'A.F. Leach on the Reformation: II', *BJES*, 4/1 (1955), 48. See also Martin, 'Neglected women historians', 554.
25 J. Simon, 'The state and schooling at the Reformation and after: From pious causes to charitable uses', *History of Education*, 23/2 (1994), 157.
26 J. Simon, 'An "energetic and controversial" historian of education yesterday and today: A.F. Leach (1851–1915)', *History of Education*, 36/3 (2007), 367–89.
27 A.V. Judges (ed.), *Pioneers of English Education*, London, Faber and Faber, 1952.
28 Sir P. Morris, 'The English tradition of education', in Judges (ed.), *Pioneers of English Education*, 42–63.
29 Sir J. Maud, 'The twentieth-century administrator', in Judges (ed.), *Pioneers of English Education*, 227–47.
30 Anon [B. Simon?] 'Book notes: Educational pioneers "interpreted"', March–April, *Educational Review*, 1953, 11 (Simon papers, IOE, SIM/1/70).
31 Anon [B. Simon?] 'Book notes: Educational pioneers'.
32 Anon [B. Simon?] 'Book notes: Educational pioneers'.
33 R. Samuel (ed.), *People's History and Socialist Theory*, London, Routledge and Kegan Paul, 1981.

34 Maurice Cornforth, 'A.L. Morton: Portrait of a Marxist historian', in M. Cornforth (ed.), *Rebels and their Causes: Essays in honour of A.L. Morton*, Lawrence & Wishart, London, 1978, 7–19.
35 Maurice Cornforth, 'A.L. Morton', 19.
36 Maurice Dobb, *Studies in the Development of Capitalism*, London, Routledge & Kegan Paul, 1946.
37 Bill Schwartz, '"The people" in history: The Communist Party's Historians' Group, 1946–56', in *Making Histories: Studies in history-writing and politics*, Centre for Contemporary Cultural Studies in association with Hutchinson, London, 1982, 52.
38 Bill Schwartz, '"The people" in history', 66.
39 Eric Hobsbawm, 'The Historians' Group of the Communist Party', in M. Cornforth (ed), *Rebels and their Causes*, 21–47.
40 Joan Simon to James Klugmann, 18 September 1962 (CP papers, CP/CENT/CULT/8/4).
41 Simon, 'The ideological struggle'.
42 Notes, Education in the nineteenth century, February 28, 1955 (Brian Simon papers, DC/SIM/4/1/14).
43 Notes, Education in the nineteenth century, February 9, 1955 (Brian Simon papers, DC/SIM/4/1/14).
44 Brian Simon, Draft synopsis of book, March 24 [1955?] (Simon papers, DC/SIM/4/1/14).
45 Brian Simon, Draft synopsis of book, March 24 [1955?] (Simon papers, DC/SIM/4/1/14).
46 Brian Simon, Draft synopsis of book.
47 Lady Simon to Brian Simon, April 16, 1958 (Simon papers, DC/SIM/4/1/37).
48 Brian Simon to Maurice Cornforth, November 18 [1958] (Simon papers, DC/SIM/4/1/18).
49 Brian Simon to Maurice Cornforth, November 18 [1958] (Simon papers, DC/SIM/4/1/18).
50 Brian Simon, draft, 'Note to the Reader', n.d. [1958] (Simon papers, DC/SIM/4/1/18).
51 Brian Simon, draft, 'Note to the Reader', n.d. [1958] (Simon papers, DC/SIM/4/1/18).
52 Maurice Cornforth to Brian Simon, December 3, 1958 (Simon papers, DC/SIM/4/1/45).
53 Maurice Cornforth to Brian Simon, December 3, 1958 (Simon papers, DC/SIM/4/1/45).
54 Brian Simon to Maurice Cornforth, December 11, 1958 (Simon papers, DC/SIM/4/1/45).
55 James Klugmann to Brian Simon, December 22, 1958 (Simon papers, DC/SIM/4/1/45).
56 A.L. Morton to Brian Simon, March 19, 1959 (Simon papers, DC/SIM/4/1/45).
57 Brian Simon to Maurice Cornforth, May 30, 1959 (Simon papers, DC/SIM/4/1/45).
58 Simon, *Studies in the History of Education*, 15.
59 H.C. Barnard, review of Simon's *SHE*. *British Journal of Educational Studies*, 9 (1960–61): 8.
60 MI5 note, 'Joan Simon', 21 August 1964 (National Archives, KV.2/4286).
61 B. Simon, 'Memorandum', 14 June 1964 (National Archives, KV.2/4286, intercepted).
62 B. Simon, 'Memorandum', 14 June 1964 (National Archives, KV.2/4286, intercepted).
63 B. Simon, note, 'Revised synopsis, Studies in the History of Education, 1870–1940', 21 March 1961 (Simon papers, IOE, SIM/4/2/8).
64 B. Simon, note, 'Revised synopsis, Studies in the History of Education, 1870–1940', 21 March 1961 (Simon papers, IOE, SIM/4/2/8).
65 Simon, *Education and the Labour Movement*, 363.
66 Simon, *Education and the Labour Movement*, 363.
67 Maurice Cornforth to Brian Simon, January 6, 1964 (Simon papers, DC/SIM/4/2/8).
68 Maurice Cornforth to Brian Simon, September 11, 1964 (Simon papers, DC/SIM/4/8/9).
69 Maurice Cornforth to Brian Simon, February 3, 1964 (Simon papers, DC/SIM/4/2/14).
70 Maurice Cornforth to Brian Simon, February 3, 1964 (Simon papers, DC/SIM/4/2/14).
71 Cambridge University Press anonymous review, 5 December 1960 (National Archives, KV.2/4280, intercepted).
72 J. Simon, *Education and Society in Tudor England*, CUP, Cambridge, 1966.
73 *Times Literary Supplement*, review of Joan Simon's *Education and Society in Tudor England*, 'Tudors and their tutors', 10 June 1966.
74 J.W. Tibble (ed.) *The Study of Education*, London, Routledge and Kegan Paul, 1966.
75 B. Simon, 'The history of education', in Tibble, *The Study of Education*, 95.
76 B. Simon, 'The history of education', 92.
77 B. Simon, 'The history of education', 95–6.
78 J. Chenhallis, MI5 note, 27 February 1962 (National Archives, KV.2/4184).
79 See B. Simon, 'Education: The new perspective', in P. Gordon (ed.), *The Study of Education: Inaugural lectures*, volume 2, The Last Decade, London, Woburn Press, 1980, 71–94.

6
Chairman of the National Cultural Committee of the Communist Party

Brian Simon's communist affiliation is not unknown. Indeed, as has been seen, he wrote in his autobiography about joining the party in Cambridge in 1935, when it enjoyed considerable appeal among intellectuals.[1] However, this involvement was not confined to those alluring years but continued throughout the dull decades following. Simon did not follow his fellow students in their progressive disenchantment and subsequent abandonment of the party to join the New Left, but remained loyal. In fact, he was one of the main players in the party's strategy to counteract the effect of the dissidents and regain its lost influence. In the following decade, Simon played a decisive role in the ideological shaping of the party as head of its cultural committee. However, this seems not to be widely recognised. Simon is only a vague reference in books on the British Communist Party and he himself preferred to consign his role to oblivion. In his published memoir there are barely two post-war references to the Communist Party, in both cases significantly coupled with the Labour Party.[2] Even in his unpublished memoirs, the pages devoted to his organic work in the party seem to be limited to the Executive Committee,[3] avoiding any reference to his long-lasting position of responsibility for the cultural activity of the party. The following pages aim to shed light on this less-known, but historically significant, facet of Brian Simon's contribution.

In April 1957 Brian Simon became a member of the Executive Committee (EC) of the Communist Party of Great Britain (CP), a level just below the party's highest organ, the Political Committee (PC).[4] The timing is highly significant, since his election occurred in the midst of the turbulent 25th Special Congress, marked by the devastating crisis unleashed within the party following the invasion of Hungary by the Soviet Union in 1956.[5] Not only did the party lose one quarter of its members, perhaps more importantly, it lost its ideological hegemony within the Marxist left, a result of the emergence of the New Left. Simon persevered down a path in the opposite direction to that of many of his intellectual colleagues, and instead of reacting with disillusionment and abandoning the party, he closed ranks and, as a faithful, disciplined member, offered himself to the party's service in its time of greatest need.

Simon was one of the small group of intellectuals that the party could depend on to respond to the challenge posed by the New Left and to recover, at least in part, its waning prestige and influence. This was the explicit goal behind the launching of the party's new theoretical journal, *Marxism Today*, which took place three weeks before the 1957 Special Congress.[6] Although he ultimately was not included in the board, his name figured among those being considered for the hardcore inner circle in charge of the publication, along with his wife Joan, James Klugmann, Arnold Kettle, Alan Bush, Maurice Cornforth and John Lewis, among others. This cast included various figures that would accompany Simon in his work over the following decades and with whom he had consolidated a network of relations and friendship dating back to his days at Cambridge and even earlier. Klugmann, one of the party's official intellectuals and director of the new journal, had introduced Simon to communism at Cambridge, having previously attended secondary school (Gresham's) with him and his brother Roger. Maurice Cornforth, director of the party's editorial house, Lawrence & Wishart, was Klugmann's brother-in-law. Other members of the Cambridge network of colleagues included the professor of literary criticism at Leeds, Arnold Kettle – whose wife Margot Gale was Simon's secretary at the National Union of Students (NUS) – along with George and Betty Matthews and Jack Cohen, who went on to become party workers.[7]

A second line in the offensive strategy undertaken by the party in response to the Hungary crisis involved reactivating the Cultural Committee. In May 1957, after the designation of Brian Simon, James Klugmann and Arnold Kettle,[8] the intellectual nucleus that was to lead it out of its difficulties and give it a new direction arrived in the committee. This group of intellectuals would go on to play an important role in the ideological renovation of the party in the following decade. At a time of rapid social and political change, Simon and his colleagues proved receptive to the renewal trends within the party and offered their support and protection to the forces which were challenging the inherited orthodoxy of Stalinism: the youth, students and feminists.[9] In retrospect, these alliances show Simon to have served as a link between the ideals of the 1930s and the veritable explosion of changes that began in the 1960s over the dark years of Stalinism and its legacy. This represents the final victory of the socialist humanists, the term given by Geoff Andrews to this group.[10]

The National Cultural Committee

The National Cultural Committee (NCC) was one of the six subcommittees that advised the party's Executive Committee in specific areas (international, women's, youth, economic and social-service matters).[11] The committee was created in 1947 to further the cause of the cultural struggle for socialism under the leadership of the young economist Sam Aaronovitch.[12] The difficulties in having professionals from the world of culture and thought adhere to party orthodoxy soon became apparent. The group of scientists, headed by the prominent geneticist and biochemist John Haldane, was dissolved in 1949 as a consequence of its refusal to accept the theories of Lysenko. In the cultural realm, the official policies of socialist realism led to the defection of numerous writers and artists as well as the disappearance of the journal *Arena* in 1952. The group of historians, in contrast, achieved considerable influence in their field, launching new journals such as *Our History* and *Past and Present* (1952), thus contributing decisively to the rise of social history.[13]

In the 1950s the committee's situation only grew worse. With the Hungary crisis of 1956 the constant defection of collaborators turned into a veritable haemorrhage, while the dissolution and paralysis of specialised groups was exacerbated by a lack of leadership. In 1955 Sam Aaronovitch was replaced by Bill Wainwright, who shortly afterwards became secretary to the party's new General Secretary, John Gollan. In 1959 the committee went on to name as chairwoman Nora Jeffery, secondary-school teacher and organiser of the League of Women Communists.[14]

In this context, Simon, who had just published his *Studies in the History of Education, 1780–1870,* had become a figure of reference for the party's intellectuals, or at least this is implied in the fact that he was chosen to give a conference on 'Intellectual and Professional People' in the 1961 congress, where his presentation put on display the party's internal contradictions at the time.[15] On the one hand, Simon offered a strictly orthodox discourse, one that generated its own evidence based on a wilful diagnosis of the state of the revolt by intellectuals and professionals, concluding with a radical rejection of the notion of adopting a less rigid approach to appeal to these sectors ('Such an approach would be fatal'). His call to close ranks, in the name of ideological rearming, was explicit: 'On the contrary, our aim must be to state our position more effectively'. However, on the other hand, and notwithstanding this orthodoxy, Simon could barely conceal his interest in appealing to these social groups – intellectuals and professionals – which he considered to be a strategic objective. Citing his colleague Arnold Kettle, he acknowledged that this group wielded an influence that was disproportionate to its number. In 1961, therefore, the elements of the difficult challenge facing Simon as head of the Cultural Committee were already laid out: that of making orthodoxy attractive for intellectuals.

Brian Simon was named Chairman of the Cultural Committee in May 1962.[16] The committee's composition at this point revealed the profound rupture in personnel brought on by the crisis, with only three members remaining from 1954. With its renovation in 1961 a stable group of members was established that would remain throughout the 1960s and well into the following decade. The committee's intellectual core, which would continue to serve until 1976, included Simon, James Klugmann and Arnold Kettle, together with the veteran Bill Carritt. Alongside this group, but at an ever-growing ideological distance, was the musician and composer Alan Bush. Also in the Committee, until 1972, were the art professor Ray Watkinson and the painter Barbara Niven, organiser and columnist with the *Daily Worker* and the *Morning Star*. In the mid-1960s the former chair, Nora Jeffery, and the legendary Margot Heinemann both left the Committee.

In September 1962, a few months after his appointment, Simon outlined the main points of an ambitious programme of initiatives in a document titled 'The ideological Struggle'.[17] After the usual, positive diagnosis juxtaposing the Soviet Union's achievements against capitalism's ever-deepening crisis, Simon clamours for an ideological rearmament: 'the struggle for peaceful co-existence [...] does not imply any soft pedaling of the ideological struggle'.

Simon believed that this struggle should focus on four areas. The first was philosophy, 'the first and most important area' and the traditional realm for the articulation of Marxism. Simon follows this up immediately by insisting on the need to go a step further and move into the 'direct field of economics and politics and the connected social sciences'. He then announced his principal line of work for the next several years: cultivating Marxism in disciplines such as sociology, psychology, education and history (the fields of medicine, health and urban planning, which he had included initially, failed to prosper). Work in the cultural realm would include literature, film, theatre and television on the one hand, and art and music on the other, along with a general reflection on the relationship between culture and society. Simon acknowledged the prevailing disorientation in the cultural realm resulting from the failure of socialist realism and the subsequent interest in the possibilities offered by Raymond Williams's *Culture and Society*, a key work that has come to be considered the starting point for cultural studies. Finally, with his inclusion of an area dedicated to science, Simon showed his interest in the philosophy of science, while highlighting the Marxist contribution to its history.

In this first exposition, Simon made clear that his priority was the theoretical reorientation of the committee, an objective that was at odds with the committee's original mission, which was of a cultural nature. In fact, of the four areas outlined by Simon, only one had to do with the cultural activity for which the committee was named. The others (philosophy, social science and science) were clearly theoretical as was, without a doubt, the notion of a 'reflection' that he added to the cultural area. We see here, from the very start, the conflict between cultural action and theory that would mark Simon's leadership of the committee. While ideology could have found a space in which to bring together both elements, Simon was quick to identify the ideological realm with theory and not with cultural activity. This prioritising of theory led to a clash with the official purpose of the committee, whose ideological work was restricted to the field of culture and which was meant to be organising cultural activities, incentivising creation in the arts and sciences, stimulating the party's cultural life and supporting cultural groups. Such cultural initiatives waned under Simon's mandate, ceding ground to ideological priorities that ranged far beyond the confines of the cultural sphere. We could even go so far as to say that Simon nourished the hope of transforming the cultural committee into the motor of a theoretical-ideological renovation, one that would give a key role to intellectuals who at the time played such a minor role in the British CP, which was essentially a workers' party.[18]

Throughout his mandate Simon was never comfortable within the institutional constraints, which were hardly conducive to furthering his longed-for intellectual offensive, even proving detrimental to his cause. A comparison with what was occurring in the main communist parties of western Europe at the time helps us to understand Simon's frustration.[19] As in the UK, the invasion of Hungary by the USSR had enormous consequences for the Italian PCI and the French PCF in terms of intellectual disaffection and loss of members. In both cases, the parties enacted strategies to try to recover some of their lost intellectual influence. But in France as well as in Italy, specific institutional instruments were designed for this purpose, while maintaining their respective cultural committees in charge of cultural activities and policies. In Italy this offensive was led by the Istituto Gramsci, created in 1950 but relaunched in 1957 with prestigious intellectuals at the forefront such as Ranuccio Bianchi Bandinelli and Franco Ferri; in France the Centre d'Études et de Recherches Marxistes (CERM) was created in 1959 under the leadership of the philosopher Roger Garaudy.[20] In Great Britain, by contrast, Simon had to make do with a cultural committee that had been designed to coordinate the party's ever-diminishing cultural activity, which even at the best of times did not come close to having the kind of influence that its French and Italian counterparts enjoyed.

If the limited cultural influence of the British party painted a depressing picture to begin with, its room for improvement in the theoretical realm was even more dismal. In Britain the party was characterised by a marked 'working class ethos' that afforded no special role to intellectuals.[21] Reticence towards the idea of establishing an institution dedicated to theory was, as we shall see, obstinate and permanent. Simon therefore had no choice but to practise a complex juggling act in order to establish a programme of intellectual development within an institutional framework that seemed designed to impede this very type of initiative.

The NCC had carried out, in its early days, no cultural activity worthy of its name. As mentioned, the groups of writers and artists who were already in crisis mode at the start of the 1950s were unable to withstand the 1956 crisis, with the exception of the area of music. Yet the NCC had no choice but to resume its work in the cultural realm after the crisis, for at least two reasons. The first was the need to establish some sort of cultural policy to fill the vacuum left by the moribund socialist realism. And secondly, because, regardless of the crisis, the committee had inherited cultural institutions that could not simply be abandoned.

The elaboration of a political statement about the party's position regarding culture was begun in the early 1960s under the leadership of the artist Barbara Niven, who wrote up a report on the principal institutions involved in cultural policy in Britain and who published an article in *Marxism Today*.[22] However, more than three years went by before any definitive document was produced. 'Policy for Leisure' proposed a sweeping cultural policy based on an increase in grants and a decentralisation of cultural and sports facilities, accompanied by a regionalisation of the Arts Council and the creation of regional radio and television stations. This was to be complemented by a democratisation of the advisory committees of BBC and ITV.[23] Funding, decentralisation and democratisation, then, were the pillars upon which communist cultural policy was to be articulated. The document was circulated among some sixty people in early Autumn of 1963,[24] but the minutes of the Executive Committee do not reflect its being submitted for debate in the committee as planned, nor is there any trace of the pamphlet that had been planned for.

A second focus of the committee's cultural activity had to do with institutions associated with or close to the party. The oldest of these was the Unity Theatre, created in 1936 by workers' groups and active in Camden Town and whose financial difficulties were handled by the committee during the sixties.[25] Centre 42 was a newer group that took its name from a resolution featuring this same number, approved by the Trades Union Congress of 1960 on the initiative of Ralph Bond. The resolution called for involving unions in the promotion of workers' cultural activities. After six festivals celebrated in different cities the project managed to attract the interest of the NCC, although in a report from 1971 Simon acknowledges its decline.[26]

A third centre of the party's cultural influence was to be found in the folk song revival, led by the communists Ewan McColl and Bert Lloyd. The ideological implications of this movement of traditional music are brought to the fore by Lloyd when he contrasts the sterility of commercial popular art with this type of music, which offers a vision of life – one including sexual relations – 'touching on the true dignity of man'.[27] This constituted a traditionalist, moralist avowal against the 'brain-softening' pop-rock musical revolution of the 1960s that was electrifying youth at the time and which the Young Communist League embraced.[28]

A fourth and final line of activity, which constituted one of the NCC's objectives, was the bolstering of cultural activities in the party's local branches, a matter that Simon had addressed in his 1964 work plan.[29] A report by Bill Carritt on this issue shows just how hard it was at the time for British communists to conceive of a cultural activity removed from the prevailing, rancorous ideological debate.[30] Invariably, the discussion would move into the terrain of 'controversial ideological questions of our day', preferably pitting them against non-Marxists. Moreover, this 'ideological activity' approach came into conflict with the Department of Organization and with the district committees responsible for the branches. The conclusion was reached that 'it is not particularly a task for the Cultural Committee', an affirmation conveying the relief felt by Simon in being able to free himself of the whole mess.[31]

Despite his presiding over a committee defined as cultural, and despite the fact that the 1960s were witness to a bona fide cultural revolution,[32] Brian Simon's interests did not lie in culture, but were unapologetically directed to the realm of theory. A report from early 1964 tells us that under his mandate seventeen meetings and four full-day conferences were held and that eleven and three of these, respectively, were dedicated to ideological matters.[33] These included an agenda of intellectual concerns very close to the essence of communist orthodoxy, such as the relationship between base and superstructure, socialist realism, literary criticism and alienation.

However, the central focus of the NCC's work during the first years of Simon's leadership was the organisation of the Weeks of Marxist Debate. The closest and most direct precedent for this initiative was the series of conferences planned by the National Union of Students (NUS) for November 1962, which showcased the students' vitality. The programme was made up of the reduced group of intellectuals who had stayed in the party after the haemorrhage of 1956: George Thomson (professor of Greek at Birmingham), Sam Aaronovitch (economist and Secretary of Central London), Arnold Kettle (professor of literary criticism at Leeds), John Desmond Bernal (professor of physics at Birkbeck) and Maurice Dobb (professor of economics at Trinity College, Cambridge). A cast representing the purest orthodoxy of the CP.

In June of 1962, a few months before the course organised by the students, the committee decided to appropriate the event – which it had not been involved with – and to organise a Week of Marxist Debate (sometimes 'Thought').[34] Simon's main objective here was to bring the party out of its isolation. In order to reach beyond the party's orthodox circles, he planned to open the event and create a forum for debate between Marxists and non-Marxists. This was an ambitious project, meant to involve a broad spectrum of intellectuals, British and foreign, including E.H. Carr, the historian Christopher Hill, C.P. Snow, author of *The Two Cultures,* Raymond Williams and Roger Garaudy. The event would culminate with a dialogue on *War and Peace,* between the Soviet journalist Ilya Ehrenburg and Bertrand Russell.

Despite the ambitious programme, which included many parallel discussion panels (history, economics, music, film, modern theatre, folk song),[35] it was not long before difficulties arose in bringing together the figures that the event was counting on. Among the obstacles, a committee report alludes to the reticence of some of these individuals to appear in an event organised under the auspices of the party.[36] The ambitious plans dissipated and ultimately Simon had no choice but to resort to the traditional cast of party intellectuals and to essentially repeat the programme offered by the students, with the addition of Hobsbawm in History and Maurice Cornforth (editor at Lawrence & Wishart) in

Philosophy. Finally, the week-long event was held in London from 14 to 22 November 1963, with an attendance in the plenary conferences of between 130 and 180 persons.[37]

For all the huge chasm that existed between the intellectual forum that had been planned and the party gathering in which the event resulted, Simon's assessment of the affair was highly favourable.[38] He saw it as a first attempt at organising a global, concentrated event, one that showed the communists capable of presenting Marxism in a nonsectarian light and echoing the cooperation envisaged in the classic popular front period of the late 1930s. In Simon's view, they had succeeded in resolving the contradictory objective of broadening the area of debate between Marxists and non-Marxists while making it clear that the party had something to say in these different fields. It would seem, then, that the goal of breaking out of their isolation had been achieved. Maurice Dobb was considerably more sceptical, caustically asserting that the communists were so desperate to have someone debate with them that they were willing to let their principles become watered down to nothing.[39]

Undaunted by Dobb's scepticism, Simon persevered in his faith in this kind of opening, promoting a new edition of the Week of Marxist Debate for January of 1966. So anxious was he to broaden the party's reach that he even proposed suspending its usual reticence regarding non-party intellectuals through a joint organisation with the *New Left Review*, later reduced to 'some left journals'.[40] After the Labour general election victory in October 1964, the week was refocused on pressuring the government – from a broad leftist front that included 'leftwing Labour party members, left intellectuals, and etc' – to follow the path towards socialism laid out by the party.[41]

Over the following months, the difficulties involved in carrying out this programme became clear.[42] The lack of a response or the refusal of some invitees take part, together with the difficulties in attending on the part of others, led to a non-stop switching of names; once again, the ambitious initial programme was reduced to the traditional nucleus of party intellectuals. The Week, celebrated in January 1966, received scant attendance and meagre coverage. After the intense shuffling of names and figures that took place in the months leading up to it, eight activists and five non-party participants took part. The final session, in which General Secretary John Gollan spoke, brought together some 250 attendees. The opening session, which Brian Simon himself had to take charge of in a last-ditch emergency, had around 180 attendees, while the rest of the sessions averaged 80. Surprisingly for the organisers, the most successful session was the one on art. The participation of John

Berger created considerable expectation, drawing some 450 attendees as well as various artists and writers. Berger's attempt to conceive Marxism from the point of view of the artist, described by Simon as honest and creative, received harsh sectarian criticism. Nonetheless, the general tone of the interventions, along with the presence of artists and writers such as Edna O'Brien, Kenneth Tynan and others, emboldened Simon to 'consider in particular how to follow up this discussion in terms of bringing artists of all kinds closer to the Party and the working class', reinforcing his optimistic notion that at this point it would be easier to involve intellectuals from outside of the party than it had been previously. Simon applauded the fact that the invitations to the event had been so well received by professors A.J. Ayer, Morris Carstairs, and Raymond Williams, and that their non-attendance had been due to other circumstances and not to a refusal to engage with the party. In any case, Simon's conclusion after the experience was that the party must persevere in this direction, to 'break out of our isolation and to begin to act again as a centre of focus of Marxist discussion leading to action'. At the same time, he was perfectly aware of the internal reticence that such an opening gave rise to: 'One noticeable feature was the tendency towards a dogmatic approach on the part of a few comrades which, if unchallenged, is particularly unhelpful when we are trying to establish new relations with the Left.'

Simon's goal of bringing the party out of its intellectual isolation meant tackling head-on the matter of the role of artists and intellectuals, an issue that had become a commonplace in communist party debates. In the case of a party with a 'working class ethos', as was the case of the CP,[43] this posed a considerable challenge. As alluded to previously, in a report from the congress of 1960 Simon had acknowledged the difficulty of bringing intellectuals into the party, while at the same time refusing to accept less rigid positions in order to do so. As chairman of the NCC, however, Simon's priority was to seek out a more flexible, open position, conducive to overcoming intellectuals' reticence towards the party. After the 1966 Week he could hardly contain his enthusiasm at the presence of recognised writers at the art session. Similarly, he was hard put to contain his displeasure at the sectarian attitudes that doomed this attempted new direction to failure.

Simon's ambition to appeal to intellectuals was particularly challenging in Great Britain. The scant influence of the British CP in the realm of culture meant that the NCC's approach to art and culture was increasingly theoretical. Unlike in Italy, France or even Spain – despite its dictatorship – in Great Britain the relationship between artists and intellectuals and the party could never be approached from cultural practices for the simple reason that the party played no role at all in the world of culture. This barrier left the cultural question in a merely speculative plane, with no possibility of practical modulation. Such a framework allowed for little flexibility and quickly led to the adoption of dogmatic postures or, alternatively, at the other extreme, to completely renouncing the establishment of criteria in cultural questions, as will be seen below.

The professor of literary criticism at Leeds, Arnold Kettle, was the committee member to most vigorously study the role of the artist – and, by extension, the intellectual. In a 1960 booklet[44] Kettle proposes a quite simple, clear solution to this complex predicament: the obedience of intellectuals to the party. Needless to say, coming from a university specialist in literary criticism, this dogmatic conclusion was preceded by a convoluted theoretical exposition. In a similar direction, a year earlier Kettle had defended in *Marxism Today* the prohibition of Pasternak's *Doctor Zhivago*,[45] which had triggered a heated debate among western communists and leftists and had led to the influential Italian editor Feltrinelli abandoning the PCI.[46] While Kettle conceded that writers should not be told what to write, that did not mean that they should have free license to act irresponsibly, and that society did not have a legitimate right to pressure the writer to abandon such attitudes. In summary, there was no place in socialist society for the publication of a work that misrepresented or opposed the ideals of the socialist revolution. Kettle added that only those who also opposed the end of exploitation could oppose this conclusion. Citing *A Painter of our Time* by John Berger, Kettle argued that artists should only feel different from others in the sense that they are able to express what others feel. The central idea, once more, was the submission of the artist to the collective, in the name of the struggle for emancipation.

With this closing reference to Berger, committee intellectuals seemed to be indicating that, notwithstanding the dogmatism of their recent stances, they were actually quite interested in exploring new approaches to culture from the left. One unequivocal sign of this was the weekend seminar that Simon organised in October of 1961 in Leicester, where he lived, for the purpose of debating, from a Marxist perspective, the most important recent theoretical contribution to the field of culture: the work *Culture and Society,* by Raymond Williams.[47] As principal lecturer, Simon resorted to Kettle, who, in an article meant to serve as a basis for the discussion,[48] maintained an inflexible position in both the theoretical and political spheres. With regard to the former, he refuted the autonomy of culture, precisely one of the questions that had made Williams' book a foundational milestone in cultural studies; as for the political element, Kettle defended state control – which according to Williams only kept artists away from socialist culture – with the argument, again, of the socialist state's responsibility. He finished off his critique by accusing Williams of an insularity more in keeping with the New Left. In the end, Kettle illustrated the contradictory position in which the committee's intellectual core found itself with regard to the party's opening up: a trepidation brought on by a mixture of attraction and fear.

And yet, despite these theoretical obstacles, changes were quick to come. In February 1963 the Political Committee's General Secretary seemed to be inclined to take the opposite view to Kettle and to refrain from establishing criteria in the cultural sphere. Thus, it announced that 'we do not intend to issue any directives at all or to exercise any control over the direction of the comrades' work'.[49] This pronouncement put to rest once and for all the application of Lysenkian arguments in the scientific realm as well as socialist realism in the arts. However, the party still reserved the right to establish its point of view when a work touched upon the political sphere. It was clearly a declaration resting on shifting pillars; how was one to discern clearly between a merely cultural and a political context? And how does one separate a general cultural activity from its concrete products? Be this as it may, the declaration did attest to the party leaders' desire to move beyond the rigid cultural and scientific control, inherited from Stalinism, which had constituted a part of their identity.

A lucid, forceful report by local historian Lionel Munby and presented to the cultural committee in January 1965 gives a good idea of the speed and import of the changes taking place in the heart of the party. It also made clear that no one was being fooled any longer on the issue of artists and intellectuals.[50] Munby began by corroborating the mistrust that professional workers felt towards the party and towards communism, along with the futility of the party's attempts to overcome this mistrust. 'There is no hope of bludgeoning intellectuals into an acceptance of Marxism nor of winning them by a sleight of hand trick which evades the issues as they see them.' When professional intellectuals looked towards socialist countries, they saw travel restrictions, dogmatic party declarations and the control of publishing, performances and exhibits, all carried out by illiberal, partisan figures. Munby did not deny the existence of certain areas that needed censure, although he disdained the sexual puritanism of socialist countries. The question came down to where the line should be drawn. While acknowledging the state's responsibility in culture – so dear to Kettle – he also recognised the problems in applying it, asking himself just who should be in charge of hanging this painting or exhibiting that sculpture. For Munby, resorting to the people was pure demagoguery, as it skipped over the lead-up question of how popular taste was formed in the first place. Far from the communist dogma of overcoming all contradictions, it seemed that socialism was still a long way from resolving the problem of art.

Munby proposed two ways out of this conundrum. The first, and certainly the most original, as well as probably the most viable in practice, was to decentralise the cultural activity of the socialist society. Having numerous institutions active in the cultural field would bring a plurality that contrasted starkly with the uniformity of real socialism. His second line of action, a consequence of the party's new policy of not establishing directives, involved the necessary struggle for ideas as a way for the Marxist vision to gain favour in society. This formulation had unquestionable Gramscian connotations. The dismantling of the rigid party control served to open up the field of hegemony to all contenders; for Munby, this realisation went a good way in explaining how the achievements of western communists and intellectuals towered over those of their counterparts in socialist countries. And this call to action also had a bearing on the intellectual field of one of Simon's strategic lines: the development of Marxism in specialised academic disciplines such as aesthetics and sociology.

Questions of ideology and culture

Ultimately it was an external event that accelerated the pace and process of the revisionism of orthodox communism in Great Britain: the statement by the Central Committee of the French Communist Party regarding arts and culture. The resolution, taken in Argenteuil in March of 1966,[51] put socialist realism to rest for good, advocating at the same time for the independence of cultural and artistic production, which would be freed of the party's oversight.[52] In the absence of doctrinal truths in the area of culture and the arts, 'everything invites communist intellectuals to approach the problems open in the field of science, of philosophy and of art with boldness and independence of judgement'.[53] It was a call to bring communist intellectuals into the national culture, theoretically claiming a position of leadership that they were losing in practice.

The principles that came out of Argenteuil served to resolve, rapidly and radically, many of the debates that were taking place in the British CP.

Simon took this as an endorsement to take a qualitative step forward and push through a similar statement; ultimately, this may well have been the most notable public intellectual contribution of his entire tenure as head of the committee. The statement was approved by the Executive Committee in March 1967 and published shortly afterwards as a brochure entitled *Questions of Ideology and Culture*.[54]

Despite being directly derived from the French resolution, the British version was considerably bolder and much more groundbreaking. After announcing 'the clarification of our attitudes to such questions of ideology and culture',(4)[55] it went on to address the contentious issues directly, without working them into an elaborate, indirect subtext praising the party, as the French declaration did. Simon preferred to first tackle the questions that needed to be clarified (science, art, religion, democracy and humanism) and to leave the matter of the party for the end. The prominence of the theoretical-ideological concerns which so marked his mandate was also made clear by his choice of topics, where culture was relegated to a secondary position.

With regard to science, the new policy renounced the party's intervention in the justification of scientific theories, guaranteeing scientific communities total freedom to apply their internal criteria based on 'only experiment and practical testing'.(5) This new approach implied a return to traditional neopositivist conceptions. It is difficult to imagine that a figure as well-read and as interested in the philosophy of science as Brian Simon could not have been familiar with the key work published by Kuhn in 1962,[56] but the need to guard scientists against any infiltration of external factors that could result in a repeat of the Lysenko case, with its 'harmful results',(6) led him to ignore the historicist and sociological derivations of the Kuhnian perspective.

As for art and culture, the declaration abandoned traditional doctrinal elaborations and renounced the setting up of Marxist criteria, defending instead total freedom and independence for creators. All traces of socialist realism were erased – albeit without actually mentioning this policy itself – and even the few exceptions pertaining to political considerations that had been established by the Political Committee and had figured in some of the early drafts were eliminated. The text, to its credit, acknowledged Marxism's limitations in creating a normative theory in the field of art, something that had always constituted a concern for Simon. The communists were in essence taking a step backwards, relinquishing their aspiration to control artistic production. 'We reject the concept that art, literature or culture should reflect only one (official) school or style'.(7) Therefore, there would be no school *of* or *close to* communism, no merit accorded to a work for its being *exemplary*. In addition to this renunciation of virtually all traditional communist assumptions regarding art, the declaration implicitly dispensed with the idea that the popularisation of art was equivalent to its democratisation. And without directly addressing the subject, the text recognised that understanding was not possible without study,(6) which would seem to acknowledge the acquired, specialised nature of art. The abandonment of the old concepts of commitment and popularisation was followed by praise for the one principle, aside from freedom and plurality, that the declaration embraced in the field of art and culture: innovation. To be sure, 'not every innovation will lead to positive results, but without it culture will be stifled and stultified'.(7)

In the religious realm, the statement made reference to the dialogue with Christians that western communists had undertaken after Vatican II. British communists, who recognised the potential that faith could have as a stimulus for progressive causes, also proposed a reinterpretation highlighting common values such as justice and solidarity.(8)

The most openly political section of the declaration was unquestionably that dealing with democracy. Here the party ratified the pacifist, democratic strategy of transition to socialism that had been established in 1951 in its *British Road to Socialism*. Now, however, it went beyond this parliamentary path, appropriating the liberal-democratic tradition and presenting its achievements as the fruit of the working class, but from a plural vision that included other political forces such as the Labour Party and the unions. Its defence of democracy not only rejected the concept of the single party but took the bold, unprecedented step of accepting that socialism could consist of a multiparty system in which other parties could include those opposing socialism.

In truth, these policies were not new in Brian Simon's case. In a pamphlet from 1960 in which he questioned the capitalist concept of freedom,[57] Simon was careful to avoid twisting the meaning of the word or resorting to duplicitous concepts of real or socialist democracy. While acknowledging that freedom could be subordinated to class and to individuals' real possibilities of acting, the enforced restrictions of individual and group freedoms in socialist countries seemed to Simon to denote a lack of faith in the people themselves, who had brought socialism in the first place.(21) And Simon was explicit in affirming that the single-party model did not constitute a part of communist doctrine but that it had arisen in response to a specific historical situation, that is, Russia's lack of a parliamentary tradition, which was aggravated by the treason of Mensheviks and Social-Revolutionaries.(22) In Great Britain, by contrast, socialism's advocacy of the right to vote seemed to make sense, representing the culmination of a long process of fighting for rights (Habeas Corpus, trial by jury, the right to strike...).(23) For Simon, and for the party after the statement, the dictatorship of the proletariat became a metaphor, not a constitutional prescription of communism.

The section of the resolution dealing with humanism clearly echoed its French counterpart. As in the original, the British declaration held that not only was socialism a humanism, but that it was the genuine humanism, stripped of bourgeois deceit. 'We, who are Marxists, claim to be the most consistent humanists of our time.'(11) The stance opposed the antihumanist conception of Marxism defended by Louis Althusser in France[58] and followed in the tradition of British committee intellectuals, reproducing Kettle's formula from a few years earlier. Actually, Andrews describes the nucleus of committee intellectuals (Simon, Klugmann, Cornforth and Kettle) as the socialist humanists.[59] John Lewis, another prominent member of the committee, would later debate with Althusser from the pages of *Marxism Today*.[60]

All of these principles announced in the statement reach their culmination in the section on the communist party. The first several paragraphs deal with Marxism, understood as the principal theoretical instrument for understanding the world in a general way – with no discredit to the work of scientists and artists. In fact, the incorporation of theoretical work from different Marxists' perspectives and fields was applauded. This was where Simon showed his determination to wage the theoretical battle in the academic world through the specialised development of Marxism, as Munby had proposed. But theoretical work in itself was not enough; achieving socialism required a political organisation that could be none other than the Communist Party. As a way of highlighting the importance of the practical struggle, the resolution concludes with paraphrasing of Marx's famous sentence on Feuerbach: 'if there is to *be* a world to be *interpreted* it will have to be *changed*'.(12)

The declaration reflected a determined stand in favour of ideological renovation arrived at after years of committed activism by the group of intellectuals making up the cultural committee under the leadership of Brian Simon. The positions were much more radical on every point than those of their French counterparts, and, even more importantly, were not attributable to any sort of political strategy or positioning, given that, unlike the French Communist Party and its *union des gauches*, the British CP was not participating in any electoral strategy whatsoever. The British declaration openly defended a multiparty democratic socialism, with none of the convoluted clauses and exceptions worked into the fine print of the French declaration. The truly significant difference with regard to the French version, however, was that it proposed extending freedom of discussion to the realm of theory, whereas the French only applied it to the domain of culture, zealously reserving the control of theory to the Communist Party. The party, thus, became a collective intellectual that produced theory together with the contributions of intellectuals and the working class.[61]

Notwithstanding its ideological audacity, the text was not without its weaknesses, reflecting certain internal contradictions and discrepancies. Over the course of the debate Maurice Cornforth, editor at Lawrence & Wishart, levelled stinging criticism against the theoretical inconsistencies of the stance towards artistic and cultural matters.[62] John Lewis was even more radical – and political – in his critique of what he called an opportunistic and instrumental declaration,[63] going as far as to appeal to the Political Committee.[64] However, during the entire process, Brian Simon enjoyed the support and complicity of General Secretary John Gollan, who demonstrated his faith in the party intellectuals explicitly.[65] In fact, the statement was approved during a session of the Executive Committee that dealt with many other matters, with a tempered debate far removed from the dramatics that had flourished at Argenteuil.[66]

The Gramscian bastion

Simon had played a key role in the ideological renovation of the British Communist Party in the 1960s, leading to its adopting more flexible ideological formulas and accepting democracy. A new theoretical framework had been established and the only thing that seemed to be missing was a new name. While it came to be known as Eurocommunism, many prominent renovators in the British party were reticent to use the new term, preferring to define themselves as Gramscians, a choice that attests to the influence that the Italian thinker had in this ideological evolution.[67]

As Forgacs has pointed out, Gramsci's reception in Great Britain was both partial and unbalanced, with certain areas having been overdeveloped to the detriment of his broader legacy.[68] But beyond the theoretical and political coherence of his reception, Gramsci's ideas addressed the concerns and yearnings for renovation of an important sector of the British left.[69] Ultimately, within the party, being a Gramscian meant being critical of the status quo and aspiring to something better, even if this something had not yet been coherently articulated. It is not surprising then that the appropriation made of Gramsci was inconsistent, depending mostly on the particular needs of those resorting to him. In any case, if there was one institution in the party that was notably affected by the Gramscian turn it was undoubtedly the NCC, owing to how Gramsci had always defended the independence of culture, rejecting its traditional reduction to a mere superstructure rigidly determined by an infrastructure. This revaluation of the field of culture, and especially the Gramscian concept of hegemony, offered a promising horizon for the committee and its activities. Furthermore, the Gramscian concept of the organic intellectual allowed committee intellectuals to affirm not only their autonomy but also the central role that had always been denied them in the British party.[70] Under Simon's leadership, the NCC sought to make the best possible use of the opportunities offered by the new ideological framework and to claim their spot at the forefront of the struggle for hegemony.

Following upon the publication of *Questions of Ideology and Culture* in 1967, Simon undertook the reorganisation of the National Cultural Committee. At this point, he dispensed with some of the earlier subterfuge, openly proposing the creation of a committee of intellectuals focused on ideology that would be separate from the cultural committee. The obedient activists who a decade earlier had closed ranks with the party against its dissidents were now clamouring for a role of their own. In July 1968 Simon presented to the General Secretary a report calling for a thorough overhaul of the committee's work, including the reconsideration of the committee's relationship with *Marxism Today* and with the publisher Lawrence & Wishart. The two principal means of ideological expression of the party had, until now, maintained no more than an informal, personal relationship with the NCC.[71] After an exchange of impressions at the party's summer school with James Klugmann and Jack Cohen, his two old friends from Cambridge,[72] Simon decided to give up on indirect strategies and propose the constitution of a small group whose role would be to advise the EC on ideological matters. The group would be made up of two or three members of the EC, the hard core traditional intellectual nucleus of the committee (James Klugmann, Maurice Cornforth and Brian Simon) plus Nora Jeffery, Jack Cohen and Betty Matthews, the latter also an old friend from Cambridge who had replaced Cohen at the head of the education department. However, by September this initiative had lost steam, mired in a never-ending attempt to clarify the work perspectives and in a vague project to publish a number of articles in *Marxism Today* that would kindle the theoretical debate.[73] The slackening of this bold new project of Simon's over the summer is not so surprising if we take into account the Soviet Union's invasion of Czechoslovakia in August, an event that shook the party from top to bottom and offered the spectre of a new haemorrhage of militants.

Two years later, in January of 1971, Simon again proposed, in an internal document, a strategic reorientation of the committee towards the theoretical-ideological domain.[74] While aware that the direction ratified by the Political Committee in 1968 was aimed at placing emphasis on the cultural domain, Simon nonetheless pushed in the opposite direction, openly proposing a shift away from this cultural realm, his idea being to turn the committee into a 'centre for the encouragement of Marxist studies, with a view to clarifying and reinstating Marxism as the dominant philosophical outlook'. He was essentially going back to the old idea of the Weeks of Marxist Debate, albeit from an approach that was more academic than ideological. He believed that the committee's mission should be 'assisting the development of Marxism and of Marxist cadres covering modern knowledge'. Marxism, in his view, needed to be applied and developed in different academic disciplines, especially the social sciences, without relinquishing its traditional application in science, philosophy, culture and literature. The ideological changes that Simon himself had overseen within the party were what allowed for this more flexible approach to Marxism, which coincided with the evolution of these academic disciplines. Ultimately, he was advocating unabashedly for the new academic Marxism that was beginning to take shape in the 1970s.[75]

Simon's stance in support of academic Marxism reflected a significant change in intellectuals' makeup. Tony Judt has pointed out how, as of the late 1960s, the traditional public intellectual – a philosopher or a novelist for the most part – was ceding ground to a new type of academic who intervened in the public sphere from his or her specialised field.[76] In a similar vein, Di Maggio remarks on how intellectuals in the French CP, who had traditionally operated on the margins, were beginning to occupy prominent academic positions. Academia was, after all, the domain in which the institutions created by the French and Italian communist parties engaged in theoretical debate. The Istituto Gramsci aspired to be the seed of a Marxist university and was in fact the principal force behind the valued historical journal *Studi Storici*, while the most important work carried out by the Centre d'Études et de Recherches Marxistes (CERM), in Di Maggio's opinion, dealt with linguistics, psychoanalysis, anthropology and the Asian mode of production.[77]

The main obstacle facing Simon in developing this line of work was the profound reticence of his colleagues in the party's core. This resistance did not stem merely from the markedly working-class tradition of the

British PC. The idea of creating a committee that moved independently from the leadership organs and appropriated the theoretical discussion could only be viewed with suspicion, and not only by the British party. Di Maggio points out that the French declaration was based on the agreement to recognise total freedom for artists but to jealously restrict the elaboration of theory to the party, which developed it as a collective intellectual through its organisations.[78] The party's refusal to create a specific institution for theory, even in an academic sense, meant that Simon had to continue operating within the confines of a more generalist institution designed for other objectives, as was the cultural committee. Simon, however, opted to pay the price and to steer the committee in the direction that he himself was determined to take it.

While working on this reorientation, Simon also focused considerable energy on the renewal of the committee. In January 1968 he had managed to have the EC name two figures who would play an important part in the party's Gramscian evolution: Betty Matthews[79], a friend from Cambridge who was now in charge of the department of education, and Martin Jacques.[80] Jacques, a recent graduate, had led the student movement before being promoted to the EC by Simon and Klugmann in 1967.[81] He eventually became successor to both: to Simon as head of the committee and to Klugmann as director of *Marxism Today*, to which Jacques gave new life in the 1980s.[82] By the mid-1970s Jacques had become one of the party's prominent figures in the Eurocommunist sector. He represented perhaps the most outstanding example of the alliance forged by Simon and other veteran party intellectuals with the reform currents of the 1970s, although he was not the only one. Another notable incorporation of the committee's was Monty Johnstone, a veteran anti-Stalinist militant who had been 'isolated and ostracised by the party'.[83] The committee also attempted to recruit Mick Costello, former student leader in Manchester, future national union organiser and editor of the *Morning Star*, but the EC forbade his incorporation on the grounds of a technical incompatibility.[84]

The renovation gained traction in 1971. In keeping with his determination to develop Marxism in specialised disciplines, Simon's report from this year included the recommendation that new recruits should 'ideally consist of young or youngish cdes [comrades] working in the fields of the social sciences and humanities (and science) who have themselves achieved a definitive level of Marxist thinking in their own fields'. Youth and academic specialisation were the new criteria, promptly embodied in the incorporation of young researchers such as sociologist Alan Hunt, a partner of Martin Jacques in the leadership of the Radical Student Alliance since 1966,[85] social psychologist Tony Agathangelou and the specialist in literature Jeremy Hawthorn. All of these figures helped in consolidating the Gramscian turn of 1968.

At the same time that he was renewing the committee, Simon, undaunted by the storm unleashed by the Czechoslovakia invasion, moved forward with his reformist roadmap, which offered him a good view of how easily the cup could flow over. In April 1969 he organised a committee event on 'Intellectuals and their role today', which sought to update the party's position on this classic topic and to publicly present the party's new intellectual beacon, who was none other than Gramsci.[86] In charge of this presentation was Roger Simon, who had shown an interest in the Italian thinker for quite some time and was responsible for the English publication of his *Quaderni del Carcere* – edited by Quintin Hoare and Geoffrey Nowell-Smith[87] – and Martin Jacques, who was consolidating his position as leader of ideological renewal.

But Simon was to find that it was no easy matter keeping the newly liberated forces on the path he had mapped out, which was essentially theoretical. Tempers were running high after the Czechoslovakia invasion, and news of Dubček's removal as General Secretary only fanned the flames, directing anger towards 'much wider issues [...] not properly the province of Cultural committee', as Simon bemoaned.[88] A number of young members were calling vehemently for greater freedom of discussion and for the suppression of the Stalinist legacy, which they claimed was responsible for the party's intellectual failure and its scant intellectual appeal in general.[89] Among these critics were the Young Turks[90] of the Economic Committee, Pat Devine and Bill Warren. Faced with a barrage of blatantly political censure, veteran committee members sought a safe harbour in the theoretical terrain in which they had traditionally moved, with Simon attempting to divert the focus of the debate towards the publication of contributions in *Marxism Today*. In this context of heated debate, the silence of the young leader Martin Jacques, purported spokesman for the party's reformist voices, was conspicuous.[91]

Judging by his notes from this event, Simon felt overwhelmed at the direction that the discussion had taken.[92] His main concern at this point was to save the party from a radical, generalised censure. In his notes we sense a profound unease with what he saw as an individualist, liberal tack – although he was very careful in not using these adjectives – which he considered as incompatible with collective commitment to the party. From his own position of loyalty, he was not afraid to engage in spirited combat with those who held that democratic centralism scared-off intellectuals, vehemently defending the need for it. While acknowledging that the EC had avoided or limited internal debate in day-to-day practice, he went after his critics harshly. First of all, he expressed his concern about a return to a liberal interpretation of democracy which was reinforced by the anarchist, assembly-driven tendencies. He then reproached those who were critical of the party's intellectual weakness, their scant individual contributions to a collective study that could help the party to find its way out of this situation. Finally, he warned against repeating mistakes committed on the heels of the 20th congress by those who 'in order to live with themselves they had to make a declaration of position'. Against this sentiment, which he professed to understand, Simon appealed to the communists' judgement and their ability to comprehend the consequences that their individual actions had on the collective struggle. In this sense, he pointed out how the articles published by Hobsbawm in *Black Dwarf* and *New Left Review* were not merely writings – interesting as they may have been – but that they constituted political actions with consequences. It seems clear that, in the face of a new challenge, Simon was vindicating his option taken in 1956, and for the first time we sense a profound irritation on his part for the incomprehension of the price he had paid in terms of personal conscience and public prestige. Beyond loyalty to the party, however, Simon's misgivings reflected the quandary – one that even today affects intellectuals who consider themselves committed – between commitment to a collective political action and commitment to the principles of autonomy from which intellectual prestige and authority derive. For Simon, there was no doubt that the former had to prevail. We should see this as his taking a stance, but in a sense quite contrary to the majority.

Simon was quick to compose himself and to find a pragmatic way of redirecting the youthful rebellion in favour of his principal demand from several months earlier, the creation of a committee in charge of theory.[93] Although this demand did not appear explicitly in the final version of the report handed to the party,[94] Simon was clearly channelling the newly liberated forces towards traditional objectives of his own.

A new episode, one that put the reformists in an even more uncomfortable position, came with the expulsion of the novelist Aleksandr Solzhenitsyn from the Writers' Union of the USSR and the prohibition of his work. This time, Simon's reaction was direct, public and forceful. On 29 November 1969 he sent a harsh letter to the *Morning Star*[95] that opened with an insidious, rhetorical interrogation about the Soviet authorities' fears regarding the autonomous judgement of Soviet citizens who had been through fifty years of socialist education.

After pointing out that the Stalinist practices written about by Solzhenitsyn had been condemned by the Communist Party itself, Simon lamented the fact that censorship had been reinstated in Czechoslovakia as an essential ingredient of socialism. He also criticised the cases of Soviet citizens who were jailed for expressing their opinion, something supposedly allowed by their constitution. With this allusion, Simon was taking a qualitative leap: suggesting the betrayal of socialism by Soviet authorities. Finally, and as a way of ratifying the legitimate communist orthodoxy of his harsh recriminations, he insisted on signing the letter not in an individual capacity but rather as Chairman of the party's Cultural Committee. It seems that at this point Simon's tolerance for decrepit Soviet authoritarianism had reached its absolute limit.

Paradoxically, the Marxist renewal in academic disciplines that Simon had been yearning for came about not as a result of committee initiatives but rather from developments well on the periphery. The Communist University of London (CUL) sprang up in the environment of young students who were playing such an important role in the renewal of the party. There is a broad consensus as to the success and the considerable influence of the CUL in ideological and intellectual circles.[96] Martin Jacques defined it retrospectively, a decade later, as 'the most interesting and sophisticated school of thinking on the Left';[97] for Forgacs it represented one of the crowning achievements of the Gramscian renewal of the party.[98]

The CUL came into being in 1969 outside of the committee, in the heart of the National Union of Students (NUS) and with the limited format of party school.[99] With 159 participants that year and more than 200 in the following gathering, the CUL soon caught the committee's attention. In late 1970 the committee, while recognising that it was not its responsibility, nonetheless demanded to be informed about its activities. Two years later Simon stressed the importance of their working together.[100] The organisation of the subsequent edition was followed closely by the committee, and finally in 1975 the organisers found themselves answering to the committee.[101] In 1976 the party institutionalised its organisation with representatives from different committees and departments and with *Marxism Today*. At this point the event had taken on proportions that would have been unimaginable just a few years earlier. In 1974 the CUL had left the party and opened to the general public with structured courses. The apex of its success came in 1977 and 1978, with more than a thousand students and some seventy courses.[102]

The CUL appeared to be the culminating achievement of Simon's efforts. As Andrews has indicated, it became the platform from which the considerations addressed in 1967's *Questions of Ideology and Culture* could finally be developed. To be sure, the CUL left few areas unexplored; numerous courses were offered on the most diverse subjects while traditional boundaries, both political and academic, were expanded fearlessly with the incorporation of new theoretical fields such as feminism, the family, sexual policy, and gays and lesbians.[103] It seemed that finally Marxism – together with the party – had something to say about theoretical topics with real social implications, Simon's main concern from the very start of his mandate. Marxism could therefore finally consolidate its position as a source for social disciplines.

The coincidences between the CUL and the approaches that Simon had been defending for years were numerous. In fact, the principles guiding the 1976 CUL, presented to the committee by John Bloomsfield, could be seen as, more than a new route for the young students, a logical development of the points addressed in Simon's first Weeks of Marxist Debate. Emphasis was placed on the idea of attracting 'broad sectors' to the opportunities for knowledge offered by Marxism, but also on its close link to the struggle for democracy and a 'non-dogmatic approach', both of these principles being literal reiterations of points from Simon's 1964 report, more than a decade earlier.[104] As Bloomsfield himself acknowledged, none of these ideas were new, but it was only with the CUL that they were finally able to 'take off'.[105] Another sign of the miraculous qualitative leap achieved by the CUL was its ability to find common ground with the New Left,[106] another of Simon's perennial aspirations, embodied in Gramscianism.

Beyond the theoretical domain, in practice the CUL and the NCC managed to establish, despite their formal independence, a relationship of mutually beneficial positive feedback. From the time of its first courses the CUL provided the NCC with a list of specialists in diverse academic fields, something the committee had always coveted.[107] The CUL also brought greater dynamism to the specialised groups of the committee, which became one of the principal providers of courses. While the activity of these groups was directed towards the CUL, their work took place within the committee.

In the mid-1970s, with more than a thousand participants, the CUL embodied the triumph of the intellectual path defended by Simon from his position at the head of the committee, confirming just how judicious his strategies had been. Analysts at the time attributed the CUL's success to two lines of work that Simon had advocated unceasingly. The first of these was the capacity for the new academic Marxism to encourage a profound renovation of contents and methods, one of the main functions of the specialised courses. The second was its ability to create a common space for debate among leftist forces, something the Labour Party had been unable to accomplish.[108]

It seemed that Simon's long-sought dream had finally come true. Actually, it even looked like he may have felt that he had completed his mission. After its renewal in 1972 Simon was no longer a member of the party's Executive Committee. In November 1975, overloaded with various academic obligations, he also seemed ready to give up his leadership of the Cultural Committee, which he chose to delegate to Martin Jacques, the young Gramscian student leader whose trajectory he had been supporting for years.[109]

Epilogue: the committee's division

Simon's long yearned-for goal of overcoming the tension between culture and theory by splitting the committee finally came to pass in 1976. However, this did not come about due to pressure from the chairman, who had given up on the idea after the last attempt in 1971, but as a result of an initiative by the party's central authorities, who in 1975 had asked the committee to redefine its functions.[110] Simon was not about to let such an opportunity pass, despite the opinion of secretary Betty Reid, who felt it would be madness to undertake such a thing in March without a prior exchange of opinions between the PC and the EC.[111] In its following session the Cultural Committee agreed unanimously to split in two; the Committee of Arts and Entertainment would deal with traditional arts, film and popular culture, while the Committee of Ideology and Theory (a 'non-determined' title) would focus on theoretical aspects of Marxism.[112]

With the pretext of academic commitments abroad, Simon left the negotiations about the configuration of future committees in the hands of Martin Jacques. The debate was postponed until May,[113] and in the interim Simon actively supported Jacques' initiatives. At the end of April, Simon wrote to express his support for the draft that Jacques had written up and to offer his services for the preparation of strategies for the upcoming EC session.[114] At the same time he worked to dispel some of the suspicion still felt by some party members towards the idea of a committee that had the audacity to debate ideological questions. On this point, Simon was careful to point out to the EC secretary that the ideological matters at issue were related to academic disciplines (of social sciences, science, law, medicine, psychology, education, etc.); in no way did they concern major political considerations, which were not the domain of a such a committee anyway. Simon concluded by affirming that no one really called it an ideological committee to begin with,[115] underscoring the mistrust that the committee's equivocal name had given rise to. Curiously, the final obstacle in the way of the committee's division came not from the committee itself, 'which (so far) "dares not speak its name"' – as Monty Johnstone remarked ironically – but from the lack of leadership of the other committee, which was finally given the name Arts and Leisure and whose profile and mission seemed perfectly innocuous to all.[116] In mid-May the EC secretary proposed that Martin Jacques take charge of it provisionally, maintaining his position in the other committee as well, for which he hoped, as he commented half-jokingly, to 'be able to think up a respectable name'.[117] In August Jacques presented to the Political Committee his proposal for the division of the NCC into two. The proposal contemplated an Arts and Leisure Committee, presided over by Jacques whose mission would be to 'develop policies on the arts, leisure and recreation and, in particular, on the provision of facilities in these areas,' and what was finally called a Theory and Ideology Committee, whose mission was 'to encourage and promote the development of Marxist theory and the study of ideological problems'. This committee was to be presided over provisionally for six months by Brian Simon, after which time Jacques would take over.[118]

With the constitution of the Theory and Ideology Committee in the summer of 1976 a cycle came to a close, one that had begun twenty years before under the difficult circumstances of 1956. Simon, at the head of a core of socialist-humanist intellectuals, had steered the course from rigid Stalinist orthodoxy to a Eurocommunist opening. He had accomplished this by establishing alliances and complicities with the renovating forces that had shaken-up the party in the sixties, backing and placing in positions of leadership young reformists like Martin Jacques. Simon and his group served as a bridge between the brilliant communist ideals of the 1930s and the democratising forces of the seventies, over the bleak years of Stalinism and its legacy. The disciplined militant who in 1957 had sacrificed his natural preference as an intellectual to 'take a stand' and had renounced the praise of his peers to close ranks in defence of the party, eventually, ended up playing a far more significant role in the renewal of communism than many of those who left the party in anger. It was, however, a grey and discreet work, far from the intellectual laurels that Simon never received outside his field of expertise in the history of education.

Notes

1 Brian Simon, *A Life in Education* (London: Lawrence & Wishart, 1998), 12.
2 Brian Simon, *A Life in Education*, 29 and 75.
3 Brian Simon, [Unpublished autobiography], chapter 9. 'Politics and the Communist Party', SIM/4/5/2/16, IOE Archives.
4 EC Minutes, 11–12/5/1957 CP/CENT/EC/4/5.
5 John Callaghan, *Cold War, Crisis and Conflict: The CPGB 1951–68* (London: Lawrence & Wishart, 2003), 76–7.
6 'Proposals for new theoretical journal' (3 April 1957), CP/CENT/EC/4/7.
7 Simon, *A Life*, 10, 33 and 70.
8 EC Minutes, 11–12/5/1957, CP/CENT/EC/4/8.
9 Geoff Andrews, *Endgames and New Times: The final years of British Communism, 1971–1991* (London: Lawrence & Wishart, 2004), 16.
10 Andrews, *Endgames and New Times*, 77–8.
11 'National Committees and groups' [1958] CP/CENT/EC/5/6.
12 For the committee before the 1956 crisis, see Callaghan, *Cold War*, 87–105.
13 Miguel Angel Cabrera, *Postsocial History: An introduction* (Oxford: Lexington Books, 2004).
14 CP/CENT/EC/6/6, https://www.theguardian.com/news/2006/feb/02/obituaries.mainsection.
15 Brian Simon, 'Political Trends among intellectual and professional people'. [March, 1961] CP/CENT/CONG/13/3.
16 NCC Minutes, 11–12/5/1963. CP/CENT/EC/9/5.
17 Brian Simon, 'The ideological struggle', September, 1962. CP/CENT/CULT/3/8.
18 Richard. J. Evans, *Eric Hobsbawm: A life in history* (London: Abacus, 2020), 132 and Eric Hobsbawm, *Interesting Times: A twentieth-century life* (New York: Pantheon Books, 2002), 131.
19 Nello Ajello, *Intellutuali e PCI, 1944–1958* (Bari: Laterza, 1979); Albertina Vittoria, *Togliatti e gli intellettuali. Storia dell'Istituto Gramsci negli anni Cinquanta e Sessanta* (Rome: Editori Riuniti, 1992); Marco Di Maggio, *Les intellectuels et la stratégie communiste. Une crise d'hégémonie (1958–1981)* (Paris: Les éditions sociales, 2013); Marco Di Maggio, *The Rise and Fall of Communist Parties in France and Italy: Entangled historical approaches* (Basingstoke: Palgrave Macmillan, 2021); Nello Ajello, *Il lungo addio: Intellettuali e PCI dal 1958 al 1991* (Bari: Laterza, 1979); Manuel Aznar Soler, 'Los intelectuales y la política cultural del Partido Comunista de España (1939–1956)', in *Nosotros los comunistas: Memoria, identidad e historia social*, edited by Manuel Bueno and Sergio Gálvez (Madrid: Fundación de Investigaciones Marxistas, 2009), 367–87; Giaime Pala, *Cultura clandestina: Los intelectuales del PSUC bajo el franquismo* (Granada: Comares, 2016).
20 Vittoria, *Togliatti*, 129–130; Di Maggio, *The Rise*, 52.
21 Evans, *Hobsbawm*, 132; Hobsbawm, *Interesting*, 131. Andrews, *Endgames*, 23–8.
22 Barbara Niven, 'Proposals for the arts', *Marxism Today*, April, 4 (4): 1960, 117–22.
23 'Policy for Leisure' [September, 1963] CP/CENT/CULT/3/9.
24 NCC Minutes, 13/9/1963 CP/CENT/CULT/3/9.
25 'Unity theatre' [1963] and NCC Minutes, 8/3/1966, CP/CENT/CULT/3/8, NCC Minutes, 13/11/1964 CP/CENT/CULT/3/11, NCC Minutes, 9/9/1966, CP/CENT/CULT/3/12.
26 'Centre 42 Movement' [1963] and NCC Minutes, 11/01/1063, CP/CENT/CULT/3/8 and 1/5. Brian Simon, 'Cultural work of the party' [September 1971] CP/CENT/EC/13/14.
27 'Discussion on the folk song revival', 21/7/1962. CP/CENT/CULT/1/4.
28 Mike Waite 'Sex 'n' drugs 'n' rock 'n' roll (and communism) in the 1960s', in *Opening the Books: Essays on the social and cultural history of the British Communist Party*, edited by Geoff Andrews, Nina Fishman and Kevin Morgan (London: Pluto, 1995), 210–24, 215.
29 'The work of the Cultural Committee, for the Political Committee', 23/1/1964 CP/CENT/CULT/18/1.
30 Bill Carritt, 'Notes in preparation for a discussion on the cultural activity of branches', 5/1/1965. CP/CENT/CULT/3/9.
31 'From: National Cultural Committee' [January 1965], CP/CENT/ CULT/3/9.
32 Hobsbawm, *Interesting*, 261.
33 'The work of the Cultural Committee', 23/1/1964, CP/CENT/CULT/3/10.

34 NCC Minutes, 15/6/1962 CP/CENT/CULT/1/4 y Committee for week of Marxist Thought. Minutes of first meeting' 24/7/1962. CP/CENT/CULT/3/10.

35 'Challenge of Marxism. Sub-committee minutes of fifth meeting', December 14, 1962 CP/CENT/CULT/3/10.

36 NCC Minutes, 11/9/1964. CP/CENT/CULT/3/9.

37 Brian Simon, 'The challenge of Marxism' and 'Week of Marxist debate, November 1963', [January 1964] CP/CENT/CULT/3/10CP/CENT/CULT/3/10.

38 Simon, 'Week of Marxist debate, November 1963', [January 1964] CP/CENT/CULT/3/10.

39 Simon, 'Week of Marxist debate, November 1963', [January 1964] CP/CENT/CULT/3/10.

40 NCC Minutes, del 11/9/1964, CP/CENT/CULT/1/7 and 3/9.

41 CP/CENT/CULT/3/9.

42 NCC Minutes, 11/6, 9/7, 10/9, 8/10 and 5/11/1965. CP/CENT/CULT/1/8 and 3/9.

43 Evans, *Hobsbawm*, 132; Hobsbawm, *Interesting*, 131.

44 Arnold Kettle, *Communism and the Intellectuals* (London: Lawrence & Wishart, 1960).

45 Arnold Kettle, 'The artist and politics', *Marxism Today*, May 1959, 139–45.

46 Ajello, *Intelletuali,* 444.

47 NCC Minutes, 5/9/1961 CP/CENT/CULT/3/8.

48 Arnold Kettle, 'Culture and revolution: A consideration of the ideas of Raymond Williams and others', *Marxism Today*, October 1961, 301–7.

49 'The Political Committee wants to make perfectly clear to all comrades engaged in cultural and scientific spheres that the position of our Communist Party is that we do not intend to issue any directives at all or to exercise any control over the direction of the comrades' work. If, however, in a painting or a story or poem a direct political theme was dealt with, we reserve the right to state our view on the politics of that theme'. NCC Minutes, 11/2/1963, CP/CENT/CULT/3/8.

50 Lionel M. Munby, 'For discussion at Cultural Committee, January 8th, 1965', 5/1/1965.

51 'Résolution sur les problèmes idéologiques et culturels adoptée par le comité central du parti communiste français', [13 March 1966]. CP/CULT/3/11.

52 Roger Martelli, *Une dispute communiste: Le comité central d'Argenteuil* (Paris: Les Éditions sociales, 2017). Di Maggio, *Les intellectuels*, 88.

53 'The communist party, intellectuals and culture' [typewritten translation, 1966], CP/CENT/CULT/3/11.

54 EC Minutes, 11–12/3/1967, CP/CENT/EC/11/09. *Questions of Ideology and Culture* (London: Communist Party, 1967). Also published in *Marxism Today*, 11, 5, 1967: 134–7.

55 Numbers in brackets refer to the pages of *Questions of Ideology and Culture*.

56 Thomas S. Kuhn, *The Structure of Scientific Revolutions* (Chicago, IL: University of Chicago Press, 1962).

57 Brian Simon, *Freedom* (London: Communist Party, [1960]). Following numbers in brackets in this paragraph refer to this work.

58 For the humanist polemic, Di Maggio, *The Rise*, 72–80.

59 Andrews, *Endgames*, 77–8.

60 John Lewis, 'The Althusser Case' (parts I and II). *Marxism Today*, January and February 1972, 23–7 and 43–7; Louis Althusser, 'Reply to John Lewis' (parts I and II). *Marxism Today*, October and November 1972, 310–17 and 343–49.

61 Di Maggio, *The Rise,* 81.

62 [Letter from Maurice Cornforth to Ted Ainley], 8/2/1967, CP/CENT/CULT/3/11.

63 [Letter from John Lewis to Ted Ainley], 5/12/1966. CP/CENT/CULT/3/11.

64 [Letter from John Lewis to John Gollan], 27/2/1967. CP/CENT/PC/5/14.

65 [Letter from Brian Simon to John Gollan], 5/9/1966, 19/9/1966, 29/10/1966, 2/3/1967, [Letter from John Gollan to Brian Simon], 20/9/1966, 23/9/1966, 1/11/1966, 4/11/1966. CP/CENT/EC/3/11 and CP/CENT/PC/05/04.

66 EC Minutes, 11–12/3/1967, CP/CENT/EC/11/09.

67 Geoff Andrews, 'Young Turks and old guard: Intellectuals and the Communist Party leadership in the 1970s'. In *Opening the Books: Essays on the social and cultural history of the British Communist Party,* edited by Geoff Andrews, Nina Fishman and Kevin Morgan (London: Pluto, 1995), 225–50, 237.

68 David Forgacs, 'Gramsci and Marxism in Britain', *New Left Review* 1, no. 176 (1989): 70–88, 70.

69 For the reception of Gramsci by the New Left, see Tom Steele, 'Hey Jimmy! The legacy of Gramsci in British cultural politics', in *New Left, New Right and Beyond: Taking the sixties seriously*, edited by Geoff Andrews, Richard Cockett, Alan Hooper and Michael Williams (London: Palgrave MacMillan, 1999), 26–41. For the lines of gramscian criticism inside the party, see Andrews, *Endgames*, 141–53.

70 Andrews, 'Young Turks', 226.

71 'Cultural Committee. Some points for the discussion on August 4th 1968', [15/7/1968], CP/CULT/CENT/18/2.

72 Hobsbawm, *Interesting*, 118.

73 'Cultural Committee', 18/8/1968, CP/CULT/CENT/18/2.

74 'Cultural Committee Draft Memo', 1/1971 Brian Simon.

75 Geoff Eley, 'Reading Gramsci in English: Observations on the reception of Antonio Gramsci in the English speaking world 1957–82', *European History Quarterly* 14 (1984): 441–77, 442.

76 'The correspondence between the decline of the great public intellectuals and the resurrection of the professors is thus no mere coincidence', Tony Judt, *Past Imperfect: French intellectuals, 1944–1956* (Berkeley: University of California Press, 1992), 296.

77 Vittoria, *Togliatti*, 75. Di Maggio, *Les intellectuels*, 215.

78 Di Maggio, *The Rise*, 88.

79 Forgacs, 'Gramsci', 81.

80 EC NCC Minutes, 13–14/1/1968, CP/CENT/EC/12/06.

81 Andrews, 'Young Turks', 228.

82 Hobsbawm, *Interesting*, 273 and 276.

83 Andrews, 'Young Turks', 228.

84 CP/CENT/CULT/18/3.

85 Andrews, *Endgames,* 53.

86 Betty Reid [To all NCC members], March 1969. CP/CENT/CULT/18/2.

87 *Selections from the Prison Notebooks of Antonio Gramsci*. Edited and translated by Quintin Hoare and Geoffrey Nowell Smith (London: Lawrence & Wishart, 1971).

88 [Brian Simon] 'Intellectuals and their role' [April 1969], CP/CENT/CULT/1/12.

89 Betty Reid 'Points made in discussion at NCC meeting on "Intellectuals and Their Role",' 18th April 1969' CP/CULT/CENT/1/12.

90 Andrews, 'Young Turks'.

91 Betty Reid, 'Points made in discussion at NCC meeting on "Intellectuals and Their Role",' 18th April 1969' CP/CULT/CENT/1/12.

92 [Brian Simon] 'Intellectuals and their role' [April 1969], CP/CENT/CULT/1/12.

93 'Cultural Committee', 15/6/1969, CP/CENT/CULT/18/2.

94 'Draft of statement to Political Committee', 30/6/1969, CP/CENT/CULT/18/2.

95 [Letter from Brian Simon to *Morning Star* editor] 29/11/1969 CP/CENT/CULT/18/3.

96 Geoff Eley, 'Reading Gramsci in English: Observations on the reception of Antonio Gramsci in the English speaking world 1957–82', *European History Quarterly* 14 (1984): 441–77, 444. Andrews, *Endgames,* 52–9. Francis Beckett, *Enemy Within: The rise and fall of the British Communist Party* (London: John Murray, 1995), 170.

97 Martin Jacques, 'The last word', *Marxism Today*, December (1991): 28–9.

98 Forgacs, 'Gramsci', 79.

99 Andrews, *Endgames* 55; Andrews, 'Young Turks', 228 and 233; 'Background notes' [1982], CP/CENT/CULT/18/5.

100 NCC Minutes, 10/11/1970, CP/CENT/CULT/2/2; Notas de Simon, 11/10/1972 CP/CENT/CULT/1/13.

101 NCC Minutes, 7/2/1975 y 1/1/1976. CP/CENT/CULT/2/5.

102 'Background notes' [1981], CP/CENT/CULT/18/5.

103 CP/CENT/CULT/7/3, 7/4 y 7/5.

104 Brian Simon, 'Week of Marxist debate, November 1963', [January 1964], CP/CENT/CULT/3/10.

105 [John Bloomsfield] 'Notes on the development of the work of the specialist groups', [January 1976], CP/CENT/CULT/2/5.

106 Michael Kenny, 'Communism and the New Left'. In *Opening the Books: Essays on the social and cultural history of the British Communist Party*, edited by G. Andrews, N. Fishman & K. Morgan (London: Pluto, 1995), 195–209, 206.

107 CPGB. *32nd National Congress. Report of the Executive Committee, August 1969–July 1971*, 7 CP/CENT/CONG/18/01 and NCC Minutes, [end of 1970], CP/CENT/CULT/1/13.

108 Colin MacCabe, 'Britain's Communist University', *New Statesman,* 20 May 1977, 673.

109 [Letter from Brian Simon to Betty Reid], 18 January 1976. CP/CENT/CULT/4/7.

110 14/1/1976 Carta de Reuben Falber, Assistant Secretary del Executive Committee CP/CENT/CULT/2/5.

111 [Letter from Betty Reid to Brian Simon], 5 February 1976. CP/CENT/CULT/4/7.

112 NCC Minutes, 13/2/1976 CP/CENT/CULT/2/5.

113 NCC Minutes, 12/3/1976 y 7/5/1976 CP/CENT/CULT/18/4.

114 NCC Minutes, 24/4/ 1976 CP/CENT/CULT/4/7.

115 CP/CENT/CULT/18/4.

116 [Letter from Monty Johnstone to Brian Simon], June 15, 1976. CP/CENT/CULT/4/7.

117 'EC Assistant Secretary to Martin Jacques', 18 May 1976. CP/CENT/CULT/18/4.

118 'For Political Committee', 5/8/1976. CP/CENT/CULT/2/5.

7
Campaign for comprehensive education: 1951–79

Brain Simon was a Marxist activist in the comprehensive education movement in the UK. For Simon, the demand for the comprehensive school was 'a rallying point in the class struggle on the educational front'.[1] He thought of education as part of the 'struggle for social change'.[2] Therefore, in the struggle for socialism, he argued that: 'It is necessary to act both on the political and educational plane.'[3] Instead of acting on the political plane, Simon was directly involved in the politics of education, as he claimed.[4] Immediately after the Second World War, as a member of the Communist Party, Simon threw himself with considerable enthusiasm into being an advocate for the comprehensive school.[5] As Simon pointed out in his unpublished autography, he found no contradiction between his membership of the Communist Party and his pursuit of educational objectives, but such membership was 'a positive source of support for those activities I felt to be of over-riding importance'.[6] Within three months of Stalin's death in 1953, popular revolts broke out in some Eastern European countries. In 1956, the rebellion in Hungary was brutally suppressed by Soviet military forces. The fact that the leadership of the British Communist Party supported the Soviet intervention was criticised by many intellectuals and trade unionists and led to their resignation from the party.[7] Nevertheless, Simon chose to stay in the party since he was 'convinced of the need for Communist politics and international solidarity', even though in his later life he admitted that this standpoint had been wrong.[8]

From 1958 to 1972, Simon served on the Executive Committee of the party.[9] In the summer of 1962 the Cultural Committee of the party was reorganised and Simon became its chair (until 1975).[10] In 1977, Simon joined the party's Education Advisory Committee and had a great impact on the party's education policies.[11] Meanwhile, Simon was an academic at the University of Leicester from 1950. In 1958, he cofounded a journal, *Forum*, which became a significant vehicle for promoting a common secondary education for all.[12] In 1977, as a historian and educationist, he was honoured as the president of the British Educational Research Association (BERA), the biggest independent educational research organisation in Britain. By means of the Communist Party, *Forum* and BERA, Simon was able to campaign for his Marxist ideal of comprehensive education.

As outlined in chapter 4, from a Marxist perspective, Simon especially challenged the functions and technology of intelligence testing, which, in his view, provided an ideological support for a tripartite system – grammar, technical and modern school.[13] As Simon himself stated, this 'was my own first contribution to establishing a clear theoretical foundation for the comprehensive school'.[14] Based on his criticisms of intelligence testing and the concept of 'intelligence' itself, in the late 1940s, when the Labour government (1945–1951) continued to consolidate a tripartite system of secondary education, Simon had already attempted to set forth his ideal pattern of comprehensive education. In 1949, Simon stressed that the comprehensive school was a school to which '*all* [emphasis in the original] children from a given locality would automatically proceed'.[15] In other words, the comprehensive school must be a 'neighbourhood school'. Moreover, in line with his Marxist belief in the educability of man, Simon argued that, in a comprehensive school, all children would follow a common core of subjects during the first few years.[16] With his ideal of comprehensive education in view, Simon was vigorously involved in the politics of education, never compromising in terms of a genuine comprehensive education from the 1950s to the 1970s.

The Conservative governments (1951–64)

In 1951, the Conservative Party was returned to power. Foreseeing that the Conservative government would sabotage the establishment of the comprehensive school, in 1953, Simon made a further statement that the comprehensive school should provide every child with the opportunity of following the same basic curriculum up to the age of fourteen or fifteen.[17] Only at this age should differentiation of subject matter for specifically vocational purposes begin, though Simon stressed that the greater part of the curriculum should still remain common to all pupils.[18] In the autumn of 1953, Florence Horsbrugh, the new Minister of Education, interfered with the London school plan, in which Kidbrooke, London's first, purpose-built comprehensive school, was to absorb a grammar school (Eltham Hill Grammar School for Girls), two technical and two modern schools.[19] In March 1954, the Minister announced that she was unable to approve the closure of the girls' grammar school.[20] In January 1955, soon after David Eccles took office, he also made his position clear, that he would never agree to the 'assassination' of the grammar schools.[21] Three months later, Eccles stated that comprehensive schools could be approved only when they were developed 'as an experiment' and when 'no damage is done to any existing school'.[22]

Against this background, Simon published another book, *The Common Secondary School* (1955), to propose his reform agenda which would help the establishment of the comprehensive school. First, because streaming was inimical to the development of a common curriculum, streaming in junior schools and secondary schools must be eliminated.[23] Second, the General Certificate Examination (GCE), which was mainly for grammar school pupils, must be replaced by an examination for all pupils.[24] Thirdly, the school-leaving age must be raised in order to provide a systematic education for every child up to the age of 18.[25] Fourthly, the semi-independent schools (direct-grant schools) and the fully independent schools (private 'public' schools) must be abolished and be brought into the control of the local education authorities (LEAs).[26] On this account, Simon's Marxist ideal of comprehensive education was to establish a state system of comprehensive schools and, more importantly, that no selection and differentiation between and within comprehensive schools would exist.

With the reform agenda as criteria, Simon critically examined various reports and official documents in relation to secondary education. For instance, in 1955, Simon remarked on *Early Leaving* (1954), a report by the Central Advisory Council for Education. This report was mainly concerned with the problem that children left grammar schools before completing the full course.[27] However, the committee disregarded the comprehensive school since, as it explained, 'Very few comprehensive schools existed at present and these are hardly beyond the experimental stage.'[28] For Simon, the council by-passed the solution to the problem since, in the existing comprehensive schools, the proportion of children staying on beyond fifteen had nearly doubled. By contrast, in Simon's view, grammar schools presented their pupils with a narrow overspecialised course leading to university and often ignored the study of technology, which was desired by working-class children. No wonder that many children were anxious to leave earlier. On these grounds, Simon believed that only through the establishment of the comprehensive school could the crisis in education be solved.[29] One year later, Simon gave a speech in Derbyshire in which he reiterated that 'specialization is not a function of the secondary school, especially below sixteen, but that a broad general education should be given at this age on which a more specialized or vocational education can later be built'.[30] Furthermore, he added, 'science and technique [sic]' should become an integral part of the education of all pupils.[31]

Simon's proposal was actually influenced by Marx's idea. Marx argued that all pupils should receive a technical education, which should familiarise them with the basic principles of the processes of production as well as with the utilisation of the most common tools of production.[32] This was what Marx called 'polytechnical teaching', which was not narrow vocational training, but the acquisition by the pupil of a wide understanding of science and its application in technology.[33] While Simon visited Poland in the spring of 1952, he had observed that Marx's idea was implemented there. The grammar schools (Lyceum) provided a well-balanced scientific and humanist education for all pupils and this would become the prototype of the general schools developed in the future.[34] In the same vein, in his visit to the Soviet Union in 1955, he also noticed that polytechnical education was being fostered and its purpose was to give a broad general education to all children from seven to seventeen.[35] Undoubtedly, the Soviet educational system provided Simon with an educational ideal different from English education.[36] In May 1957, Simon became a member of the Executive Committee of the Communist Party and delivered a speech organised by the East Midlands District of the Communist Party.[37] In his speech, Simon urged other communists to 'stand for [the] fullest human development of all'.[38] To this end, Communists must support the common school, which was 'the condition for developing a full, general, human, many-sided and all-round education', he emphasised.[39]

In December 1958, the Conservative government published the white paper, *Secondary Education for All: A New Drive* (1958). While the Joint Committee of the Four Secondary Associations (headmasters, headmistresses, assistant masters, assistant mistresses) gave the white paper the most enthusiastic welcome, Simon wrote an article in a new journal, *Forum*, to criticise it.[40] *Forum* was founded in autumn 1958 by Simon, Robin Pedley and Jack Walton. They felt that a journal devoted specifically to encouraging comprehensive secondary education was imminently needed.[41] In his article, Simon criticised the white paper for describing the extension of a grammar school to become comprehensive as forcibly 'bringing to an end an existing grammar school' and as 'completely abolishing' parents' freedom of choice.[42] Thus, the government only permitted experiments with comprehensive schools in country districts with sparse populations and in new housing estates where there were no existing schools.[43] In addition, the white paper also suggested the building up of advanced (examination) courses in separate modern schools.[44] For Simon, the development of such courses had exposed the futility of selection.[45] Simon concluded that the white paper was 'a challenge to local authorities wishing to abolish selection by developing comprehensive schools'.[46]

In 1959, another official document, the Crowther Report on 15 to 18, was published. For Simon, the report's main point was that the raising of the school-leaving age to 16 should take place between 1966 and 1968, and that an exact date for this should be given.[47] In order to achieve a balance between economic issues and political considerations, in March 1960, the government reaffirmed the principle of the raising of the school-leaving age but did not announce a date for the policy to be implemented.[48] In view of this Simon called for 'a broad campaign initiated by the Labour movement and drawing in teachers and others to force the government to reverse its decision and implement Crowther [Report]'.[49] In August 1963, when the Newsom Report, *Half Our Future*, which proposed the raising of the school leaving-age to 16 by 1970, was submitted to the Minister of Education, Edward Boyle, *Forum* also expressed its support for the report.[50] Eventually, in January 1964, due to a large element of electoral opportunism, the Conservative government announced that the school leaving-age would be raised to 16 from the academic year 1970/71.[51] Aside from this, the Crowther Report also strongly held that less than 50 per cent of modern school children should receive a systematic education leading to some form of external examination.[52] In an article in *Forum*, Simon and Pedley opposed this by emphasising that 'we just do not know about the potentialities of the large majority of the pupils in the schools'.[53]

Following the Crowther Report, the Beloe Committee, which was appointed by the Secondary Schools Examinations Council (SSEC) in July 1958, published its report in 1960 and proposed the establishment of a new examination for less academic fifteen-year-olds, to run alongside the existing GCE O Levels. The proposed new examination was eventually introduced in 1962 and known as the Certificate of Secondary Education (CSE).[54] Since Simon had been campaigning for a common examination accessible to all children, he highlighted that there was no evidence for the assumption of the Beloe Report that only the top 20 per cent in ability were capable of taking GCE O level.[55] Hence, he made a plea for a public inquiry into the GCE and reiterated his proposal that the standard of the GCE should be lowered so that it could become a general school-leaving examination.[56] He insisted that a test like this would allow schools to develop a broad general education up to and including the sixth forms.[57]

Whereas the Conservative government sought to consolidate a tripartite system, in effect, once Hugh Gaitskell was elected as Labour Party leader and Michael Stewart was chosen as shadow minister, the Labour Party in opposition began to identify a viable approach to develop comprehensive education.[58] In 1958, after one year's study, the party published a report, *Learning to Live* (1958), proposing that a Labour government would 'require' the LEAs to 'adopt the comprehensive principle'.[59] In reviewing the report, Simon expressed his satisfaction with the fact that the Labour Party finally admitted the educational advantages of the comprehensive school and of broadening opportunity for all children.[60] Despite this, in line with his insistence on a common core-curriculum for all up to 15 or 16, he accused the report of 'an intentional vagueness about the definition of a comprehensive school', since it spoke of the comprehensive principle as involving 'a wide range of courses' in each secondary school.[61] Apart from this, Simon was also dissatisfied with the report's policy on the 'public' school, since it proposed to 'steadily reduce the influence of the privileged fee-paying schools on public life' through improving the nation's schools.[62] In the light of this, Simon reiterated that the 'public' schools must be brought under the control of local authorities. Without this, Simon stressed, 'few areas can establish a genuine system of comprehensive secondary schools'.[63] Simon's criticism of the Labour Party's report revealed the differences between his purist approach and the Labour Party's pragmatic approach.

In addition to commenting on various reports and official documents, Simon also participated in the policy-making process, seeking to influence the formation of educational policies. In February 1961, the Robbins Committee was appointed to review the pattern of full-time higher education.[64] Simon and Pedley published an open letter to the committee in *Forum*.[65] They indicated that the growing competition for university entry was turning education more and more into a conscious race which buttressed the whole competitive system of streaming and selection, down to and including the infant school.[66] They held that: 'To open up higher education much more widely is the only positive solution to this problem.'[67] In 1963, the Robbins Report was published. It suggested a requirement of about 560,000 places for full-time students in all higher education in 1980/81.[68] *Forum* welcomed the Report and recommended that its main proposal should be implemented.[69]

Similarly, when the Plowden Committee was appointed in 1963 to consider primary education and its transition to secondary education, the editorial board of *Forum* also submitted evidence to the committee.[70] In its evidence, the board suggested that, in the junior school, 'it is of first importance that the movement towards non-streaming, and all that it implies, be encouraged'.[71] Moreover, the board urged the Central Advisory Council to 'give a strong lead in favour of the abolition of all forms of selection for secondary education'.[72] Simon and two experienced junior schools heads (G.C. Freeland and Eric Linfield) also presented oral evidence to the committee.[73] During the meeting, Simon successfully convinced A.J. Ayer that both the bright children and the more backward children would not suffer in a non-streaming classroom.[74] In the end, the Plowden Report on *Children and Their Primary Schools* was published in 1967, in favour of unstreaming in the junior school.[75] Simon recalled in his biography that this was the only occasion in his life that he was involved in an official policymaking process.[76]

Half way there? (1964–70)

In October 1964, a Labour government was elected to office and promised to introduce comprehensive education.[77] In July 1965, Anthony Crosland, now Secretary of State for the Department of Education and Science (DES), issued Circular 10/65. Unlike the proposal of *Learning to Live*, the circular simply 'requested' rather than 'required' the LEAs to submit plans to the secretary of state for the reorganisation of secondary education in their areas, on comprehensive lines, within one year.[78] Two months after the issuing of the circular, the Comprehensive Schools Committee (CSC), a well-organised pressure group of comprehensive supporters, was formed to monitor developments and to press for radical changes.[79] At a press conference, as sponsor of the CSC, Simon emphasised that 'the committee's first task should be to find out what schemes the local authorities were putting forward in response to the government's circular – and which of these were receiving ministerial sanction'.[80]

Therefore, on 12 October 1965, Simon wrote to Caroline Benn, who was the driving force of the CSC, to urge the CSC to express its opinion on the schemes Crosland was passing and rejecting.[81] Simon observed that Crosland passed schemes submitted by Doncaster, Middlesbrough, Wakefield and Cardiff. These schemes were similar – each achieved the abolition of the 11-plus exam by developing a common school for the age group 11–13. At 13, parents had to choose whether they were prepared to promise that their children were to stay at school to 18. In the former case, their children would proceed to a 'grammar school'; if not, they would stay in the lower schools, or move to a parallel 'modern' school. For Simon, these schemes were worse than the tripartite system since they would be primarily socially selective. After all, middle-class parents would choose the grammar school at 13 and working-class parents would not be prepared to give the required promise. Simon emphasised that: 'I imagine that masses of Tory authorities will be submitting plans of this type – the sad thing is that Doncaster is ... Labour.'[82] Hence, different from the Labour government's pragmatic approach towards comprehensive education, Simon proposed that 'the CSC should consider seriously coming out against the Doncaster type scheme on principle, since it does not measure up to our agreed criteria'.[83]

Shortly afterwards, CSC published the first issue of its bulletin, *Comprehensive Education*. In it, Simon wrote the editorial and emphasised that for children over 13, the Doncaster scheme was simply 'a means of preserving the grammar schools as separate schools'.[84] Since the pattern of comprehensive education in the future would be determined by the secretary of state's decision, Simon contended that: 'The actions of the DES in accepting or rejecting these schemes deserve the closet attention.'[85] Similarly, Simon published another article in *Forum*.[86] He pointed out: 'The key question is whether a deliberate attempt is now being made to build into the state system of education, under the umbrella of the comprehensive school, a clear principle of social selection.'[87] Beyond doubt, the Doncaster plan 'presents working-class parents with no genuine choice at all since these, in general, are not in a position to make the promise required'.[88] In order to ensure that new obstacles were not set in place of the old, Simon stressed that 'all local schemes need the most careful scrutiny'.[89]

In March 1966, Circular 10/66 was issued, which announced that capital grants for new secondary buildings would be available only for projects compatible with comprehensive reorganisation.[90] Despite this, Surrey County Council and 20 other LEAs still decided to defy the government's policy on comprehensive education.[91] In view of this, Simon stressed that: 'Clause one of the 1944 Education Act quite definitely gives the Secretary of State the power to insist that local authorities carry out this policy.'[92] Moreover, on 31 March 1966, the Labour Party won the election and had the opportunity for developing the educational system as a genuinely unified system.[93] Hence, Simon wrote an article in *Forum* to call for a new legislation.[94] He suggested that in the new Education Act, the concept of 'age, abilities, and aptitudes' on which the secondary clause of the 1944 Education Act was based should be deleted and clauses related to voluntary-aided grammar schools and 'parents' choice' also needed remodelling. Besides, the new Act should include some form of democratic control over the so-called 'independent' schools, which, as Simon insisted, should be brought under the control of the LEAs.[95]

In December 1965, Crosland had appointed a commission chaired by John Newsom to 'advise on the best way of integrating the public schools with the state system of education'.[96] In 1967, *Forum* submitted its evidence to the commission.[97] In the evidence, it stressed that the term 'to integrate' should mean 'bringing the "public" schools into the national system of education' and exclude any inference that 'they can be "integrated" by recruiting a proportion of non-paying pupils to produce a "social mix"'.[98] In this view, *Forum* suggested that the 'public' schools should be brought fully into the national system of education.[99] In July 1968, the Public Schools Commission's report (a second Newsom report) was published.[100] It proposed a 'public' school willing to enter an integrated sector must admit assisted pupils from maintained schools to at least one half of its places and all assisted pupils, whatever their parents' means, should be entitled to free tuition.[101] The government decided not to accept this proposal.[102] Simon also wrote in the press to advocate a definitive solution to the 'public' school problem, that is 'to abolish the public schools by taking them over'.[103] Despite this, as Simon noted, before the Conservative Party returned to office in 1970, the Labour government did not initiate reform in this sector.[104]

Apart from this, as Simon indicated, the position of the direct-grant schools became anomalous once the government had announced its decision to go comprehensive.[105] Thus, Simon also restated his argument that: 'No truly comprehensive system of education is possible if these schools refuse to co-operate and remain outside the schemes.'[106] Simon stressed the fact that in many LEAs, many children still enter direct-grant grammar schools, which underlined 'the need for new steps, including legislation, to make the evolving system of comprehensive secondary education fully effective'.[107] Hence, after the secretary of state, Edward Short, stated his intention to introduce legislation for the introduction of comprehensive secondary education, in March 1969, *Forum* urged Short to ensure that the direct-grant schools must be integrated into local-authority plans for secondary education.[108] Meanwhile, *Forum* also published its evidence to the Public Schools Commission, which received a further reference covering these schools in October 1967.[109] *Forum* proposed 'the abolition of the direct grant list', which implied 'bringing to an end the method of financing these schools by central government'.[110]

CAMPAIGN FOR COMPREHENSIVE EDUCATION

In March 1970, the Public Schools Commission, now chaired by David Donnison, published its report. The commission proposed that the direct-grant schools should participate in the movement towards comprehensive reorganisation and the present direct-grant arrangements should therefore be discontinued.[111] Since the Donnison report was in line with Simon's position, *Forum* demanded that the government should 'take steps to implement it immediately'.[112]

In February 1970, Short finally introduced his Bill in the House of Commons. Simon believed that 'Although this Bill had certain weaknesses, allowing selection in certain fields and giving no final date for the submission of the plans demanded – its general effect would certainly have been to impose the duty of developing non-selective systems on all local authorities in England and Wales.'[113] However, due to Harold Wilson's decision to call a general election in June 1970, the Bill fell, to be followed by the defeat of the Labour Party.[114] This result led Simon to criticise the Labour Party for remaining tentative in its approach to comprehensive education since gaining power in 1964.[115] One week before the election, Simon and Caroline Benn published a book, *Half Way There* (1970), to put forward some recommendations for further development of comprehensive education.[116] Since the Bill failed, Simon and Benn suggested that 'a clear and positive national decision be taken in favour of a comprehensive system up to the age of 18 years and that legislation to implement this decision be introduced'.[117] Moreover, they emphasised, 'To be effective, legislation must do three things – ensure (i) that every authority plans ahead in respect of every single one of its secondary schools; (ii) that these plans are compatible with a non-selective comprehensive system of secondary education throughout that authority; and (iii) that plans are worked out to be operable within a named and definite period of time.'[118]

The indictment of Margaret Thatcher (1970–4)

As mentioned above, although Circular 10/65 did not imply any legal sanction to establish comprehensive schools, pressure was further applied through the issue of Circular 10/66, which laid down that resources would not be forthcoming for any building in secondary education which did not contribute to a scheme of comprehensive reorganisation.[119] In this situation, between 1965 and 1970, the total number of comprehensive schools increased between four to five times, to 1,145.[120] Between 1970 and 1974, the Conservative government attempted to reverse the progress of comprehensive reorganisation. Once the Conservative Party was returned to power in June 1970, within a month, Margaret Thatcher, Secretary of State for Education and Science, issued Circular 10/70, signifying that Circular 10/65 was withdrawn and parents and LEAs would be freer to decide on the shape of secondary provision in their areas.[121]

Not long after the Conservative Party took office in 1970, Simon's mother, Shena wrote to him, pointing out that: 'It seems to me that all of us who believe in comprehensive education now will have to depend upon propaganda amongst teachers and parents so that local demands can be stimulated.'[122] Following his mother's advice, in *Morning Star*, Simon stressed that the aim of Conservative policy was 'to put the clock right back and maintain a privileged sector in education at all costs'.[123] In fighting this, Simon urged that 'the widest possible mass movement comprising teachers, the Labour movement, parents and children must be created'.[124] Similarly, at a conference organised by the CP, Simon also argued that what was needed was to bring together such organisations as the National Union of Teachers (NUT), the Trades Union Congress, the Council for Educational Advance, the Comprehensive Schools Committee, and the Confederation for the Advancement of State Education.[125]

The Conservative government's determination to retain selective schools in secondary education also created a significant obstacle to the comprehensive education movement. At the Conservative Party annual conference, Thatcher claimed to support a whole system of independent and direct-grant schools and envisaged a mixed system of both comprehensive and grammar schools alongside each other. One week before the general election, Simon had already indicated in *Half Way There* that the Conservative Party accepted the principle of comprehensive reorganisation of secondary education with provisos 'directed to preserving a privileged area, whether in terms of selective schools within the state system or the fee-paying "public" schools'.[126] Thus, in opposition to Thatcher's policy, Simon emphasised that the CP's objective was 'a universal system of comprehensive schools', namely 'an end to the ideal of co-existence and all the implications of that policy'.[127]

Following the Conservative conference, Simon continued to argue that comprehensive schools could not coexist with independent schools, direct grant schools and grammar schools.[128] As he put it, at another conference in London, voluntary-aided grammar schools still took about 16 per cent of entrants at the age of 11, and in Coventry, 12 per cent of entrants to secondary education were snapped up by independent and direct-grant boys' schools.[129] In view of this, in 1972, Simon and Caroline Benn republished their book, emphasising that 'the object [sic] of a comprehensive reform is … a changeover from a two-sector system … to a comprehensive system of schools where selection by ability is no longer necessary'.[130] To achieve this they reiterated the necessity for new legislation, to ensure 'a non-selective comprehensive system of secondary education'.[131] In December 1972, far from meeting Simon's demand, the Conservative government published a white paper, *Education: A Framework for Expansion*. As far as secondary education was concerned, it merely proposed to improve school building, staffing standards and teacher training.[132] In a *Forum* editorial, Simon deplored the white paper for its ignoring of 'this continuing in-built injustice and the various selective devices within semi-comprehensive schemes'.[133]

Meanwhile, from the Summer of 1972, since Circular 10/70 could not stop the development of comprehensive schools, Thatcher started using her power of veto to intervene in plans submitted by the LEAs and to preserve selective grammar schools against the wishes of the LEAs.[134] In response, Brian urged Joan, his wife, to write an article entitled 'Indictment of Margaret Thatcher', which was printed in September 1973 by the publishers of *Forum* – Robin Pedley, Brian Simon and Jack Walton.[135] As Joan explained to Alan Evans, a member of the NUT, 'It seems to me that it is mainly LEAs that will have grounds for taking the woman [Thatcher] to court' and this paper was to provide background information.[136] In her article, Joan accused Thatcher of concentrating on Section 13 of the 1944 Education Act, which was amended by the 1968 Education Act.[137] Section 13 stipulated that 'where a local education authority intend to make any significant change in the character … of a county school, they shall submit proposals for that purpose to the Secretary of State'.[138] After any proposals were submitted to the secretary of state, the authority should give public notice of the proposals and any ten or more local government electors for the area might within two months submit to the secretary of state objections to the proposals.[139] After making such modifications as appeared to the secretary of state to be desirable, the proposals might be approved by the secretary of state.[140] As Joan indicated, based on Section 13, Thatcher argued that her proper duty was fulfilled by 'examining each school covered by a plan individually, taking any statutory objections into full account, while ignoring the overall plan of the elected LEA'.[141]

For Joan, Thatcher's interpretation of Section 13 was seemingly 'respect for the law and democratic rights', but was in fact 'carefully framed to encourage objections to aspects of reorganization plans'.[142] Indeed, as Joan pointed out, at the Conservative Party conference in October 1972, Thatcher herself even openly incited those present to be 'vocal' in defence of selective grammar schools.[143] According to Joan's records, in order to retain selective schools, Thatcher turned down plans submitted by Bromley, Havering, Dudley, Teesside, Harrow, and Birmingham by appealing to 'local objections'.[144] In Surrey, Thatcher even considered objections 'out of time'.[145] Subsequently, Joan condemned Thatcher's behaviour to be 'so unreasonable, so capricious, so irrelevant to any proper considerations as to mark the Minister in question as unfit to assume the powers vested in the office of Secretary of State'.[146] Brian Simon also argued that Thatcher was 'actively undermining local authority planning in order to carry through the undeclared policy ... of preserving a proportion of selective places in any reorganization plan'.[147] This, for Simon, was 'a clear attempt at an extension of executive power, on "legalistic grounds", to the detriment of the rights of democratically elected local authorities'.[148] When Joan's article was published, Simon explained clearly to the press that if Thatcher would not change her policy, 'she should resign'.[149]

Apart from ensuring the establishment of a universal system of comprehensive schools, Simon was also concerned with innovations within comprehensive schools themselves, in particular inner organisation of the schools. As mentioned above, as early as the mid-1950s, Simon had already advocated for a common curriculum for all. In his article in 1970, Simon explained that since the comprehensive school was essentially a means by which the need for early selection could be overcome, 'It seems ... to be a contradiction ... to continue to differentiate between children ... through streaming.'[150] He indicated that comprehensive schools in the USSR, Japan, Sweden and a high proportion of such schools in the United States did not stream their pupils.[151] By contrast, Simon observed that, in Britain, 'ideas derived from "intelligence" testing still have considerable force' as, in 1968, 19.5 per cent of the schools investigated by Simon and Benn still utilised streaming by ability in the first school year.[152] As Simon indicated, streaming was based on the theory that 'intellectual potential was largely determined by heredity, that it was fixed and unchanging and that it could be accurately assessed at an early age', which had been challenged by himself from the late 1940s.[153] However, in 1969, the American psychologist Arthur Jensen published an article in the *Harvard Educational Review* to reinstate the view that genetic factors had a dominant influence on intellectual development.[154]

In September 1969, in an article for a Communist Party conference on Marxism and Science, Simon stated that Jensen specifically set out to 'rehabilitate the hereditarian [sic] theory of intelligence in terms not only of class but "race"'.[155] Echoing Jensen's key contentions, in *Black Paper Two* published in October 1969, Cyril Burt and Hans Eysenck, two British psychometricians, stressed the necessity for streaming and selection.[156] Indeed, Burt argued that: 'If, with classes of thirty or more, the curriculum and teaching-methods are adapted to the pace of the majority, it is impossible to do justice to the latent capacities either of the dull or of the bright.'[157] Eysenck also maintained that 'it is impossible for everyone to go on to A-levels, and selection is necessary'.[158] Apart from this, Burt and Eysenck also 'launch into a lengthy defence of intelligence testing as instrument of selection'.[159] They all claimed that intelligence tests were 'instruments of social justice'.[160] On these accounts, Simon criticised them for attempting to 'ascribe human development largely to biological factors'.[161] One year later, at a Communist Party conference on the 'Battle for Educational Opportunity', Simon also noted that *Black Paper Two* 'brings in a so-called element of science in defenceless policy'.[162] He emphasised that since it is impossible on any scientific basis to predict any individual child's future development, 'logically we are bound to fight ... against streaming in the comprehensive schools'.[163] It was against this background, in 1971, Simon reprinted his book, *Intelligence Testing and the Comprehensive School* (1953), with the addition of other papers on the same topic.[164] In the epilogue of the reprinted book, *Intelligence, Psychology and Education: A Marxist Critique*, Simon expected that the comprehensive school would move towards unstreaming.[165]

Simon also called for radical reform in examinations. As stated, in 1962, accepting the Beloe Committee's proposal that a new examination for less academic fifteen-year-olds should be established alongside the existing GCE O-Level, the government brought in the CSE.[166] For Simon, the existence of two parallel school examinations was 'an historical product', based on 'tripartism'.[167] As he explained, GCE O-Level was specially designed for grammar schools and CSE was mainly for modern schools.[168] Within comprehensive schools, there was also a reproduction of the old divisions, the GCE for the top 20 per cent of pupils, the CSE for the next 40 per cent and non-examination for the rest.[169] Since this could not be considered in line with comprehensive school ideas, Simon argued for 'a single exam for all as objective at 16'.[170] In *Half Way There*, Simon also recommended substituting CSE for the very rigid GCE examination and, under Mode III, the CSE examination could be adapted to work in schools and be under the control of the teachers themselves.[171]

In 1971, the Schools Council for The Curriculum and Examinations published a report, *A Common System of Examining at 16+*. The report contended that a common examination system should be developed in place of GCE and CSE.[172] However, it recommended that 'the common system of examining should be designed to assess performance, subject by subject, from the 40th percentile to the top of the range of ability' considering the fact that 'methods of assessment that collectively are effective over the percentile range 40–100 are well established'.[173] Since the proposed examination catered only for 60 per cent of pupils, Simon argued that this did not go far enough and pressed for 'an examination appropriate to all pupils in the comprehensive school'.[174] In 1972, when the school-leaving age was finally raised to 16, a *Forum* editorial put forward that in order to make possible the development of a unified course for all between the ages of 11 and 16, one further step was: 'the provision of a single system of examination … catering for all at the age of 16'.[175] As Simon argued: 'It is essential for the success of comprehensive education that a unified five-year secondary course, leading to a single examination at the same point in time for all … should be provided for all pupils.'[176]

Simon and the great debate (1974–9)

Due to Margaret Thatcher's resolution to adopt a policy of coexistence, from 1970 to 1974, although the actual number of comprehensive schools more than doubled, catering for more than 50 per cent of children of secondary school age, at least half of these schools were in no sense 'genuinely' comprehensive.[177] Hence, in March 1974, once the Labour Party came into government, Reg Prentice, now Secretary of State for Education and Science, decided to consult the LEAs and teacher associations in advance on the terms of the new circular.[178] In a letter to Caroline Benn, Simon expressed his concern that 'things get held up because of this'.[179] Therefore, Simon emphasised that 'the sooner a new circular goes out the better, followed by effective legislation'.[180] In April 1974, the government issued Circular 4/74, showing their intention of developing a fully comprehensive system of secondary education.[181] Circular 10/70 was accordingly withdrawn. Moreover, in the case of voluntary-aided schools, the governors could not continue to receive substantial financial aid if they were not prepared to cooperate with the LEAs in settling their schools' place in a local comprehensive system.[182] In a *Forum* editorial, Simon welcomed Circular 4/74 for 'its promise of a tougher line towards those voluntary aided schools which refuse to participate in comprehensive reorganization'.[183] However, considering the fact that the direct-grant schools continued to prevent many areas from reorganising along fully comprehensive lines, Simon argued that the new circular was 'unlikely to achieve a fully comprehensive system'.[184]

Months later, another *Forum* editorial also urged the Labour government to take 'definite action to introduce genuinely comprehensive education once and for all', which implied 'passing the necessary legislation to enable all grammar schools to come fully into local systems' and 'putting an end to the direct grant list'.[185] In July 1975, the Direct Grant Grammar Schools Regulations were eventually laid before parliament, whereby the direct-grant schools would no longer receive grant and would become maintained by the LEAs.[186] In April 1976, James Callaghan succeeded Harold Wilson as Prime Minister. In November the 1976 Education Act eventually empowered the government to require the LEAs or governors of voluntary schools to submit proposals for effecting the comprehensive principle.[187] Despite this, in a Communist Party pamphlet produced in collaboration with Charles Godden, Simon indicated that too many loopholes remained in the 1976 Education Act, and thus he held that a Bill must be introduced to ensure that the LEAs were given 'full powers' to bring voluntary-aided schools into local comprehensive systems.[188] Moreover, he stressed that: 'The final objective must be the inclusion of the so-called independent schools.'[189]

In addition, from the mid-1970s, because of the Conservatives' success in placing 'educational failure' and 'low standards' at the centre of popular debate, there was a tendency towards central control in educational procedures in Labour government policy.[190] As Simon indicated, the mass media publicised widely the idea that comprehensive education was a disaster and standards in schools were non-existent.[191] When the Tyndale affair broke in the press in 1974, the impression that teaching methods or teachers in primary schools featured 'progressive education' and were getting out of hand was also promulgated.[192] Additionally, employers and industrialists also blamed schools for their failure to prepare pupils for entry into the world of work, especially after the world-wide economic recession in 1974–75.[193] Faced with all this, Labour ministers did little to counter the critics.[194] Instead, in July 1976, a confidential document, *School Education in England: Problems and Initiatives* (The Yellow Book), prepared for the prime minister, James Callaghan, by a group of civil servants within the DES, reached the prime minister.[195] The Yellow Book suggested that the government should 'explore the case and scope for the introduction of a common core curriculum in all schools' in order to ensure improved standards and to meet the needs of the economy.[196] In line with this, in October 1976, James Callaghan delivered a speech at Ruskin College in Oxford and initiated the 'Great Debate' on education. In this speech

Callaghan also made a strong case for the so-called 'core curriculum' of basic knowledge and skills such as literacy and numeracy, and advocated for improved relations between industry and education.[197]

For Simon, the most positive aspect of the cry for a core curriculum was that the concept of 'education for all' was beginning to be accepted.[198] Despite this, the government intervention in the curriculum implicit in Callaghan's initiative was opposed by Simon. As Simon indicated, in Britain, 'Neither state nor central government lays down by law what should be taught, nor how it should be taught.'[199] Facing the increasing demand for centralisation of power over the process of education, Simon stressed that although Marx realised that the only means by which effective public provision could be made was by utilising the power of the state, this was something quite different from appointing the state as 'educator of the peoples'.[200] Therefore, Simon argued that 'every means must be found to strengthen local democratic control of the schools and school systems, and to provide scope for teachers, parents and school students to participate effectively in the government and control of the schools'.[201] Meanwhile, he also accused neo-Marxists of evaluating the whole system of education as a function controlled by the state, and reducible to the simple reproduction of existing social relations.[202] After all, as Simon observed, Marx did not conceive education as part of the oppressive apparatus of the state, not open to any influences which could bring about its transformation. This kind of thinking, Simon added, was contradictory to the dialectical and historical nature of Marx's thinking.[203]

In July 1977, the government issued its green paper, *Education in Schools: A Consultative Document*. Following this, Simon published an article in *Forum*, indicating that 'the Green Paper marks a new phase in its clear assertion of an active (leadership) role for the DES in relation to educational (as apart from administrative) matters'.[204] First, in relation to the curriculum, the green paper asserted that the secretaries of state could not 'abdicate from leadership' on this issue.[205] Moreover, it proposed that curricular arrangements in each local authority must be reviewed.[206] The circular initiating this review would list a wide range of issues for report.[207] For Simon, this meant that 'options are kept wide open for further central government action on this highly sensitive issue'.[208] Thus, in a Communist Party pamphlet, Simon reiterated the party's opposition to such centralising tendencies and argued that: 'the internal organization and curriculum of schools should certainly be a matter in which the teachers, because of their professional expertise, have a decisive role to play'.[209]

Additionally, Simon emphasised that: 'the main immediate impact of the Green Paper will undoubtedly be felt in the area of standards and assessments'.[210] The green paper made a clear assertion of 'the need for schools to demonstrate their accountability to the society', and this required 'a coherent and soundly based means of assessment for the education system as a whole, for schools, and for individual pupils'.[211] Indeed, the green paper indicated that the Assessment of Performance Unit (APU) of the DES was developing 'tests suitable for national monitoring in English language, mathematics and science' and 'its programme of national assessment will start in 1978'.[212] For Simon, the effect of this would be disastrous as this would lead to 'the imposition of mass testing of a limited and restrictive type covering the three Rs'.[213] Moreover, Simon held that the proposal would result in 'a sharp restriction on the teacher's power to provide educational experiences of a broad and varied character'.[214] In September 1977, at the annual conference of the British Educational Research Association (BERA), as the president of BERA, Simon also stated to the members that: 'if the Great Debate, and various reports in the pipeline, operate to cabin and confine individual and group initiative on the part of teachers, then I hope we will be prepared to raise our voices in opposition'.[215] In November 1978, at a public lecture commemorating Shena Simon's work with Manchester City Council, Simon posed a basic question to the audience: 'To whom do schools belong?'[216] In answering the question, he argued that 'the strength and vitality displayed historically through the forms of local control and initiative' was one specific feature of the English tradition in education and 'needs today to be strengthened against attempts to erode it'.[217]

Conclusion

This chapter illustrates Brian Simon's Marxist ideal of comprehensive education and his involvement in politics, campaigning for a genuine comprehensive education, from the 1950s to the 1970s. For Simon, the comprehensive school should be a school for all children. Moreover, a common core of subjects as well as a general and all-round education should be provided to all, up to the age of 15 or 16. Simon believed that only this way could a real educational opportunity be guaranteed for all children. Between 1951 and 1964, facing constant hindrance from the Conservative government, Simon continued to advocate for the comprehensive school and push for reforms, including unstreaming in junior and secondary schools, a common examination for all children at the age of 16, the raising of the school-leaving age to 18, and the elimination of direct-grant schools and public schools. With this reform agenda in mind, Simon remarked critically on various reports and official documents, such as *Early Leaving* (1954), *Secondary Education for All: A New Drive* (1958), *Learning to Live* (1958), the Crowther Report (1959), the Beloe Report (1960) and the Newsom Report (1963), to put pressure on the Conservative government and the Labour Party in opposition and hasten the pace of reform. Additionally, seeking to influence the formation of educational policies, Simon also wrote an open letter in *Forum* to the Robbins Committee and gave written and oral evidence to the Plowden Committee.

Between 1964 and 1970 a Labour government held office and eventually decided to introduce comprehensive education. Following the issue of Circular 10/65, which 'requested' rather than 'required' the LEAs to submit plans on comprehensive lines, working with the CSC, Simon also monitored the developments and criticised the Doncaster scheme. Meanwhile, through *Forum*, Simon also urged the Public Schools Commission to abolish the public schools and the direct grant list. In early 1970, after Short's Bill failed, Simon also called for new legislation to impose the duty of developing comprehensive education on all local authorities. Between 1970 and 1974, since the Conservative government was determined to preserve selective grammar schools, Simon insisted on a comprehensive system of secondary education and criticised Thatcher's intervention in local authority planning. Facing attacks from *Black Paper Two*, in which Burt and Eysenck rehabilitated the theory of hereditary intelligence and argued for streaming and selection, Simon reiterated his opposition to the ideology of intelligence testing and called for non-streaming in comprehensive schools along with a single examination for all pupils up to the age of 16.

After the Labour Party was returned to office in 1974, again, Simon pressed for a new Act to ensure a complete reform of comprehensive education. Eventually, in 1975, according to the Direct Grant Grammar Schools Regulations, the direct-grant schools would no longer receive funding from central government and would become maintained by the LEAs. The 1976 Education Act empowered the government to require the LEAs or governors of voluntary schools to submit proposals in line with the comprehensive principle. Despite this, for Simon, many loopholes remained in the new Act and, more importantly, the public schools were also not included in it. Hence, Simon continued to campaign for a Bill to be introduced. Additionally, followed by James Callaghan's

Ruskin Speech and the Great Debate in 1976, Simon was opposed to the centralising tendency in education, from his Marxist perspective, although his ideal of a common core curriculum was finally recognised by the Labour government.

Overall, in Simon's view, development in the 1970s was 'downhill all the way'.[218] Apart from resisting all the challenges to the comprehensive schools outlined in this chapter, Simon also noticed the rise of market philosophy in the Conservative Party. With the oil crisis of 1973–74, the 'golden age' of sustained economic growth, full employment and reasonably stable prices in Britain ended.[219] In 1974–75, GDP at constant factor cost fell for the first time since 1946, by 3.5 per cent. In 1974–1977, the rate of unemployment rose from 2.6 per cent to 6.2 per cent. In 1975, the rate of inflation reached 26 per cent.[220] Since the welfare-state societies were unable to sustain economic growth, low rates of inflation or high levels of employment, market philosophies emerged.[221] By applying neoliberal thoughts to educational policies, as will be shown in the next chapter, the Thatcher governments in the 1980s caused greater damage to the comprehensive system of education. Again, Simon was involved in the politics of education and played an important role in defending the comprehensive schools.

Notes

1 Brian Simon, 'The comprehensive school', *Communist Review*, April 1949, 486–91, 490.
2 Brian Simon, 'Speech made by Brian Simon to the "Battle for Educational Opportunity Conference"', 1971. Simon papers, IOE UCL Archives, Simon 1/17.
3 Brian Simon, 'Education! The socialist perspective', May 1978. Simon papers, IOE UCL Archives, Simon 1/41.
4 'Professor Brian Simon in conversation with Ruth Watts', *History of Education Research*, no. 71 (May 2003): 3–13, 9. Simon papers, IOE UCL Archives, Simon 4/9/1. It should be noted that from the 1950s, the British Communist Party endeavoured to develop its own policy and spoke of a conquest of power through parliamentary means in its programme called 'The British Road to Socialism'. This was quite different from Marx's advocacy of social revolution carried out by trade unions. See Henry Pelling, *The British Communist Party: A historical profile* (London: A&C Black, 1975), 161; M. Beer (ed.), *A History of British Socialism (Vol. II)* (London: Routledge, 2002), 218–20.
5 Brian Simon, Autobiography Vol. II (1945–1994), [n.d. 1993?]. Simon papers, IOE UCL Archives, Simon 4/5/2/16. Simon joined the Communist Party in 1935. See Brian Simon, *A Life in Education* (London: Lawrence & Wishart, 1998), 10.
6 Brian Simon, Autobiography Vol. II (1945–1994), [n.d. 1993?].
7 James Eaden and David Renton, *The Communist Party of Great Britain since 1920*, 118–21.
8 Brian Simon, Autobiography Vol. II (1945–1994), [n.d. 1993?].
9 Brian Simon, Autobiography Vol. II (1945–1994), [n.d. 1993?].
10 National Cultural Committee, *Cultural Work*, no. 5 (February 1964). Communist Party's paper, CP/CENT/CULT/3/1.
11 Matthew R. Kavanagh, 'British communism and the politics of education, 1926–1968' (PhD diss., University of Manchester, 2005), 211.

12 Simon, *A Life in Education*, 88.
13 It should be noted that even Cyril Burt, a well-known British psychologist advocating intelligence testing, did not support a tripartite system. He argued that 'any scheme of organisation which proposes to classify children at the age of eleven or twelve according to qualitative mental types rather than according to general intelligence is in conflict with the known facts of child psychology'. See Cyril Burt, 'The education of the young adolescent: The psychological implications of the Norwood Report', *British Journal of Educational Psychology* 8, part III (November 1943): 126–40, 140.
14 Brian Simon, Autobiography Vol. II (1945–1994), [n.d. 1993?].
15 Brian Simon, 'The comprehensive school', *Communist Review*, April 1949, 486–91, 486.
16 Brian Simon, 'The comprehensive school', 490.
17 Brian Simon, 'Intelligence testing and the comprehensive school', in *Intelligence, Psychology and Education: A Marxist critique*, 29–121, 114.
18 Brian Simon, 'Intelligence testing and the comprehensive school', 114.
19 Brian Simon, *Education and the Social Order, 1940–1990*, 171–2.
20 Brian Simon, *Education and the Social Order, 1940–1990*, 172.
21 Brian Simon, *Education and the Social Order, 1940–1990*, 183.
22 Brian Simon, *Education and the Social Order, 1940–1990*, 184.
23 Brian Simon, *The Common Secondary School*, 99–100, 105.
24 Brian Simon, *The Common Secondary School*, 110.
25 Brian Simon, *The Common Secondary School*, 114.
26 Brian Simon, *The Common Secondary School*, 126.
27 Brian Simon, 'Early leaving – why?', *Education Today and Tomorrow* 7, no. 5 (May–June 1955): 5.
28 Central Advisory Council for Education (England), *Early Leaving* (London: HMSO, 1954), 12.
29 Simon, 'Early leaving – why?', 5.
30 Brian Simon, 'Derbyshire Teacher Bulletin', June 1956. Simon papers, IOE UCL Archives, Simon 1/71.
31 Brian Simon, 'Derbyshire Teacher Bulletin', June 1956.
32 Brian Simon, 'Karl Marx on education', in *Intelligence, Psychology and Education*, 177–99, 197.
33 Brian Simon, 'Karl Marx on education', 197.
34 Brian Simon, *Education in the New Poland*, 26.
35 Brian Simon, 'Polytechnical Education in the USSR', *The Vocational Aspect of Education* 7, no. 15, 1955, 135–41, 135.
36 Brian Simon, *Education: The new perspective*, 12–13.
37 Minutes of Executive Committee Meeting held on 11–12 May 1957. Communist Party's paper, CP/CENT/EC/4/8; Teachers' Weekend Residential School, 25–26 May 1957. Simon papers, IOE UCL Archives, Simon 5/7.
38 Brian Simon, 'The present stage in the struggle for educational advance', Matlock School, May 1957. Simon papers, IOE UCL Archives, Simon 1/4.
39 Brian Simon, 'The present stage in the struggle for educational advance'.
40 David Rubinstein and Brian Simon, *The Evolution of the Comprehensive School, 1926–1972* (2nd edition, London: Routledge & Kegan Paul, 1973), 72; Brian Simon, 'The Government's White Paper', *Forum* 1, no. 2 (1959): 75.
41 Brian Simon, 'Robin Pedley 1914–1988: Comprehensive pioneer', [n.d., 1988?]. Simon papers, IOE UCL Archives, Simon 2/53.
42 Simon, 'The Government's White Paper'; Ministry of Education, *Secondary Education for All* (White Paper) (London: HMSO, December 1958), 6.
43 Ministry of Education, *Secondary Education for All*, 5.
44 Ministry of Education, *Secondary Education for All*, 6.
45 Simon, 'The Government's White Paper'.
46 Simon, 'The Government's White Paper'.
47 Brian Simon, 'Crowther Report must be implemented', 1960. Simon papers, IOE UCL Archives, Simon 1/72; Ministry of Education, *15 to 18* (London: HMSO, 1959) (Crowther Report), xxx.
48 Gary McCulloch, Steven Cowan & Tom Woodin, 'The British Conservative government and the raising of the school leaving age, 1959–1964', *Journal of Education Policy* 27, no. 4 (2012): 509–27, 516–17.
49 Simon, 'Crowther Report must be implemented'.
50 Simon, 'Crowther Report must be implemented'; Ministry of Education, *Half Our Future* (London: HMSO, 1963) (Newsom Report of 1963), xvi.

51 McCulloch, Cowan & Woodin, 'The British Conservative government and the raising of the school leaving age, 1959–1964', 523.
52 Crowther Report, 88.
53 Robin Pedley and Brian Simon, 'Has Crowther wasted his time?', *Forum* 2, no. 3 (1960): 84–91, 87.
54 Simon, *Education and the Social Order*, 304; Ministry of Education, *Secondary School Examinations other than the GCE* (London: HMSO, 1960) (Beloe Report), 46–7.
55 'Public Inquiry into GCE: Mr Simon's Proposal', *Times Educational Supplement*, 3 February 1961. Simon papers, IOE UCL Archives, Simon 1/72. See also Beloe Report, 47.
56 'Public Inquiry into GCE: Mr Simon's Proposal', 47.
57 'Call for abolition of 11-plus exam in ten years', *Nottingham Evening News*, 28 January 1961. Simon papers, IOE UCL Archives, Simon 1/72.
58 Gary McCulloch, 'British Labour Party education policy and comprehensive education: From Learning to Live to Circular 10/65', *History of Education* 45, no. 2 (2016): 234–7.
59 Gary McCulloch, 'British Labour Party education policy and comprehensive education', 241.
60 Brian Simon, 'Labour's education policy', *Labour Monthly*, September 1958, 418–21, 418.
61 Brian Simon, 'Labour's education policy', 418.
62 Brian Simon, 'Labour's education policy', 421; Labour Party, *Learning to Live: Labour's policy for education* (London: Labour Party, 1958), 60.
63 Simon, 'Labour's education policy', 420–1.
64 Ministry of Education, *Report of the Committee on Higher Education* (London: HMSO, 1963) (Robbins Report), iii.
65 Robin Pedley and Brian Simon, 'Open letter to the Robbins Committee', *Forum* 4, no. 1 (1961): 3–11.
66 Robin Pedley and Brian Simon, 'Open letter to the Robbins Committee', 3.
67 Robin Pedley and Brian Simon, 'Open letter to the Robbins Committee', 3.
68 Robbins Report, 268.
69 [No Author, editor Brian Simon?], 'Robbins, Newsom and Plowden', *Forum* 6, no. 2 (1964): 39.
70 DES, *Children and Their Primary Schools* (London: HMSO, 1967) (Plowden Report), 1; 'The case for non-streaming' (Evidence submitted by the Editorial Board of *Forum* to the Central Advisory Council for Education (England) The Plowden Committee), in *Non-streaming in the Junior School*, ed. B. Simon (Leicester: PSW (Educational) Publications, 1964), 7–28.
71 DES, *Children and Their Primary Schools*, 24.
72 DES, *Children and Their Primary Schools*, 24–5.
73 Simon, *A Life in Education*, 92–3.
74 Simon, *A Life in Education*, 93–4.
75 Plowden Report, 474.
76 Simon, *A Life in Education*, 94.
77 Rubinstein and Simon, *The Evolution of the Comprehensive School*, 93.
78 DES, *Circular 10/65* (London: HMSO, 1965).
79 Simon, *Education and the social order,* 281.
80 Leaflet for 'Comprehensive Schools Committee', [n.d., 1965?]. Simon papers, IOE UCL Archives, Simon 4/4/35; Shirley Toulson, 'Polishing that public image', *Teacher*, 1 October 1965. Simon papers, IOE UCL Archives, Simon 1/74.
81 Brian Simon, Obituary of Caroline Benn, [n.d., 2001?]. Simon papers, IOE UCL Archives, Simon 2/18; Brian Simon to Caroline Benn, 12 October 1965. Simon papers, IOE UCL Archives, Simon 4/4/35.
82 Simon to Caroline Benn, 12 October 1965.
83 Simon to Caroline Benn, 12 October 1965.
84 Caroline Benn to Brian Simon, 11 November 1965. Simon papers, IOE UCL Archives, Simon 4/4/35; 'Editorial: What sort of schools does Mr Crosland want?', *Comprehensive Education*, November 1: Autumn 1965. Simon papers, IOE UCL Archives, Simon 4/4/35.
85 'Editorial: What sort of schools does Mr. Crosland want?'.
86 Brian Simon, 'Social selection and the Doncaster Plan', *Forum* 8, no. 2 (1966): 39–42.
87 Brian Simon, 'Social selection and the Doncaster Plan', 40.
88 Brian Simon, 'Social selection and the Doncaster Plan', 41.
89 Brian Simon, 'Social selection and the Doncaster Plan', 41.
90 Simon, *Education and the Social Order*, 283; DES, *Circular 10/66* (London: HMSO, 1966).

91   Brian Simon, 'Sharp eye on your council's comprehensive school scheme', [*Morning Star?*], 3 June 1966. Simon papers, IOE UCL Archives, Simon 1/ 74.
92   Brian Simon, 'Sharp eye on your council's comprehensive school scheme'.
93   Simon, *Education and the Social Order*, 284.
94   Brian Simon to Caroline Benn, 9 May 1966. Simon papers, IOE UCL Archives, Simon 2/12; [No Author, editor Brian Simon?], 'National policy in education', *Forum* 8, no. 3 (1966): 75–6.
95   [No Author, editor Brian Simon?], 'National policy in education', 75–6.
96   Public Schools Commission, *First Report* (London: HMSO, 1968)(Newsom Report of 1968), vii.
97   'Public Schools Commission' (Evidence submitted by the Editorial Board of *Forum* to the Newsom Committee on the Public Schools), *Forum* 10, no. 1 (1967): 2–3.
98   'Public Schools Commission', 2.
99   'Public Schools Commission', 3.
100 Simon, *Education and the Social Order*, 323.
101 *Newsom Report* of 1968, 8, 12.
102 Simon, *Education and the Social Order*, 326.
103 Brian Simon, 'Note on public school', newspaper cuttings. [n.d., 1968?]. Simon papers, IOE UCL Archives, Simon 4/4/40.
104 Brian Simon, review of *The Labour Party and the Organization of Secondary Education, 1918–1965* by Michael Parkinson, 1970. Simon papers, IOE UCL Archives, Simon 1/17.
105 Simon, *Education and the Social Order*, 320.
106 Simon, 'Sharp eye on your council's comprehensive school scheme'.
107 Brian Simon, 'Changing complex of our schools', 24 October 1968. Simon papers, IOE UCL Archives, Simon 1/5.
108 [No Author, editor Brian Simon?], 'For genuine comprehensive schools', *Forum* 11, no. 3 (1969): 75.
109 Simon, *Education and the Social Order*, 328; 'Direct grant grammar schools' (Evidence submitted to the Public Schools Commission by the Editorial Board of *Forum*), *Forum* 11, no. 3 (1969): 76–7.
110 'Direct grant grammar schools', 77.
111 Public Schools Commission, *Second Report* (London: HMSO, 1970)(Donnison Report), 11–12.
112 [No Author, editor Brian Simon?], 'The long lurch to comprehensive education', *Forum* 12, no. 3 (1970): 75.
113 Simon, *Education and the Social Order*, 301.
114 Simon, *Education and the Social Order*, 301.
115 Simon, review of *The Labour Party and the Organization of Secondary Education, 1918–1965* by Michael Parkinson, 1970.
116 Simon, *Education and the Social Order*, 408.
117 Caroline Benn and Brian Simon, *Half Way There: Report on the British comprehensive reform* (1st edition, Maidenhead: Mc-Graw Hill, 1970), 347–8.
118 Benn and Simon, *Half Way There*, 348–9.
119 Rubinstein and Simon, *The Evolution of the Comprehensive School*, 107.
120 Rubinstein and Simon, *The Evolution of the Comprehensive School*, 108.
121 DES, *The Organization of Secondary Education* (Circular 10/70) (London: HMSO, 1970).
122 Shena Simon to Brian Simon, 6 July 1970. Simon papers, IOE UCL Archives, Simon 5/1/5.
123 Brian Simon, 'Opportunities for education: A matter of national survival', *Morning Star*, July 13, 1970, 4. Simon papers, IOE UCL Archives, Simon 1/6.
124 Brian Simon, 'Opportunities for education: A matter of national survival'.
125 Betty Reid to Brian Simon, [n.d., between 16 September and 17 October 1970]. Communist Party's paper, People's History Museum Archives, CP/CENT/CULT/3/12. Brian Simon, 'Speech made by Brian Simon to the "Battle for Educational Opportunity Conference"' (working paper, 1970). Simon papers, IOE UCL Archives, Simon 1/17.
126 Benn and Simon, *Half Way There* (1st edition), 5.
127 Simon, 'Speech made by Brian Simon to the "Battle for Educational Opportunity Conference"'.
128 Brian Simon, 'Wyggeston parents' (lecture, November 18, 1970). Simon papers, IOE UCL Archives, Simon 1/37; Brian Simon, 'On Comprehensive' (lecture, Watford, May 1971). Simon papers, IOE UCL Archives, Simon 1/38.

129   Brian Simon, 'Half way there' (lecture, Glasgow EIS, March 1972). Simon papers, IOE UCL Archives, Simon 1/43.
130   Caroline Benn and Brian Simon, *Half Way There: Report on the British comprehensive reform* (2nd edition, Harmondsworth: Penguin, 1972), 491–2.
131   Caroline Benn and Brian Simon, *Half Way There* (2nd edition), 492.
132   DES, *Education: A framework for expansion* (The White Paper) (London: HMSO, 1972), 1, 3.
133   Editorial, '16–19', *Forum* 15, no. 2 (1973): 35.
134   Editorial, 'A Summer's Outrage', *Forum* 16, no. 1 (1973): 1.
135   Brian Simon to Jack Walton, 17 August 1973. Simon papers, IOE UCL Archives, Simon 4/4/45.
136   Joan Simon to Alan Evans (NUT), 9 September 1973. Simon papers, IOE UCL Archives, Simon 4/4/48.
137   Joan Simon, *Indictment of Margaret Thatcher* (Leicester: PSW (Educational) Publications, 1973), 26. Simon papers, IOE UCL Archives, Simon 4/4/58.
138   DES, *Education Act 1968* (London: HMSO, 1968), Section 13 (1).
139   DES, *Education Act 1968*, Section 13 (3).
140   DES, *Education Act 1968*, Section 13 (4).
141   Joan Simon, *Indictment of Margaret Thatcher*, 26.
142   *Indictment of Margaret Thatcher*, 26.
143   *Indictment of Margaret Thatcher*, 31.
144   *Indictment of Margaret Thatcher*, 20–3.
145   *Indictment of Margaret Thatcher*, 29.
146   *Indictment of Margaret Thatcher*, 28.
147   Brian Simon, 'Letter to the editor of the *Guardian*' (working paper, September 9, 1973). Simon papers, IOE UCL Archives, Simon 4/4/45.
148   Brian Simon, 'Letter to the editor of the *Guardian*'.
149   Hilary Brook, 'Mrs Thatcher indicted', *The Teacher*, 12 October, 1973. Simon papers, IOE UCL Archives, Simon 4/4/45.
150   Brian Simon, 'Streaming and the Comprehensive School', *Secondary Education* 1, no. 1 (1970): 3–5, 3. Simon papers, IOE UCL Archives, Simon 1/6.
151   Brian Simon, 'Streaming and the comprehensive school', 4.
152   Benn and Simon, *Half Way There* (1st edition), 24, 146.
153   Brian Simon, 'Streaming and unstreaming in the secondary school', in *Education for Democracy*, 142–50, 143.
154   Brian Simon, 'Streaming and unstreaming in the secondary school', 143.
155   National Committee (working paper, September 8, 1969). Communist Party's paper, People's History Museum Archives, CP/CENT/CULT/1/12; Brian Simon, 'Intelligence, race, class and education', in *Intelligence, Psychology and Education*, 237–63, 243. (Reprinted from Marxism Today, November 1970).
156   Brian Simon, 'Intelligence, race, class and education', 245.
157   Cyril Burt, 'The Mental Differences between Children', in *Black Paper Two: The crisis in education*, 16–25, 20.
158   H. J. Eysenck, 'The rise of the mediocracy', in *Black Paper Two: The crisis in education*, 34–40, 34.
159   Brian Simon, 'The Black Paper' (working paper, [n.d., 1970?]). Simon papers, IOE UCL Archives, Simon 1/6.
160   Burt, 'The mental differences between children', 20; Eysenck, 'The rise of the mediocracy', 36.
161   Simon, 'Intelligence, race, class and education', 247.
162   Simon, 'Speech made by Brian Simon to the "Battle for Educational Opportunity Conference"'.
163   Simon, 'Speech made to the "Battle for Educational Opportunity Conference"'.
164   Brian Simon, 'Introduction', in *Intelligence, Psychology and Education*, 9–27, 9.
165   Brian Simon, 'Epilogue: Comprehensive school organization in the 1970's', in *Intelligence, Psychology and Education*, 264–76, 272.
166   Simon, *Education and the Social Order*, 304; Beloe Report, 46–7.
167   Brian Simon, 'Examinations and the comprehensive school' (lecture, Sydenham, May 7, 1970). Simon papers, IOE UCL Archives, Simon 1/37.
168   Brian Simon, 'Examinations and the comprehensive school'.

169 Brian Simon, 'Examinations and the comprehensive school'.
170 Brian Simon, 'Examinations and the comprehensive school'.
171 Benn and Simon, *Half Way There* (1st edition), 174, 354.
172 Schools Council, *A Common System of Examining at 16+*, 7.
173 Schools Council, *A Common System of Examining at 16+*, 9–10.
174 Simon, 'Half way there'.
175 Editorial, 'ROSLA and de-schooling', *Forum* 14, no. 3 (1972): 69.
176 Benn and Simon, *Half Way There* (2nd edition), 497–8. See also Editorial, 'Comprehensive reform', *Forum* 15, no. 1 (1972): 1.
177 Simon, *Education and the Social Order*, 430; Clyde Chitty, *Towards a New Education System: The victory of the New Right?*, 55.
178 Editorial, 'Advice to Reg Prentice', *Forum* 16, no. 3 (1974): 67.
179 Brian Simon to Caroline Benn, 17 March 1974. Simon papers, IOE UCL Archives, Simon 2/17.
180 Brian Simon to Caroline Benn, 17 March 1974.
181 DES, *The Organization of Secondary Education* (Circular 4/74) (London: HMSO, 1974).
182 DES, *The Organization of Secondary Education*.
183 Editorial, 'Advice to Reg Prentice'.
184 Editorial, 'Advice to Reg Prentice'.
185 Editorial, 'The politics of education', *Forum* 17, no. 1 (1974): 2–3.
186 DES, *The Direct Grant Grammar Schools Regulation* (London: HMSO, 1975).
187 DES, *Education Act 1976* (London: HMSO, 1976), Section 2.
188 Brian Simon and Charles Godden, *The Comprehensive School* (London: Communist Party of Great Britain, 1978), 8. Communist Party's paper, People's History Museum Archives, CP/CENT/IND/10/2.
189 Brian Simon and Charles Godden, *The Comprehensive School*.
190 Ken Jones, *Education in Britain: 1944 to the present* (Cambridge, UK: Polity, 2003), 100.
191 Brian Simon, 'What School is for' (working paper, December 28, 1976). Simon papers, IOE UCL Archives, Simon 1/18.
192 Brian Simon, 'The Primary School Revolution: Myth or reality?' (working paper, October 21, 1980). Simon papers, IOE UCL Archives, Simon 1/15. The Tyndale affair occurred in 1974 in a small ILEA primary school, in which a few teachers adopted an extreme version of child-centred education and caused conflicts between teachers and parents. For more details on the Tyndale affair, See Simon, *Education and the Social Order*, 444–5.
193 Chitty, *Towards a New Education System*, 60.
194 Peter Gordon, Richard Aldrich and Dennis Dean, *Education and Policy in England in the Twentieth Century* (London: Woburn Press, 1991), 197.
195 Chitty, *Towards a New Education System*, 40.
196 DES, *School Education in England: Problems and initiatives* (The Yellow Book) (London: HMSO, 1976), 22.
197 James Callaghan, 'A rational debate based on the facts' (The Ruskin Speech).
198 Simon, 'What school is for'.
199 Brian Simon, 'Marx and the crisis in education', *Marxism Today* (July 1977): 195–205, 198–9.
200 Brian Simon, 'Marx and the crisis in education', 198.
201 Brian Simon, 'Marx and the crisis in education', 204–5.
202 Brian Simon, 'Marx and the crisis in education', 199.
203 Brian Simon, 'Marx and the crisis in education', 199.
204 Brian Simon, 'The Green Paper', *Forum* 20, no. 1 (1977): 18; See also DES, *Education in Schools: A consultative document* (Green Paper) (London: HMSO, 1977), 12.
205 DES, *Education in Schools*, 12.
206 DES, *Education in Schools*, 13.
207 DES, *Education in Schools*, 13.
208 Simon, 'The Green Paper', 18.
209 Simon and Godden, *The Comprehensive School*, 6.
210 Simon, 'The Green Paper', 18.
211 DES, *Education in Schools*, 16.
212 DES, *Education in Schools*, 17.
213 Simon, 'The Green Paper', 18.
214 Simon, 'The Green Paper', 18.

215 Brian Simon, 'Educational research: Which way?', *Research Intelligence* 4 no.1 (1977): 2–7, 2. Simon papers, IOE UCL Archives, Simon 1/6.
216 Brian Simon, 'To whom do schools belong?', in *Does Education Matter?*, 55–76. Shena Simon was Brian Simon's mother. She served the Education Committee in Manchester for more than 40 years.
217 Simon, 'To whom do schools belong?', 68.
218 Simon, *Education and the Social Order*, chapter 9.
219 G. C. Peden, *British Economic and Social Policy: Lloyd George to Margaret Thatcher*, 196.
220 Peden, *British Economic and Social Policy*, 196.
221 Jones, *Education in Britain: 1944 to the present*, 106.

7 Brian Simon in girls' class, USSR, 1955.
Courtesy of UCL IOE Archives, SIM/6/1/3.

8 Staff of Abbott Street school, 1946.
Courtesy of UCL IOE Archives, SIM/5/4/4.

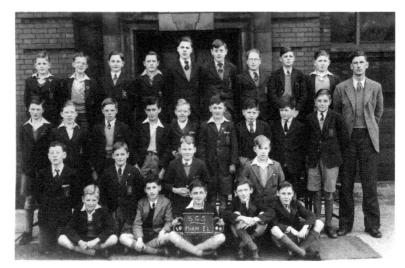

9   Brian Simon with Form 1L, Salford Grammar School, 1948.
Courtesy of UCL IOE Archives, SIM/5/4/4.

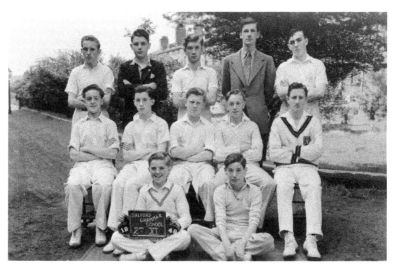

10   Salford Grammar School cricket 2nd XI, 1948.
Courtesy of UCL IOE Archives, SIM/5/4/4.

11 Salford Grammar School staff photo, c.1947–1950.
Courtesy of UCL IOE Archives, SIM/5/4/6.

12 Brian Simon in the USSR, 1955.
Courtesy of UCL IOE Archives, SIM/6/1/6.

13 Brian Simon in the USSR, 1955.
Courtesy of UCL IOE Archives, SIM/6/1/6.

14 Reflecting in later years – Brian Simon in the Sears Tower, Chicago, 1975.
© Simon family. Archive reference SIM/5/4/8.

8
Defending comprehensive education: 1979–90

By 1980, nearly 90 per cent of pupils in England and Wales were in comprehensive schools.[1] Nevertheless, as Simon indicated, from 1979 to 1990, there was an ideological offensive from the right wing, intent on 'rubbishing' the advances of the 1960s.[2] On the one hand, three successive Conservative governments continued to increase central control and destroy the partnership between central government, the LEAs and teachers, which was established after the 1944 Education Act.[3] On the other hand, government encouraged market forces to create variety within the system and to emphasise parental choice. In November 1987, the government introduced a Great Education Reform Bill (immediately dubbed the 'GERBIL') to ensure further reforms. For Simon, all these threatened the development of comprehensive education. Moreover, he strongly argued that the 1988 Education Reform Act (ERA) 'has one major target and one only: the comprehensive secondary school'.[4] Therefore, in retirement and arranging numerous overseas visits, as well as returning to his historical studies, he was still vigorously engaged with the politics of education.[5] Unlike those reformers of the Second World War, who supported the Education Bill of 1943 and endeavoured to press for further reforms, on the grounds of a consensus on 'secondary education for all' across political parties, there was now much less political consensus, while Simon himself was now a senior figure with more allies, resisting policies of the New Right, alongside other left-wing figures such as Caroline Benn.[6] Based on his Marxist ideal of comprehensive education, Simon revealed and challenged the ideology behind the policies, not only through the Communist Party and its organs (*Marxism Today* and *Education Today and Tomorrow*), but also via other outlets. These include journals such as *Forum* and *Comprehensive Education*, as well as various professional organisations. Therefore, in this chapter, Simon's response to educational policies under Margaret Thatcher's governments is explored, in particular focusing on those measures relevant to comprehensive education. In so doing, this chapter will shed some light on Simon's role and distinctive contribution to the defence of comprehensive education in the 1980s.

Comprehensive education in the 1980s

In May 1979, the first Thatcher government was returned to office. From a very difficult start, the Thatcher government retained power, with a much increased majority in the general election of June 1983, followed by another overwhelming electoral triumph in 1987.[7] In November 1990, Margaret Thatcher resigned and ended her premiership.[8] The Thatcher years, in Kenneth O. Morgan's words, 'implied the triumph of the market philosophy, the private ethic, and the imperatives of early-nineteenth-century liberalism'.[9] In 1974, influenced by the Institute of Economic Affairs (IEA), a British 'free-market' think-tank, Margaret Thatcher and Sir Keith Joseph had established the Centre for Policy Studies to develop a new conservative radicalism based on nineteenth-century free-market anti-statism.[10] After 1975, once Margaret Thatcher was elected as Conservative leader, with the party in opposition, belief in the market gradually became the motif of Conservative policy.[11] In the area of education, while Thatcher was the secretary of state, at the 1973 Conservative Party conference, she was already seeking to empower parents through choice of school.[12] Following this, support grew in the Conservative party for parental choice and education vouchers, as advocated by Rhodes Boyson and others of the right wing.[13] It was from this background that the 'new right' emerged, which included two contrasting groups, the neoconservatives and the neoliberals.[14] Whereas the neoconservatives claimed to support traditional 'Victorian values' and the increase of central control, the neoliberals advocated a completely deregulated free-market society.[15] Throughout the 1980s, the two groups competed to influence the government's policies.

As shown in chapter 6, in the mid–late 1970s, Simon had already criticised centralising tendencies in education from his Marxist perspective. From the early 1970s, Simon also questioned the concept of 'parental choice'. In his speech at the Communist Party's conference, he noticed that the IEA was asking to turn the whole state system of education into a 'private enterprise in which education is bought and sold rather like fish and chips on the voucher system'.[16] In refusing this, he stressed that a comprehensive school must be a 'neighbourhood or community school', catering for all the children living in a given area.[17] He argued that this principle was administratively the only possible solution, once comprehensive schools became universal, and was in fact adopted by the United States, USSR and Sweden.[18] Hence, he reminded other members of the party that 'we ought to be very careful about any schemes of parental choice, because the only people who gain the most … are the middle-classes'.[19] Similarly, in 1975, when Boyson advocated that a large private sector of grammar-type schools maintained by the voucher system and by fee-payers must be developed, Simon pointed out to the readers of *Marxism Today* that Boyson's essay 'reveals clearly where all this conservative ideological theorising would lead us' and thus it was worth study in order to 'know your enemy'.[20]

After the Conservative Party won the general election in 1979, the Thatcher government adopted 'supply-side' policies such as the sale of council houses, the privatisation of a wide range of nationalised industries, further cutbacks in industrial subsidies and attacks on the trade unions.[21] Apart from this, the government also reduced public-sector support for services such as housing, welfare and education.[22] Indeed, in order to reduce inflation, only three weeks after the government had been in office, it decided to adopt monetarist policy, with a sharp attack on public spending.[23] There were also cuts to educational expenditure. Whereas total educational expenditure between 1979 and 1980 rose slightly from 5.07 per cent to 5.288 per cent of GDP, it declined by 1.232 per cent from 1981 to 1990.[24] Other reforms were also rolled out by the government. In view of this, six months after the election, in *Marxism Today*, Simon published a paper entitled 'Education and the Right Offensive', to comment on the nature and impact of Conservative policy, in line with his ideal of comprehensive education.[25]

In Simon's view, it was due to the Labour Party's constant failure to adopt socialist policies that the ideology of the New Right was able to win popular support.[26] Indeed, in the 1970s, there had been attacks on comprehensive schools from the Conservative party. Nevertheless, Labour ministers did little to counter the critics.[27] Moreover, the Ruskin Speech of the prime minister James Callaghan in 1976 laid an emphasis on the insufficient cooperation between schools and industry, and placed the onus on schools to produce a workforce better equipped to take its place in the world of industry rather than to achieve social justice.[28] Therefore, when the Conservatives returned to office, apart from cutting local government expenditure on education and restricting the ability of local government to fund developments through raising the rates (rate-capping), Mark Carlisle as Education Secretary introduced two bills within the first six months of office.[29] The Education (No. 1) Bill, receiving royal assent in July 1979, declared that the 1976 Education Act was repealed.[30] The Education (No. 2) Bill, which became the 1980 Education Act, brought in the 'assisted places scheme', enabling pupils form the publicly maintained system to attend independent schools and permitting the secretary of state to reimburse participating independent schools for the fees that were remitted. The Department of Education and Science (DES) could also provide grants to low-income families to meet some of the incidental costs (on travel, school uniform and school meals) of taking-up places.[31] Apart from this, the 1980 Education Act also contained a group of clauses designed to extend the scope of 'parental choice'.

For Simon, the main objectives of government policy were to 'strengthen the independent sector and to downgrade the public sector in education and starve it of resources', in particular, with an intention to 'halt the advance to the establishment of a fully comprehensive system of secondary education'.[32] Moreover, as Simon commented: 'Under the banner of slogans about "choice", new, socially based, differentiating structures are being built into the publicly provided schools system', which was also contradictory to his Marxist ideal of comprehensive education.[33] In the face of this, Simon believed that the challenge for the left was to formulate an equally definite policy and strategy in the struggle for socialism.[34] Furthermore, Simon urged imperative actions in the following main areas. First, teachers, students, ancillary workers, parents and the labour movement as a whole needed to find new and appropriate organisational forms by which joint struggles might be carried through, demanding the reversal of the cuts in education. Secondly, there was the need to fight consciously and deliberately to prevent the deliberate shift of resources towards the independent sector. Thirdly, the left should continue to fight against the implications for the 'choice' clauses in the 1980 Education Act and to 'establish genuinely comprehensive local systems of education, based on the neighbourhood principle'.[35]

In effect, the 1980 Education Act did not meet the ideals of the radical right. In September 1981, Thatcher embarked on an extensive reshuffle of cabinet members, and Sir Keith Joseph replaced Carlisle as secretary of state.[36] It was expected that there would be radical changes in Conservative education policy, with the succession of Joseph as Education Secretary and Rhodes Boyson as Junior Education Minister, but this was not the case. According to Knight's analysis, Joseph's education team comprised two major schools of right-wing educational thought.[37] One was the centralisers (paternalist-right), opposed to the voucher, including Robert Rhodes James and Lord Beloff. They were members of the Conservative Research Department Advisory Board. The other was the decentralisers (market-right), proponents of the voucher, including William Shelton (junior minister), Rhodes Boyson and Stuart Sexton (special adviser).[38] Initially, Joseph was sympathetic to vouchers, but from 1981 he was convinced by the civil servants in his department that there would be practical difficulties in implementing an education voucher scheme.[39] Therefore, by the end of 1983, the idea had been dropped and Joseph turned to support the centralisers, although he did not support a National Curriculum.[40]

While Joseph was in office, central control of education was continuously strengthened, not only through the DES, but also other departments such as the Department of Employment. The Schools Council was abolished in April 1982, to be superseded by two nominated bodies, one concerned with curriculum, the other with overseeing public examinations.[41] Furthermore, there was the imposition of the new vocational exam at the age of seventeen (Certificate of Pre-Vocational Education, CPVE) alongside the existing GCE at the age of sixteen and the Certificate of Secondary Education (CSE) mainly for less academic fifteen-year-olds, and the massive growth of the Manpower Services Commission (MSC).[42] The MSC was created in 1973 and directly accountable to the Department of Employment.[43]

For Simon, the MSC, concerned with education and training of young workers, represented a new type of state apparatus, since it was developed outside the DES, directly funded and with considerable powers. In view of this, Simon argued that the Schools Council should not be abolished and should have responsibility for both curriculum and examinations, although the new body should include community representatives (teachers, labour-movement representatives, and so on) rather than being overly teacher-dominated.[44] Indeed, for some in the DES, the Schools Council was a power base for teacher unions.[45] Furthermore, Simon stressed that, under socialism, the planning function of the DES must be made available for democratic discussion through systematic procedures of publication.[46] As Simon pointed out in another article, 'Marx held the view that it was entirely objectionable, from the point of view of the working class, if the State in capitalist society arrogated to itself the right directly to control the education of the people.'[47]

In November 1982 the Thatcher government continued to exert further central control on education. The Technical and Vocational Education Initiative (TVEI), which was administered by the MSC rather than the DES, was introduced to develop new forms of vocationally and technically orientated curricula for the fourteen-to-eighteen age group.[48] As Stephen Ball indicates, the fact that the TVEI was sponsored by the MSC and the speed its implementation demonstrates the potential for quick, radical, top-down reform.[49] Aside from this, in January 1983, Joseph also announced the Lower Achieving Pupils Project (LAPP), which was directed at those pupils in secondary schools Joseph designated as the 'bottom 40 percent'.[50] In late 1983, a number of Conservative-controlled local authorities, such as Solihull, Berkshire, Wiltshire and Redbridge failed to reintroduce selective schooling because of a clear rejection by the majority of the people living in the areas.[51] Following this, Joseph became more determined to impose differentiation within schools through the TVEI and the LAPP. As Simon analysed in a speech to the National Union of Teachers (NUT) in April 1984, the Conservative government's tactic was to enhance differentiation within schools through introducing a threefold division within all comprehensive schools, with an academic track to GCE O and A Levels for those being prepared for universities and professions, a technical/vocational track for the middle group, and a criterion referenced track for the 'bottom 40 percent'.[52] As mentioned above, this was contradictory to Simon's ideal of comprehensive education. On this account, Simon argued that all forms of early differentiation within individual comprehensive schools must be countered. This, he added, involved 'the construction of curricula appropriate and relevant for all'.[53]

Simon also published an article in *Education Today and Tomorrow*, to urge comprehensive teachers and parents to support the unification of the school and the achievement of a common or core curriculum.[54] Simon emphasised that this should involve 'radical examination reform in line with these aims'.[55] As he indicated in another article in *Marxism Today*, from the late 1960s there had been a long battle for the fusion of GCE O Level with the CSE.[56] The objective was the creation of a single exam which could provide an attainable perspective for all students.[57] Nevertheless, in June 1984, instead of implementing a single exam, Keith Joseph announced that there would be 'a system of examinations', consisting of 'differentiated papers and questions in every subject'.[58] Moreover, there would be seven sets of 'grade-related criteria', in the attempt to define precisely what should be taught at each level. For Simon, this implied the imposition of a differentiated system and, above all, 'the winnowing out of an élite will remain a primary function of comprehensive schools'.[59]

Indeed, as Simon put it, in the early 1980s, 'the world economic recession together with the Thatcher government's de-industrialization policies resulted in a sharp contraction of employment possibilities for young people'.[60] Against this background, the DES officials believed that the solution was the deliberate restructuring of the system embodying processes of continuous differentiation and selection, with each level in the age cohort assimilated to acceptance of its fore-ordained lot, both on the labour market and in the social order.[61] As Simon stressed, the government arrogated centralised powers with a view to using the educational system as 'a means of social control', that is to educate everyone 'to know their place'.[62] In a similar vein, the government's white paper, *Better Schools* (1985), also embodied the government's plan to impose differentiation within the schools. After discussing with members of the Education Advisory Committee of the Communist Party in June 1985, Simon published an article to criticise the white paper.[63]

The white paper stated that the government was 'supporting development work to promote this principle [differentiation]', especially through the LAPP.[64] Apart from this, the government was also considering extending the TVEI and additional resources were to be given to in-service training in TVEI, under a scheme administered by the MSC.[65] As for assessment, the white paper announced that the new General Certificate of Secondary Education (GCSE) was to have 'differentiated papers and questions' and to test success 'at different levels of attainment'.[66] On this account Simon castigated the white paper for its 'pervading emphasis on differentiation', which, for him, 'reflects a resurgence of obsolete ideas concerning fixed levels of "intelligence" (though now the in-word is "ability"), determined presumably by heredity'.[67] Therefore, Simon insisted on 'the development of a general, single system of assessment for all at sixteen, in place of the divisive and highly differentiated proposals for the GCSE'.[68]

In March 1986, there was a crisis in the Conservative party following a policy dispute among members of the cabinet.[69] In order to restore Thatcher's personal credibility, the party was seeking an issue with a wide populist appeal. As Simon observed, it was clear that the Prime Minister wanted to attack problems of education as a priority.[70] Apart from this, different groupings or individuals of the party also put forward 'manifesto' policies. Simon indicated that these policies took two main directions.[71] The first was privatisation and the second was greatly strengthened central-government control of education. Privatisation was supported by the hard right section of the Conservative party, such as Robert Dunn (Parliamentary Secretary at the DES), Arthur Seldon (Editorial Director of the IEA), and the 'No Turning Back Group' of Conservative MPs. Central control of education was proposed by Joseph and his junior minister, Chris Patten. Simon declared that some would argue that both would be opposite in origin and intention, but 'One thing both have in common is the wish to downgrade, and severely to limit the role of the local authorities.'[72] Simon observed that action was already being taken along the two lines and further measures, possibly combining both privatising and centralising objectives could even be expected.[73] In this situation, he reasoned that 'what is urgently needed is a great, popular campaign in defence of the public system of education'.[74] As outlined before, Simon's ideal of comprehensive education was that comprehensive schools should be provided by the state, but that curriculum and examinations should not be controlled by the state.

Consequently, after again meeting with the Education Advisory Committee of the Communist Party in April 1986, Simon agreed to write a pamphlet, *Defend Comprehensive Schools* (1986).[75] In the pamphlet, Simon enumerated a series of Conservative government actions threatening the development of comprehensive education and reiterated his strategies in defending the comprehensives. Moreover, in opposition to centralising tendencies in education, Simon strongly argued for a great campaign to prevent central government taking full control and using their powers to destroy the public system.[76] To this end, he restressed that there should be a broad alliance between teachers, parents and local authorities and that the Labour movement, including trade unions, the Labour and Communist parties must also unite.[77] After the publication of this pamphlet, Joan Gregory, director of the Centre for the Study of the Comprehensive School, especially congratulated Simon and the CP on their 'courageous, strong statement about a difficult subject'.[78] Furthermore, Gregory stressed that 'it is mildly ironic that the first clear, unequivocal statement on the subject of the comprehensive schools … should emanate from a political party … almost totally eschewed by the majority of voters in the UK'.[79] Gregory's comment showed that, from 1981 to 1986, Simon did play a key role in formulating a definite policy for defending comprehensive education – something which was not provided by the Labour party.

Kenneth Baker and the 1988 Education Reform Act

On 16 May 1986, followed by the Conservative party's defeat in municipal elections and parliamentary by-elections, Thatcher replaced Joseph with an educational moderniser, Kenneth Baker, to turn things around before the next general election.[80] In effect, Joseph's demise was a fillip to the educational radical right who were in favour of the market philosophy and vouchers.[81] As Clyde Chitty points out, under Carlisle and Joseph, attempts were made to create differentiation and selection within the education system, but these fell far short of the demands by the radical right.[82] The appointment of Baker meant that the government was determined to put forward a package of radical proposals. Thus, aside from increasing educational spending, at the Conservative Party conference in October 1986 Baker announced the introduction of a City Technology College (CTC) programme.[83] According to the DES's booklet, *A New Choice of School*, the government planned to establish a network of CTCs in urban areas, providing a broadly-based secondary education with a strong technological element.[84] The CTCs would be primarily sponsored by industry and commerce, educational trusts, charities and other voluntary organisations, with financial assistance from the Secretary of State for Education and Science.[85] Moreover, although the CTCs would charge no fees, they would be registered as independent schools.[86]

After Baker's announcement, a *Forum* editorial indicated that 'This tactic is clearly aimed at further disrupting, or destabilizing, locally controlled systems of comprehensive schools.'[87] It predicted that these schools would attract parents away from the locally-provided system.[88] In other words, the CTCs would hinder the establishment of a state system of comprehensive schools as envisaged by Simon. The editorial argued that 'this initiative must not be permitted to get off the ground, under any circumstances'.[89] Additionally, from January 1987, on various occasions, Baker also brought forward his plans to introduce radical reforms such as a national curriculum laid down by statute and national tests for children aged seven, eleven and fourteen.[90] As Ball suggests, in line with Joseph's ideal of the free market, his approach to curriculum change was based on exhortation rather than legislation.[91] It was Baker who pushed on towards a large-scale, radical and reforming Education Act.[92] Baker's plans were eventually included in the Conservative Party's manifesto published in May 1987.[93] On 11 June, the general election took place. With the economy improving and the Labour Party still disunited, it resulted in a further large parliamentary majority for the Conservatives.[94]

Towards the end of July 1987 the government issued a series of 'consultation papers' and asked for responses in all cases within two months.[95] With this situation imminent, Simon decided to put his work on the fourth volume of history of education studies on one side and responded to the government's plans in *Marxism Today*.[96] According to Simon's analysis, vouchers were not to be brought in, but a more subtle set of linked measures were to be relied on to push the whole system toward a degree of privatisation.[97] There was, first, the proposal to devolve financial responsibility for running schools more or less completely to the heads and governors.[98] Simon indicated that the main objective of this measure was to loosen the schools from the hands of the local authorities, and encourage them to take the first step towards more advanced forms of independence.[99] Secondly, there was the proposal to allow 'open enrolment' or 'open entry' to all schools. Schools were to have the right to admit as many pupils as parents wished to send them.[100] Under this measure, Simon believed, unpopular schools would be pushed into closure by market forces.[101] Moreover, Simon argued that the real meaning of the step was that 'Popular schools, now with more or less full financial responsibility, will soon begin to differentiate themselves from the others.'[102] According to Simon, this provided the springboard for the next step – opting out.[103]

Thirdly, the charging of fees by schools for 'extras' such as equipment and materials was to be permitted.[104] For Simon, this provided popular schools in affluent areas with the opportunity further to differentiate themselves from the ordinary run of schools, and to some extent to narrow their intake to the more affluent section of the local population.[105] Then, these schools were ready to 'opt out', which was the fourth proposal.[106] The proposal was that schools could apply to opt out of the local system and become 'grant maintained' schools.[107] These schools would become 'semi-independent', receiving the bulk of their finance directly from the state. A further direct effect of this, Simon emphasised, would be that the local system would be broken.[108] As Simon put it, open enrolment and opting out would lead to 'the enhancement of the semi-independent sector, and of depressing and downgrading ordinary people's children, which will remain – at the bottom of the pile – under local authority control'.[109] Therefore, these proposals would become a great obstacle to Simon's ideal of a state system of comprehensive schools, in which no selection and differentiation between schools existed.

Apart from structural aspects, the government also proposed a national curriculum and a series of precisely defined tests for all children at the age of seven, eleven, fourteen and sixteen. All this was to be statutorily determined through legislation.[110]

In line with his objection to central control, Simon held that the idea of a precisely defined curriculum written largely by civil servants at the DES was entirely unacceptable.[111] Simon stressed that 'if this curriculum is imposed, the scope for imaginative teaching, for instance for the integration of subjects in line with the development of modern knowledge, for independent initiative by individual schools, groups of schools, or local systems, will be tightly constricted'.[112] Moreover, Simon observed that this was a curriculum for the masses, since it did not apply to the CTCs and the independent schools.[113] This was against his ideal that all children should follow a common core curriculum up to the age of 14 or 15. On this account, he stated that: 'Its [the curriculum's] purpose is control.'[114] As for assessment, Simon agreed with Denis Lawton and Clyde Chitty, that a national curriculum must be freed from the age-related benchmark testing since, as they put it, the test 'will simply act as a straitjacket on the entire system'.[115]

Foreseeing that these measures would comprise a very real threat to the viability of comprehensive education, Simon made a plea for resistance to government plans from the LEAs, teachers and parents.[116] As he contended, even if opposition must be focused in parliament, where it would be led by Labour's new shadow spokesman on education, Jack Straw, a broad movement outside parliament needed to be developed to ensure that the significance of these proposals could be grasped by the population as a whole.[117] In view of this, in September 1987, Simon reconstituted his article 'Lessons in Elitism' and, as the elected president, delivered it in a speech to the conference of the British Educational Research Association (BERA), an independent and influential research organisation in the UK.[118] In this speech, Simon asked the members of BERA to ponder upon how BERA saw its role in the present context and how the expertise represented in the organisation could be brought to bear systematically and effectively in the discussions and debates over the coming, crucial months.[119] After his speech, BERA adopted Simon's standpoint and decided to send a letter to Baker.[120] Aside from this, Simon's analysis and criticisms on the consultation papers were also accepted by *Forum*'s editorial board and published in *Forum*.[121] The editorial board's response to the consultation papers was then sent to the press, to members of both houses of parliament, and to Baker.[122] Indeed, there were thousands of responses that reached the DES by early October, but the government chose to ignore them.[123]

On 20 November 1987 the Bill was finally published. Not long after, Simon wrote a book to 'clarify the issues at stake' and to 'strengthen resistance' to the bill.[124] In general, the Bill reflected the proposals as originally outlined in the consultation papers. In relation to structural changes, clauses 23–26 aimed to devolve financial responsibility for running individual schools to the governors. Clauses 17–22 allowed open enrolment at all schools. Opting out was also provided by clauses 37–78.[125] According to the bill, a school's governing body could resolve (by a simple majority) to hold a ballot of parents on the question of whether grant-maintained status should be sought for the school. Then, the parents' decision would be determined, once again, by a 'simple majority' of those voting.[126] Apart from those proposed in the consultation papers, the Bill also provided for the establishment of the CTCs, giving the secretary of state powers to make payments in respect of both capital and current expenditure incurred.[127]

In view of the provisions above, Simon argued that the objectives of the Bill were twofold.[128] First, 'to break the power, and the system of local government', which was contradictory to Simon's ideal that comprehensive schools should be controlled by the LEAs. Hence, the government sought a countervailing power – parents.[129] In Simon's view, '"parental power" is an ideological artefact, a creation of populist rhetoric acting as a smokescreen for pursuit of a coldly calculated political objective'.[130] Secondly, to establish (or reinforce) a hierarchical system of schooling both subject to market forces and more directly under central state control.[131] The government's aim was to establish three grades of school, including the independent schools for the upper strata, the grant-maintained schools and the CTCs for the middle strata, and schools of local authority systems for the mass of ordinary people.[132] This, Simon remarked, 'accords with the Conservative image of an educational system adapted to, or matched by, a structured, hierarchical society'.[133] As stated above, selection and differentiation between schools would be reintroduced into the education system.

With regard to curriculum and assessment, clauses 1–16 made provision for a national curriculum, including the core subjects (mathematics, English and science) and foundation subjects (history, geography, technology, music, art and physical education) for all pupils in maintained schools between the ages of five and sixteen, and sets of tests covering all subjects in the curriculum at the ages of seven, eleven, fourteen and sixteen. In response to this, Simon reiterated his opposition to a precisely defined curriculum laid down in legislative form as, in his view, the state should not control education.[134] Furthermore, Simon especially disparaged the Bill for devolving a waterproof totality of powers to determine every aspect of the curriculum and testing to the secretary of state.[135]

On 1 December 1987 the debate on the second reading began in the House of Commons. The result was that the government carried the second reading by 348 votes to 241.[136] In view of this, Simon expected that the real battles were likely to take place in the Lords.[137] He maintained that the teeth of the Bill could be drawn by amending the clauses about open enrolment and rejecting those of opting out. On open enrolment, Simon suggested that the base year for calculating the physical capacity of a school should be 1986 rather than 1979, since 1979 was a year when the secondary school population was at its maximum and so the potential destabilisation would be at its greatest.[138] Simon also proposed resisting the more rigid and backward-looking features of the national curriculum and pressed for a further amendment on assessment.[139]

Additionally, Simon also endeavoured to influence public opinion outside parliament. As he explained, when amendments in the Lords were returned to the Commons for further debate, they could be reversed. But, if by that time such amendments were seen to reflect a widespread and deeply felt movement of public opinion, such reversals might not be easy.[140] Thus, on 19 March, Simon and *Forum* helped organise a conference to lead and unite forces of opposition. As the *Guardian* reported, Simon's conference session was entitled 'The Fight Back', which was 'something he thinks the career politicians of the Labour Party have signally failed to organize'.[141] The conference, attended by over 500 people, having heard the view of official representatives of 25 parents, teachers, local authorities, trade unions, voluntary and other organisations, eventually published a statement to express its clear rejection of all the major measures in the Education Bill.[142] While the Bill was debated in the House of Lords in April, Simon also decided to reprint his book, *Bending the Rules*. He predicted that if the Bill went through unamended, 'it certainly presages another long period of struggle to ensure new, democratic advances in this area'.[143]

After the debate, Simon observed that the Bill remained essentially unchanged, particularly as regards the clauses concerning schools.[144] Moreover, the issue of charging fees for 'extras' in maintained schools was also included in the revised Bill presented to the House of Lords.[145] In light of this, Simon wrote a discussion paper for the Communist Party and stressed to his comrades that if the Bill passed through parliament, that 'will mark a new stage in the struggle on education, and one where we as a party, I think, can and should play a leading role'.[146] He held that 'we need to develop a strategy, and a set of tactics, to defend the existing system of education'.[147] Above all, 'there needs to be a continuous campaign against opting out, which is the heart of the Bill'.[148] This paper was later published in *Education Today and Tomorrow*.[149]

In early May, the Bill moved to the committee stage in the House of Lords. At this point Simon could finally resume the writing of his fourth volume of the history of education. Clearly, the progress of his historical studies had been delayed by his struggles over the Education Bill in 1987–88. Therefore, in his diary entry on 3 May 1988, he stated that 'I've done all I can' and 'intend from now [emphasis in the original] to turn again to the book'.[150] For Simon, only one victory was achieved after several weeks' debate, that is on procedures relating to opting out.[151] The amendment laid down that if less than 50 per cent of all parents registered voted in the first ballot, a second ballot had to be held within fourteen days.[152] This would help hinder the disruption of the existing state system of comprehensive schools. Despite this, other measures hampering the realisation of Simon's ideal of comprehensive education successfully passed through the House of Lords.[153] The final debates in the House of Commons took place in July but no important amendment was accepted. Eventually the Bill gained royal assent on 29 July 1988.[154] As Simon himself indicated, unlike the 1918 and 1944 Education acts, both of which were consensus measures and were passed after at least two years of consultations, the 1988 Education Reform Act was driven through by the Conservative government.[155] The government did not pay any serious attention to the original consultation process, and displayed inflexibility in the proceedings in parliament.[156]

In August 1988, since the new Act was implemented, Simon also closely monitored and critically assessed new developments. In a lecture to the conference of the British Educational Management and Administration Society (BEMAS) in September 1988, Simon highlighted that the most immediate and potentially damaging threat to comprehensive systems lay in the provisions relating to opting out and the CTCs.[157] As Simon indicated, a ban was imposed on all reorganisation proposals by the DES.[158] The objective of this 'planning blight' was to allow schools threatened with reorganisation to apply for grant-maintained status.[159] For Simon, this action was 'sharp and exceptionally aggressive'.[160] Hence, Simon argued that the fact that the Act gave governing bodies the right to apply to opt out and also gave them the right *not* to, needed to be made abundantly clear to all.[161] As for the CTCs, as Simon pointed out in his speech, leading industrialists preferred supporting the existing comprehensive system and thus the colleges were now largely financed by taxpayers.[162] Moreover, it would cause disruption and introduce selection to local systems.[163] Indeed, Roger Dale indicates that there were two mechanisms of selection at work.[164] In order to raise the levels of all, Simon argued that 'what is wanted is support for the mass of ordinary schools', providing them with new resources and curricula they needed.[165]

Following the legislation of the new Act, some individuals and groups also strongly opposed its major provisions. For example, Richard Johnson, director of the Centre for Contemporary Cultural Studies (1980–1987), wrote that the 1988 Education Act created diversity and 'these differences between schools would come to match more closely existing social (including racial) divisions'.[166] The left-of-centre Institute for Public Policy Research (IPPR), which was established in 1988 by leading figures in the academic, business and trade-union community to provide an alternative to the free market think-tanks, also claimed that the new Act's educational market would provide for 'selection by schools, not choice for parents' and, above all, 'this selection will result in the hierarchical division of schools and school populations'.[167] Similarly, the Hillcole Group, including members like Stephen Ball, Caroline Benn, Clyde Chitty and Ken Jones, also published a book, entitled *Changing the Future: Redprint for education*, in an attempt to 'develop a coherent democratic socialist alternative to the current Radical Right and Centrist perspectives on education'.[168] In this book, the Hillcole Group asserted that opting out would have the effect of 'destroying education provision that is collectively provided to meet local needs'.[169] 'The creation of CTCs', it argued, 'epitomises the neo-liberal attempt to shift from collective provision and collectivism to individualism and personal greed'.[170] All this reflected the influence of Simon's intellectual forces on a wider circle.

Aside from the structural measures, the Act also imposed a national curriculum with its accompanying assessment measures. Several months after the Bill passed through the parliament, Kenneth Baker announced the publication of the draft order for English for pupils of key stage one (5 to 7 years old).[171] The set of measures was often attributed to neoconservative thinking stressing centralised state control and was considered to be contradictory to neoliberal thinking concerning the creation of a market. However, as Simon explained, the national curriculum provided statutorily articulated tramlines along which all schools must operate and thereby it could help maintain social order in an educational market.[172] Furthermore, assessment could provide parents with data about the schools and was therefore seen as the prime means by which parental choices were informed.[173] Therefore, Simon also continued to make a plea for transformation of the National Curriculum in order to allow greater flexibility.[174] Moreover, based on his ideal of comprehensive education, the curriculum 'should become a truly National Curriculum relevant to and applying to everyone, of whatever school, public or private'.[175]

Conclusion

This chapter has explored Brian Simon's distinctive role and significance in defending comprehensive education, from 1979 to 1990. The evidence here shows that throughout the 1980s, facing the attack from the

New Right, Simon insisted on his Marxist ideal of comprehensive education and continued to reveal and challenge the ideology behind the Conservative policies through the Communist Party and its organs, as well as via journals and various professional organisations. Simon's ideal of comprehensive education was a state system in which comprehensive schools must be controlled by the LEAs and, more importantly, no selection or differentiation would exist between and within schools. While Carlisle and Joseph were in office, Simon formulated a definite policy based on his ideal. This, Simon believed, was not provided by the Labour Party in the late 1970s. For instance, Simon strongly objected to the Assisted Places Scheme and the parental choice clauses of the 1980 Education Act. For Simon, the former strengthened the independent sector and the latter brought selection and differentiation between schools into the state system of secondary education, which was against his 'neighbourhood principle'. Moreover, Simon was also opposed to Joseph's enhanced central control of education and his introduction of differentiation into curriculum and assessment. Simon emphasised that the state should not control the education of the people and, moreover, there should not be differentiation within comprehensive schools.

On the same ground, leaving his research work aside, Simon was also involved in reproaching Baker's policies, particularly pertaining to structural measures as well as the national curriculum and testing, and attempted to influence policy-makers through BERA and *Forum*. Simon was especially concerned with the development of the CTCs, the opting out, and the legislation of a national curriculum. The set-up of the CTCs and opting out would obstruct the establishment of a state system of comprehensive schools and, more importantly, selection and differentiation would be reintroduced into the existing system. Simon did not support a national curriculum which was legislated by the state. Furthermore, for Simon, the curriculum was not applied to all children and thus would cause differentiation between schools. After the publication of the Bill, as the Bill involved the provision of the CTCs and other proposals outlined in the consultation papers, Simon also published a book, *Bending the Rules*, to strengthen resistance to the bill. Aside from pointing out the necessary amendments that should be adopted in parliament, outside of parliament Simon organised a conference to unite organisations opposing the Bill in their fight, which, once again, the Labour Party failed to do. Eventually, in 1988, the Bill received royal assent. In Simon's view, except for a significant amendment on the procedure of opting out, other measures hampering the realisation of his ideal of comprehensive education were included in the new Act.

Hence, Simon continued to put forward a set of tactics in opposition to the government's actions. His critique of the new Act was also influential in provoking more opposition to the New Right from individuals like Richard Johnson and groups such as the IPPR and the Hillcole group.

Notes

1 Paul Bolton, *Education: Historical statistics*. Accessed 24 January 2021. https://researchbriefings.files.parliament.uk/documents/SN04252/SN04252.pdf.
2 Simon, *A Life in Education*, 152.
3 The 'threefold partnership' was strongly advocated by Fred Clarke immediately after the Second World War. Fred Clarke was the Director of the Institute of Education, University of London, from 1936 to 1945. He was vigorously involved in wartime educational reform. In recognition of his position and role in shaping educational policy, he was appointed as the first Chairman of the Central Advisory Council for Education (England) between 1944 and 1948.
4 Brian Simon, 'The politics of comprehensive reorganization: A retrospective analysis', *History of Education* 21, no. 4 (1992): 355.
5 Simon, *A Life in Education*, 146–8; Brian Simon, Autobiography Vol. II (1945–1994), [n.d. 1993?]. Simon retired from Leicester University in 1980.
6 Jane Martin, 'Telling stories about comprehensive education: Hidden histories of politics, policy and practice in post-war England', *British Journal of Educational Studies* 68, no. 5 (2020): 649–69.
7 Kenneth O. Morgan, *Britain since 1945: The people's peace*, 437–8.
8 Morgan, *Britain since 1945*, 505.
9 Morgan, *Britain since 1945*, 438.
10 Christopher Knight, *The Making of Tory Education Policy in Post-war Britain 1950–1986*, 90.
11 Jones, *Education in Britain: 1944 to the present*, 101.
12 Knight, *The Making of Tory Education Policy in Post-war Britain*, 75.
13 Knight, *The Making of Tory Education Policy in Post-war Britain*, 90.
14 Chitty, *Towards a New Education System*, 52; Clive Griggs, 'The New Right and English secondary education', in *The Changing Secondary School*, 101.
15 Ruth Levitas, 'Introduction: Ideology and the New Right', in *The Ideology of the New Right*, 1–24, 3–4.
16 Brian Simon, 'Speech made by Brian Simon to the "Battle for Educational Opportunity Conference"' (working paper, 1970). Simon papers, IOE UCL Archives, Simon 1/17.
17 Brian Simon, 'Speech to the "Battle for Educational Opportunity Conference"'.
18 Brian Simon, 'Whose objectives anyway?', (working paper, [n.d., 1970/1971?]). Simon papers, IOE UCL Archives, Simon 1/17.
19 Brian Simon, 'Speech to the "Battle for Educational Opportunity Conference"'.
20 Rhodes Boyson, 'The school, equality and society', in *Education, Equality and Society*, 196; Brian Simon, 'Editorial', *Marxism Today*, May 25, 1975.
21 Leslie Hannah, 'Crisis and turnaround? 1973–1993', in *Twentieth-century Britain: Economic, social and cultural change*, 342.
22 Jones, *Education in Britain: 1944 to the Present*, 108.
23 Morgan, *Britain since 1945*, 445.
24 UNESCO Institute for Statistics. *Government Expenditure on Education, Total (% of GDP) – United Kingdom*. Accessed 24 January 2021. https://data.worldbank.org/indicator/SE.XPD.TOTL.GD.ZS?end=2017&locations=GB&start=1971&view=chart.
25 Brian Simon, 'Education and the right offensive', in *Does Education Matter?*, 197–216.
26 Simon, 'Education and the right offensive', 198.
27 Gordon, Aldrich and Dean, *Education and Policy in England in the Twentieth Century*, 197.
28 James Callaghan, 'A rational debate based on the facts' (The Ruskin Speech).

29 Simon, *Education and the Social Order*, 474–81.
30 Simon, 'Education and the right offensive', 204.
31 DES, *Education Act 1980* (London: HMSO, 1980), clauses 17, 18; T. Edwards, J. Fitz and G. Whitty, *The State and Private Education: An evaluation of the Assisted Places Scheme*, 2.
32 Simon, 'Education and the right offensive', 204.
33 Simon, 'Education and the right offensive', 208.
34 Simon, 'Education and the right offensive', 210.
35 Simon, 'Education and the right offensive', 211–12.
36 Simon, *Education and the Social Order*, 482.
37 Knight, *The Making of Tory Education Policy in Post-war Britain*, 157–8.
38 Knight, *The Making of Tory Education Policy in Post-war Britain*, 158.
39 Chitty, *Towards a New Education System*, 185.
40 Chitty, *Towards a New Education System*.
41 Brian Simon, 'The democratic transformation of education and the state' (notes for discussion), July 1982. Simon papers, IOE UCL Archives, Simon 1/15.
42 Simon, 'The democratic transformation of education and the state'.
43 Gary McCulloch, 'Policy, politics and education: The technical and vocational education initiative', *Journal of Education Policy* 1, no. 1 (1986): 37.
44 McCulloch, 'Policy, politics and education'.
45 S. J. Ball, *Politics and Policy Making in Education: Explorations in policy sociology*, 162.
46 Simon, 'The democratic transformation of education and the state'.
47 Brian Simon, 'Popular, local and democratic: Karl Marx's formula', *Education*, 11 March 1983, 186.
48 McCulloch, 'Policy, politics and education: The technical and vocational education initiative', 42.
49 Ball, *Politics and Policy Making in Education*, 76.
50 Simon, *Education and the Social Order,* 495.
51 Simon, *Education and the Social Order*, 498–500.
52 Brian Simon, 'In Defence of Comprehensive Education' (NUT, Secondary Schools, Blackpool conference), 10 April 1984. Simon papers, IOE UCL Archives, Simon 1/11.
53 Simon, 'In defence of comprehensive education'.
54 Brian Simon, 'Comprehensives: Under attack by government', *Education Today and Tomorrow*, May 1984, 3–4, 4.
55 Simon, 'Comprehensives: Under attack by government'.
56 Brian Simon, 'Breaking school rules: Keith Joseph and the politics of education', in *Does Education Matter?*, 217–35, 225. (Reprinted, with slight additions from *Marxism Today*, September 1984)
57 Simon, 'Breaking school rules'.
58 Simon, 'Breaking school rules', 226.
59 Simon, 'Breaking school rules', 226.
60 Simon, 'Breaking school rules', 224.
61 Simon, 'Breaking school rules', 224.
62 'Beyond the Fragments: Brian Simon's statement to the Adult Education Conference', *NUSAC Bulletin* XIV, no. 2 (Spring 1985): 1–4, 3; Brian Simon, 'Breaking school rules' (TVEI Conference, Loughborough), May 1985. Simon papers, IOE UCL Archives, Simon 1/11; Brian Simon, 'Back to the tripartite system?', *Education Today and Tomorrow* 37, no. 2 (1985): 5.
63 Minutes of Meeting of Education Advisory Committee of the Communist Party of Great Britain, held on 6 June 1985. Communist Party's paper, CP/CENT/IND/10/1. Brian Simon, 'Imposing differentiation in schools', *Education Today and Tomorrow* 37, no. 3 (1985): 4–5.
64 DES, *Better Schools* (White Paper) (London: HMSO, 1985), 15.
65 DES, *Better Schools*, 17.
66 DES, *Better Schools*, 15.
67 Simon, 'Imposing differentiation in schools', 4.
68 Brian Simon, 'Comprehensive Ideals', *Comprehensive Education* 50 (1985): 15.
69 Brian Simon, 'Crisis in Education', *Marxism Today*, May 1986. Simon papers, IOE UCL Archives, Simon 1/14.
70 Simon, 'Crisis in education'.

71 Brian Simon, 'The battle of the blackboard', *Marxism Today*, June 1986, 20–6, 23–4.
72 Simon, 'The battle of the blackboard', 23.
73 Simon, 'The battle of the blackboard', 26.
74 Simon, 'The battle of the blackboard', 26.
75 Minutes of Meeting of Education Advisory Committee held on 23 April 1986. Communist Party's paper, CP/CENT/IND/10/1.
76 Brian Simon, *Defend Comprehensive Schools*, 35.
77 Simon, *Defend Comprehensive Schools*, 37.
78 'Comprehensive comrades: Joan Gregory acknowledges a debt to the Communist Party's education policy', *Times Educational Supplement*, 6 February 1987.
79 'Comprehensive comrades: Joan Gregory'.
80 Simon, *Education and the Social Order,* 516–17, 526.
81 Knight, *The Making of Tory Education Policy in Post-war Britain*, 179.
82 Chitty, *Towards a New Education System*, 196.
83 E. C. Bailey, 'The development of the city technology college programmes: 1980s Conservative ideas about English secondary education' (PhD diss., London School of Economics and Political Science, 2016), 166.
84 DES, *A New Choice of School* (London: HMSO, 1986), 2.
85 DES, *A New Choice of School*, 3, 6.
86 DES, *A New Choice of School*, 4.
87 [No Author, editor Brian Simon & Nanette Whitbread?], 'Enough is enough', *Forum* 29, no. 2 (Spring 1987): 31.
88 'Enough is enough', *Forum* 29.
89 'Enough is enough', *Forum* 29
90 Simon, *Education and the Social Order*, 531–3.
91 Ball, *Politics and Policy Making in Education*, 176.
92 Ball, *Politics and Policy Making in Education*, 181.
93 Conservative Party, *The Next Moves Forward*, 18–20.
94 G. K. Fry, *The Politics of the Thatcher Revolution: An interpretation of British politics, 1979–1990* (New York: Palgrave Macmillan, 2008), 26.
95 Simon, *Education and the Social Order*, 538–9.
96 Simon, *A Life in Education*, 160.
97 Brian Simon, 'Lessons in elitism', in *What Future for Education?*, 15–33, 18.
98 DES, *Financial Delegation to Schools* (London: HMSO, 1987).
99 Simon, 'Lessons in elitism', 19.
100 DES, *Admission of Pupils to Maintained Schools* (London: HMSO, 1987).
101 Simon, 'Lessons in elitism', 19.
102 Simon, 'Lessons in elitism', 19–20.
103 Simon, 'Lessons in elitism', 20.
104 DES, *Grant Maintained Schools* (London: HMSO, 1987).
105 Simon, 'Lessons in elitism', 20.
106 Simon, 'Lessons in elitism', 20.
107 DES, *Grant Maintained Schools*.
108 Simon, 'Lessons in elitism', 21.
109 Simon, 'Lessons in elitism', 22.
110 DES, *The National Curriculum 5–16* (London: HMSO, 1987).
111 Simon, 'Lessons in elitism', 25.
112 Simon, 'Lessons in elitism', 26–7.
113 Simon, 'Lessons in elitism', 26.
114 Simon, 'Lessons in elitism', 26.
115 Simon, 'Lessons in elitism', 28.
116 Simon, 'Lessons in elitism', 28.
117 Simon, 'Lessons in elitism', 30.
118 Simon, *A Life in Education*, 160–1.
119 Brian Simon, 'The Great Education Reform Bill' (a speech for BERA conference), September 1987. Simon papers, IOE UCL Archives, Simon 1/21.
120 Simon, *A Life in Education*, 161.
121 'The Education Bill: Forum Editorial Board's Response to the Consultation Papers, *Forum* 30, no. 1 (Autumn 1987).

122 Simon, *A Life in Education*, 161.
123 Simon, *Education and the Social Order*, 539–40.
124 Brian Simon, *Bending the Rules: The Baker 'reform' of education*, 1st ed., 9.
125 Simon, *Bending the Rules*, 48–51.
126 DES, *Education Reform Bill* (London: HMSO, 1987), clause 46.
127 DES, *Education Reform Bill*, clause 80. Simon, *Bending the Rules*, 1st ed., 55.
128 Simon, *Bending the Rules*, 1st ed., 15.
129 Simon, *Bending the Rules*, 1st ed., 165.
130 Simon, *Bending the Rules*, 1st ed., 165.
131 Simon, *Bending the Rules*, 1st ed., 15.
132 Simon, *Bending the Rules*, 1st ed., 55–6.
133 Simon, *Bending the Rules*, 1st ed., 56.
134 Simon, *Bending the Rules*, 1st ed., 108.
135 Simon, *Bending the Rules*, 1st ed., 134.
136 Simon, *Bending the Rules*, 1st ed., 166, 168.
137 Simon, *Bending the Rules*, 1st ed., 169.
138 Simon, *Bending the Rules*, 1st ed., 170.
139 Simon, *Bending the Rules*, 1st ed., 173–4.
140 Simon, *Bending the Rules*, 1st ed., 170.
141 Maureen O'Connor, 'Simon Pure of the Fourth', *Guardian*, 8 March 1988. Simon papers, IOE
    UCL Archives, Simon 1/57.
142 'Forum Conference: Statement of intent', *Forum* 30, no. 3 (Summer 1988): 73.
143 Brian Simon, 'Bending the rules: The Baker "reform" of education', [n.d. April 1988?]. Simon
    papers, IOE UCL Archives, Simon 1/20.
144 Brian Simon, *Bending the Rules: The Baker 'reform' of education*, 2nd ed., 184.
145 Simon, *Bending the Rules*, 2nd ed., 185.
146 Brian Simon, 'The Education "Reform" Bill' (for Communist Party), May 1988. Simon papers,
    IOE UCL Archives, Simon 1/23.
147 Simon, 'The Education "Reform" Bill'.
148 Simon, 'The Education "Reform" Bill'.
149 Brian Simon, 'The fight against the Bill', *Education Today and Tomorrow* 40, no. 2 (1988): 3.
150 Simon's diary, 3 May 1988. Simon papers, IOE UCL Archives, SIM/4/4/46.
151 Simon, *Education and the Social Order*, 547–8.
152 DES, *Education Reform Act 1988* (London: HMSO, 1988), 58 (clause 61).
153 Simon, *Education and the Social Order*, 548.
154 Simon, *Education and the Social Order*, 549.
155 Brian Simon, *Bending the Rules: The Baker 'reform' of education*, 3rd ed., 14.
156 Brian Simon, 'Maintaining progress towards a fully comprehensive system', in *What Future for
    Education?*, 34–55, 47.
157 Simon, 'Maintaining progress towards a fully comprehensive system', 41.
158 Simon, 'Maintaining progress towards a fully comprehensive system', 51.
159 Simon, 'Maintaining progress towards a fully comprehensive system', 51.
160 Simon, 'Maintaining progress towards a fully comprehensive system', 51.
161 Simon, 'Maintaining progress towards a fully comprehensive system', 51.
162 Brian Simon, 'City technology colleges' (Nottingham, Speech for the CASE), 22 November
    1988. Simon papers, IOE UCL Archives, Simon 1/23.
163 Simon, 'City technology colleges'.
164 Roger Dale, 'The Thatcherite project in education: The case of the city technology colleges',
    Critical School Policy 9, no. 27 (1989): 14.
165 Simon, 'City technology colleges'.
166 Richard Johnson, 'Thatcherism and English education: Breaking the mould, or confirming the
    pattern?', *History of Education* 18, no. 2 (1989): 115.
167 David Miliband, *Markets, Politics and Education: Beyond the Education Reform Act*, 26.
168 Hillcole Group, *Changing the Future: Redprint for education*, vii.
169 Hillcole Group, *Changing the Future*, 3.
170 Hillcole Group, *Changing the Future*, 5.
171 Brian Simon, 'Association for the Study of the Curriculum', 1 April 1989. Simon papers, IOE
    UCL Archives, Simon 1/23.

172 Brian Simon, 'The Education Reform Act: Causative factors', in *What Future for Education?*, 119–42, 135 (paper contributed to a seminar organised by the BERA Task Group on Assessment in July 1991).

173 Simon, 'The Education Reform Act: Causative factors'.

174 Brian Simon, 'The National Curriculum, school organization and the teacher', in *What Future for Education?*, 72–93, 90. (Originally published by the Lawrence Stenhouse Memorial Trust. It was delivered in August 1990.)

175 Simon, 'The National Curriculum, school organization and the teacher'.

9
Afterthoughts and last words

With the Education Reform Act now on the statute book after all his determined resistance, Brian Simon was at last free to complete the fourth volume of his history of education. He was now fully retired and in his mid-seventies as he came in 1991 to publish this final volume, *Education and the Social Order 1940–1990*.[1] Yet if his historical work ended on a high note, he faced difficult challenges in his final years. Educational reform seemed to be going in the wrong direction, with comprehensive education in particular difficulties. Marxist ideals appeared to have reached the end of their history as the Communist Party and the USSR itself were abandoned and a new world order came into being. His own history also came back to him to raise questions, as his sympathies for the Soviet Union were linked with the Cambridge spies.

As Simon approached formal retirement age at the University of Leicester, the accolades for academic leadership were not slow to arrive. He had been elected as the chairman of the UK History of Education Society, from 1975 to 1978, and in this capacity contacted overseas colleagues about support for an international seminar on the history of education.[2] This led to the first all-European seminar on the history of education, to be on the theme of 'The relations between education and society', organised by the History of Education Society at Westminster College, Oxford, in September 1978, with Simon as the conference chairman.[3] The International Standing Conference for the History of Education (ISCHE) resulted from these discussions, and Simon became its first chairman from 1978 to 1981. These links paved the way for a meeting between Simon and Professor Detlef Muller of Ruhr University, who was working with the sociologist Pierre Bourdieu in France on the stratification of education in the nineteenth century. Funding was then acquired for a series of three conferences in Leicester and at Bochum in Germany. This then resulted in an edited book based on the cases of Germany, France and England,

The Rise of the Educational System: Structural change and social reproduction, 1870–1920, edited by Muller and Simon together with Professor Fritz Ringer.[4] This collection highlighted Simon's continuing willingness to support different theoretical approaches, even though his own contribution rehearsed his own well-known perspective on English nineteenth-century education, rather than attempting the innovative concepts and hypotheses of Muller and Ringer.[5]

In another arena of research, Simon was also elected as president of the fledgeling British Educational Research Association (BERA). His presidential address in 1977 displayed his ability to tailor his message to a particular audience. While he was the foremost champion of his generation of a disciplinary approach to the history of education, he proceeded to give an interdisciplinary message, with BERA itself representing a coming together of a unitary ideal of education from the different disciplines that underpinned it, to focus on the conceptual and practical problems of education as a whole.[6]

For his own fourth volume, while he was delayed by these other commitments, Simon was making active preparations from the 1970s onwards. He insisted to his collaborator Caroline Benn: 'No – I'm not going to retire behind my desk for good – to do the history. But I'm going to try to give more time to it than I have succeeded in doing the last few years. That shouldn't be difficult.'[7] In the event, the third volume did not appear for nearly ten years after the second.[8] It restricted itself to a detailed study of the 1920s and 1930s, emphasising the notion of 'social control', which was a widely used term in Marxist sociology and history of education in the late 1960s and 1970s.[9] By 1977, his notes for the fourth volume were already well advanced, and the general structure that he envisaged was clearly set. The 1960s, he observed, 'should form the meat of the book', with the key dividing line of 1964 following political changes generally. However, he reminded himself, the Labour government of 1964–1970 'must not be presented as a success story; it should be a cool, dispassionate assessment of the position'.[10]

Changes since 1970 he already depicted as 'downhill all the way', with increasingly political and ideological conflict. He could not at this stage imagine the Thatcher government which was to consume so much of his time and remaining energies. Nevertheless, he concluded, overall: 'Analysis must show changing relations between educational opportunities (levels) and class/occupational structure – so relating educational change specifically to social change (cf. the Bourdieu thesis (??)).' Intrigued though he was by Bourdieu's ideas, he could not fully assess how to relate them to his own already well-established arguments. On the other hand, he was more confident about adopting Gramsci's ideas: 'It should also (following Gramsci!) look at the whole initiation by governing class to create hegemony, through not only the educational system, but also through adult education and similar initiatives (press, TV etc.), and the fight-back (insofar as there was one) against all this.'[11] Yet the final volume as it was published in 1991 developed none of these latter issues, and concentrated on tracing the changing in education policy that had led to the 1988 Education Reform Act. It might be considered a fairly orthodox political narrative of the period from 1940 until 1990, although it provided an opportunity to assess in detail the spread of comprehensive education and the educational issues of his own generation.

Always keen to assess his readership Simon calculated that over the quarter-century from 1960 to 1998, the first volume of the history had sold nearly 8,000 copies, and volume two nearly 7,000 between 1965 and 1990. The third volume still sold well, at over 3,500 copies, but the final volume less than 1,000. These reduced sales in the 1990s, he surmised, were partly due to the high price of the hardback volume but also 'declining interest in the history of education'.[12] New teacher education policies had greatly reduced the scope for the history of education in teacher education courses in Britain, leading also to a reorientation in this area from textbooks to specialist articles in research journals.[13]

Overall, Simon produced a historical account influenced by Marxist ideology that was a fresh and plausible way of interpreting the development of education in England. He was in many ways in the vanguard of the British Marxist historians of the mid-twentieth century, for which he has not always been given full credit.[14] At the same time, the cultural historian Peter Burke cautions against a 'people's history' that tends to simplify the past into a political struggle between two rival groups.[15] Yet Simon's history had a potent appeal because it spoke to contemporary debates and made sense in these terms. It provided an explanation for social inequalities in education that could no longer be ignored. It addressed the role of elite groups and individuals, and of the state itself, that seemed to loom ever larger in the control of the education system. It gave fresh meaning to the many disappointments and failures of reform in education over the past two centuries, while also contriving to offer hope and inspiration for the future. It was a persuasive analysis with a strong overarching theme.

There were a number of difficult challenges confronting Simon in his final years. One threat that faced him directly was an accusation made in a new book by a retired MI5 officer living in Australia, Peter Wright, that Simon had been a Soviet spy.[16] Simon took legal action to prevent this allegation being published, but it was still an unwelcome reminder of his past intellectual debts and relationships. More generally, the 1990s also witnessed the end not only of the USSR which he had once idolised, but also of the CP which he had supported against criticism for so long. For a time it seemed, as the political scientist Francis Fukuyama averred, that this was the 'end of history', with western liberal democracy decisively in the ascendancy.[17] It was not long before new geopolitical conflicts arose, and Simon lived to see the attack on the Twin Towers in New York in September 2001, the clearest portent of new and even more potent threats to humanity in the twenty-first century.

In the UK, the Conservative government finally fell in 1997, with a landslide victory for Tony Blair's New Labour government. Yet any brief optimism that this political change may have sparked in Simon was soon lost with the realisation that the new government was no less sceptical of the merits of comprehensive education than had been the previous government. Again, Simon lived long enough to witness Alastair Campbell, the press secretary for the prime minister, announcing in 2001 that 'the day of the bog-standard comprehensive school is over', and there were many references, including from the prime minister himself, to the 'post-comprehensive era'.[18] Andrew Adonis, schools minister from 1998 to 2000, turned his attention to supporting specialist schools and academies.[19] Caroline Benn and Clyde Chitty, longtime collaborators with Brian Simon, published a new survey of comprehensive schools, thirty years on from the Simon and Benn work *Halfway There,* but the subtitle of the new book summarised the uncertainty and defensive position that the comprehensive schools now found themselves in: 'Is comprehensive education alive and well or struggling to survive?'[20]

Simon himself, increasingly frail and suffering from cancer, was confined to a nursing home while being supported by Joan and his many friends and admirers, and passed away at his home in Pendene Road, Leicester, on 17 January 2002, aged 86. His brother Roger died several months later, in October 2002. Joan methodically arranged Brian's extensive papers, to donate them to the archive at the Institute of Education, London, before she died in August 2005.

Despite the difficulties of his final years, Simon remained as he had always been, an optimist for the future, even if progress might be made over the long term, as he himself suggested, in unpredictable ways. Human subjective experience, 'people's capacity for movement, for acting on the environment, for transforming it', was itself 'educative, and profoundly so'; 'the future is open and undecided, and it is, I suggest, of supreme importance that those closely involved in education recognise, and struggle consistently to realise, its potential'.[21] The struggle for education was at its broadest a fight for human educability to its maximum extent, a capacity that he had seen with all the passion of the intellectual and political activist in his lost sister, in Marxist ideology, in the comprehensive school, and as he described it on the final page of his fourth volume of the history of education, in 'the continuing endeavour to ensure access for all to a full, all-round education, embodying humanist objectives and including science and technology – and conceived, one might add, in a generous spirit involving recognition of the full mystery of human potential'.[22]

Notes

1   B. Simon, *Education and the Social Order, 1940–1990*, London, Lawrence & Wishart, 1991.
2   B. Simon, letter to history of education societies, 24 November 1977 (ISCHE archive, Paris).
3   James Lynch, advance notice, 9 February 1978 (*Paedagogica Historica* archive, Paris).
4   D. Muller, F. Ringer, B. Simon (eds), *The Rise of the Modern Educational System: Structural change and social reproduction, 1870–1920*.
5   B. Simon, 'Systematisation and segmentation in education: The case of England', in Muller et al. (eds), *Rise of the Modern Educational System*, 88–108.
6   See B. Simon, 'Educational research – which way?', *Research Intelligence*, 4/1 (1978), 2–7; and G. McCulloch, 'Educational research: which way now?', *British Educational Research Journal*, 44/2 (2018), 175–90.
7   B. Simon, letter to C. Benn, 28 March 1970 (Caroline Benn papers, IOE archive, Box 36, file 3, Correspondence 1969–1970, no. 29).
8   B. Simon, *The Politics of Educational Reform, 1920–1940*.
9   See G. McCulloch, *The Struggle for the History of Education*, 50.
10 B. Simon, memorandum, 'Volume 4', 14 September 1977 (Brian Simon papers, IOE, SIM/4/4/74).
11 B. Simon, memorandum, 'Volume 4'.
12 B. Simon, note, 'Historical books' (1995) (Brian Simon papers, IOE).
13 See G. McCulloch, 'History of education in Britain since 1960', in *Histoire de l'éducation*, 2020/2 (no. 154), 119–41.
14 See e.g. B. Schwartz, '"The people" in history: The Communist Party Historians' Group, 1946–1956', in Centre for Contemporary Cultural Studies (ed.), *Making Histories: Studies in history-writing and politics*, London, Hutchinson, 1982, 44–92; and H.J. Kaye, *The British Marxist Historians: An introductory analysis*.
15 P. Burke, 'People's history and total history', in R. Samuel (ed.), *People's History and Socialist Theory*, 4–9.
16 P. Wright, *The Spycatcher's Encyclopedia of Espionage*.
17 F. Fukuyama, *The End of History and the Last Man*.
18 See e.g. D. Crook, 'Missing, presumed dead?: What happened to the comprehensive school in England and Wales?', in G. McCulloch, D. Crook (eds), *The Death of the Comprehensive High School? Historical, contemporary and comparative perspectives*, 147–68.
19 A. Adonis, *Education, Education, Education: Reforming England's schools*, London, Biteback, 2012.
20 Simon and Benn, *Half Way There*; C. Benn and C. Chitty, *Thirty Years On: Is comprehensive education alive and well or struggling to survive?*
21 B. Simon, 'Can education change society?', in B. Simon, *Does Education Matter?*, 30, 13–31.
22 Simon, *Education and the Social Order*, 558.

Bibliography

Archival sources

Brian Simon papers, IOE (Institute of Education) Archives, UCL.
Caroline Benn papers, IOE Archives, UCL.
Communist party papers, People's History Museum Archives, Manchester.
ISCHE Archive, Paris.
Paedagogica Historica Archive, Paris.
Security files, The National Archives, Kew.
National census.

Newspapers and periodicals

Arena
Black Dwarf
Communist Review
Daily Sketch
Daily Worker
The Educational Bulletin
Education Today
Education Today and Tomorrow
Forum
The Gresham School Magazine
Journal of Education
Labour Monthly
Manchester Guardian
Marxism Today
Morning Star
New Left Review
Our History
Past and Present
Radcliffe Times
SCR Soviet Education Bulletin
Student News
Studi Storici
Teachers of the World
Times Educational Supplement
Times Literary Supplement

Official documents, policy reports and records of proceedings

Board of Education, Secondary Education, (Spens Report) (London: HMSO, 1938).
Central Advisory Council for Education (England), *Early Leaving* (London: HMSO, 1954).
DES, *Circular 10/65* (London: HMSO, 1965).
DES, *Circular 10/66* (London: HMSO, 1966).
DES, *Children and Their Primary Schools* (Plowden Report) (London: HMSO, 1967).
DES, *Education Act 1968* (London: HMSO, 1968).
DES, *The Organization of Secondary Education* (Circular 10/70) (London: HMSO, 1970).
DES, *Education: A framework for expansion* (White Paper) (London: HMSO, 1972).
DES, *The Organization of Secondary Education* (Circular 4/74) (London: HMSO, 1974).
DES, *The Direct Grant Grammar Schools Regulation* (London: HMSO, 1975).
DES, *Education Act 1976* (London: HMSO, 1976).
DES, *School Education in England: Problems and initiatives* (The Yellow Book) (London: HMSO, 1976).
DES, *Education in Schools: A consultative document* (Green Paper) (London: HMSO, 1977).
DES, *Education Act 1980* (London: HMSO, 1980).
DES, *Better Schools* (White Paper) (London: HMSO, 1985).
DES, *A New Choice of School* (London: HMSO, 1986).
DES, *Financial Delegation to Schools* (London: HMSO, 1987).
DES, *Admission of Pupils to Maintained Schools* (London: HMSO, 1987).
DES, *Grant Maintained Schools* (London: HMSO, 1987).
DES, *The National Curriculum 5–16* (London: HMSO, 1987).
DES, *Education Reform Bill* (London: HMSO, 1987).
DES, *Education Reform Act 1988* (London: HMSO, 1988).
Ministry of Education, *Secondary Education for All* (White Paper) (London: HMSO, December 1958).
Ministry of Education, *15 to 18* (Crowther Report) (London: HMSO, 1959).
Ministry of Education, *Secondary School Examinations other than the GCE* (Beloe Report) (London: HMSO, 1960).
Ministry of Education, *Half Our Future* (Newsom Report of 1963) (London: HMSO, 1963).
Ministry of Education, *Report of the Committee on Higher Education* (Robbins Report) (London: HMSO, 1963).
Public Schools Commission, *First Report* (Newsom Report of 1968) (London: HMSO, 1968).
Public Schools Commission, *Second Report* (Donnison Report) (London: HMSO, 1970).
Schools Council, *A Common System of Examining at 16+* (London: Evans/Methuen Educational, 1971).

Theses and published works

Adonis, A., *Education, Education, Education: Reforming England's schools* (London: Biteback Publishing, 2012).
Ajello, N., *Il lungo addio: Intellettuali e PCI dal 1958 al 1991* (Bari: Laterza, 1979).
Ajello, N., *Intellettuali e PCI, 1944–1958* (Bari: Laterza, 1979).
Aldrich, R. & Woodin, T., *The UCL Institute of Education: From training college to global institution* (2nd edition) (London: UCL Press, 2021).
Althusser, L., 'Reply to John Lewis' (parts I and II). *Marxism Today*, October and November, 1972, 310–17 and 343–9.
Andrew, C., *The Defence of the Realm: The authorised history of MI5* (London: Penguin, 2010).
Andrews, G., *Endgames and New Times: The final years of British Communism,' 1971–1991* (London: Lawrence & Wishart, 2004).
Andrews, G., *The Shadow Man: At the heart of the Cambridge spy circle* (London: I. B. Tauris, 2015).
Andrews, G., 'Young Turks and old guard: Intellectuals and the Communist Party leadership in the 1970s', in *Opening the Books: Essays on the social and cultural history of the British Communist Party*, ed. G. Andrews, N. Fishman & K. Morgan (London: Pluto, 1995), 225–50.

Auden, W. H., 'Honour', in *The Old School*, ed. G. Greene (Oxford: Oxford University Press, 1934/1984), 1–12.

Bailey, E. C., *The Development of the City Technology College Programmes: 1980s Conservative ideas about English secondary education* (Unpublished PhD Thesis, London School of Economics and Political Science, 2016).

Ball, S. J., *Politics and Policy Making in Education: Explorations in policy sociology* (London: Routledge, 1990).

Barnard, H. C., 'Review of Simon's *SHE*', *British Journal of Educational Studies* 9, no. 8 (1960–1).

Barnard, H. C., 'A History of English Education from 1760.' *British Journal of Educational Studies* 10, no. 1 (1961).

Beckett, F., *Enemy Within: The rise and fall of the British Communist Party* (London: John Murray, 1995).

Beer, M., *A History of British Socialism (Vol. II)* (London: Routledge, 2002).

Benn, C. & Chitty, C., *Thirty Years On: Is comprehensive education alive and well or struggling to survive?* (London: Penguin, 1997).

Benn, C. & Simon, B., *Half Way There: Report on the British comprehensive reform* (1st edition) (London: McGraw-Hill, 1970).

Benn, C. & Simon, B., *Half Way There: Report on the British comprehensive reform* (2nd edition) (Harmondsworth: Penguin, 1972).

Bennett, G., *The Zinoviev Letter: The conspiracy that never dies* (Oxford: OUP, 2018).

'Beyond the fragments: Brian Simon's statement to the Adult Education Conference', *NUSAC Bulletin* 14, no. 2 (Spring 1985): 1–4.

Bode, B. H., *Progressive Education at the Crossroads* (New York: Newson, 1938).

Bolton, P., *Education: Historical Statistics*. Accessed 24 January 2023. https://researchbriefings. files.parliament.uk/documents/SN04252/SN04252.pdf.

Boyson, R., 'The school, equality and society', in *Education, Equality and Society*, ed. B. Wilson (London: George Allen & Unwin Ltd, 1975), 155–200.

Brehony, K. J., 'Education as a "social function": Sociology, and social theory in the histories of Brian Simon', *History of Education* 33. no. 5 (2004): 545–58.

Burke, P., 'People's history and total history', in *People's History and Socialist Theory*, ed. R. Samuel, (London: Routledge, 1981), 4–9.

Burt, C., 'The education of the young adolescent: The psychological implications of the Norwood Report', *British Journal of Educational Psychology* 8, part III (November 1943): 126–40.

Burt, C., 'The mental differences between children', in *Black Paper Two: The crisis in education*, ed. C. B. Cox & A. E. Dyson (London: Critical Quarterly Society, 1969), 16–25.

Byford, A., 'Pedology as occupation in the early Soviet Union', in *A History of Marxist Psychology: The golden age of Soviet science*, ed. A. Yasnitsky (New York: Routledge, 2020), 109–27.

Cabrera, M. A., *Postsocial History: An introduction* (Oxford: Lexington Books, 2004).

Callaghan, J., *Cold War, Crisis and Conflict: The CPGB 1951–68* (London: Lawrence & Wishart, 2003).

Carpenter, H., *W. H. Auden: A biography* (London: George Allen and Unwin, 1981).

Carter, M., *Anthony Blunt: His lives* (London: Picador, 2003).

Cavanagh, M., 'Against fascism, war and economies: The Communist Party of Great Britain's schoolteachers during the Popular Front, 1935–1939', *History of Education* 43, no. 2 (2014): 208–31.

Cecil, R., *A Divided Life: A biography of Donald Maclean* (London: Bodley Head, 1988).

Chitty, C., *Towards a New Education System: The victory of the New Right?* (London: Falmer, 1989).

Clarke, F., *Education and Social Change: An English interpretation* (London: Sheldon Press, 1940).

Conservative Party, *The Next Moves Forward* (London: Conservative Central Office, 1987).

Cornforth, M., 'A. L. Morton: Portrait of a Marxist historian', in *Rebels and Their Causes: Essays in honour of A. L. Morton*, ed. M. Cornforth (London: Lawrence & Wishart, 1978), 7–19.

Crook, D., 'Missing, presumed dead?: What happened to the comprehensive school in England and Wales?', in *The Death of the Comprehensive High School? Historical, contemporary and comparative perspectives*, eds. G. McCulloch & D. Crook (London: Palgrave, 2007), 147–68.

Crowe, S., 'The Zinoviev Letter: A reappraisal', *Journal of Contemporary History* 10, no. 3 (1975): 407–32.

Cruickshank, M., 'The open-air school movement in English education', *Paedagogica Historica* 17, no. 1 (1977): 61–74.

Cunningham, P. & Martin, J., 'Education and the social order: Re-visioning the legacy of Brian Simon', *History of Education* 33, no. 5 (2004): 497–504.

Dale, R., 'The Thatcherite project in education: The case of the city technology colleges', *Critical School Policy* 9, no. 27 (1989): 4–19.

Despain, H. G., *The Political Economy of Maurice Dobb: History, theory, and the economics of reproduction, crisis, and transformation* (Unpublished PhD thesis, University of Utah, 2011).

Di Maggio, M., *Les Intellectuels et la Stratégie Communiste: Une Crise d'Hégémonie (1958–1981)* (París: Les Éditions sociales, 2013).

Di Maggio, M., *The Rise and Fall of Communist Parties in France and Italy: Entangled historical approaches* (Basingstoke: Palgrave Macmillan, 2021).

Dobb, M., *Studies in the Development of Capitalism* (London: Routledge & Kegan Paul, 1946).

Dobb, M., *The Collected Works of Maurice Dobb* (London: Routledge, 2012).

Eaden, J. & Renton, D., *The Communist Party of Great Britain since 1920* (New York, NY: Palgrave Macmillan, 2002).

Eccles, J. R., *My Life as a Public School Master* (Blackburn: The Times Printing Works, 1948).

Edwards, T., Fitz, J. & Whitty, G., *The State and Private Education: An evaluation of the assisted places scheme* (London: Falmer, 1989).

Eley, G., 'Reading Gramsci in English: Observations on the reception of Antonio Gramsci in the English speaking world 1957–82', *European History Quarterly* 14 (1984): 441–77.

Evans, R. J., *Eric Hobsbawm: A life in history* (London: Little, Brown, 2019).

Eysenck, H. J., 'The Rise of the mediocracy', in *Black Paper Two: The crisis in education*, ed. C. B. Cox & A. E. Dyson (London: Critical Quarterly Society, 1969), 34–40.

Fieldhouse, R. T., *Adult Education and the Cold War* (Leeds: University of Leeds, 1985).

Fitzpatrick, S., *The Commissariat of Enlightenment: Soviet organization of education and the arts under Lunacharsky, October 1917–1921* (Cambridge: Cambridge University Press, 1970).

Forgacs, D., 'Gramsci and Marxism in Britain', *New Left Review* 1, no. 176 (1989): 70–88.

Fraser, J. & Yasnitsky, A., 'Deconstructing Vygotsky's victimization narrative: A re-examination of the "Stalinist suppression" of Vygotskian theory', *History of the Human Sciences* 28, no. 2 (2015):128–53.

Fry, G. K., *The Politics of the Thatcher Revolution: An interpretation of British politics, 1979–1990* (New York, NY: Palgrave Macmillan, 2008).

Fukuyama, F., *The End of History and the Last Man* (London: Harper, 1992).

Gordon, P., Aldrich, R., & Dean, D., *Education and Policy in England in the Twentieth Century* (London: The Woburn Press, 1991).

Gramsci, A., *Selections from the Prison Notebooks of Antonio Gramsci*, ed. & trans. Q. Hoare & G. N. Smith (London: Lawrence & Wishart, 1971).

Greene, G. (ed.), *The Old School* (Oxford: Oxford University Press, 1934/1984)

Griggs, C., 'The New Right and English secondary education', in *The Changing Secondary School*, ed. R. Lowe (London: Falmer, 1989), 99–128.

Hannah, L., 'Crisis and Turnaround? 1973–1993', in *Twentieth-century Britain: Economic, social and cultural change*, ed. P. Johnson (Harlow: Longman, 1994), 340–55.

Hart, C., Dixon, A., Drummond, M. J. & McIntyre, D., *Learning without Limits* (Maidenhead: Open University Press, 2004).

Hill, C., *The English Revolution 1640: An Essay* (London: Lawrence & Wishart, 1940).

The Hillcole Group, *Changing the Future: Redprint for education* (London: The Tufnell Press, 1991).

History of Education, 33, no 5 (2004), 'Brian Simon', special issue.

Hobsbawm, E., 'The Historians' Group of the Communist Party', in *Rebels and Their Causes: Essays in honour of A. L. Morton*, ed. M. Cornforth (London: Lawrence & Wishart, 1978), 21–47.

Hobsbawm, E., *Interesting Times: A twentieth-century life* (London: Allen Lane, 2002).

Homes, L. E., *The Kremlin and the Schoolhouse: Reforming education in Soviet Russia, 1917–1931* (Bloomington, IN: Indiana University Press, 1990).

Jacques, M., 'The last word', *Marxism Today*, December (1991): 28–9.

Johnson, R., 'Thatcherism and English education: Breaking the mould, or confirming the pattern?', *History of Education* 18, no. 2 (1989): 91–121.

Jones, B., 'Simon, Ernest Emil Darwin', in *Oxford Dictionary of National Biography*, vol. 50 (Oxford: Oxford University Press, 1960), 653–6.

Jones, B., 'Simon, Shena Dorothy', in *Oxford Dictionary of National Biography*, vol. 50 (Oxford: Oxford University Press, 1960), 669–70.

Jones, D., *School of Education 1946–1996* (Leicester: University of Leicester, 2001).

Jones, K., *Education in Britain: 1944 to the present* (Cambridge: Polity, 2003).

Judges, A. V. (ed.), *Pioneers of English Education* (London: Faber and Faber, 1952).

Kavanagh, M. R., *British Communism and the Politics of Education, 1926–1968* (Unpublished PhD thesis, University of Manchester, 2005).

Kaye, H. J., *The British Marxist Historians: An introductory analysis* (Cambridge: Polity, 1984).

Kenny, M., 'Communism and the New Left', in *Opening the Books: Essays on the social and cultural history of the British Communist Party*, ed. G. Andrews, N. Fishman & K. Morgan (London: Pluto, 1995), 195–209.

Kettle, A., 'The artist and politics', *Marxism Today*, May 1959, 139–45.

Kettle, A., *Communism and the Intellectuals* (London: Lawrence & Wishart, 1960).

Kettle, A., 'Culture and revolution: A consideration of the Ideas of Raymond Williams and others', *Marxism Today*, October 1961, 301–7.

Kliebard, H. M., *The Struggle for the American Curriculum, 1893–1958* (New York, NY: RoutledgeFalmer, 2004).

Knight, C., *The Making of Tory Education Policy in Post-war Britain 1950–1986* (London: Falmer Press, 1990).

Kozulin, A., 'Vygotsky in context', in L. Vygotsky, *Thought and Language* (Cambridge, MA: MIT Press, 1986), xi–lvi.

Ku, H. Y., 'Education for democratic citizenship: Ernest Simon's ideals of liberal democracy and citizenship education in England, 1934–1944', *Historia y Memoria de la Educacion*, 7 (2018): 499–532.

Ku, H. Y., 'In pursuit of social democracy: Shena Simon and the reform of secondary education in England, 1938–1948', *History of Education* 47, no. 1 (2018): 54–72.

Ku, H. Y., 'Defending comprehensive education: Brian Simon and the Conservative governments (1979–1990)', *British Journal of Educational Studies*, 70 no. 4 (2022): 457–80.

Ku, H. Y., 'Ideological struggle in education: Brian Simon and comprehensive education movement (1946–1965)', *History of Education*, 51, no. 2 (2022): 266–85.

Ku, H. Y., 'The crisis in education: Brian Simon's battle for comprehensive education (1970–1979)', *Paedagogica Historica* (in press).

Kuhn, T. S., *The Structure of Scientific Revolutions* (Chicago, IL: Chicago University Press, 1962).

Labour Party, *Learning to Live: Labour's policy for education* (London: Labour Party, 1958).

Lavery, K. P., 'Youth of the world, unite so that you may live: Youth, internationalism, and the Popular Front in the World Youth Congress Movement, 1936–1939', *Peace and Change* 46 (2021): 269–85.

Leach, A. F., *English Schools at the Reformation* (London: Constable & Co., 1896).

Leach, A. F., *Schools of Mediaeval England* (London: Methuen, 1915).

Levitas, R., 'Introduction: Ideology and the New Right', in *The Ideology of the New Right*, ed. R. Levitas (Cambridge: Polity, 1986), 1–24.

Lewis, J., 'The Althusser Case' (parts I and II). *Marxism Today*, January and February 1972, 23–7 and 43–7.

MacCabe, C., 'Britain's communist university', *New Statesman* 20, no. 5 (1977): 673.

Martelli, R., *Une Dispute Communiste: Le Comité Central d'Argenteuil* (Paris: Les Éditions sociales, 2017).

Martin, J., 'Shena D. Simon and English education: Inside/out?', *History of Education* 32, no. 5 (2003): 477–94.

Martin, J., 'Neglected women historians: The case of Joan Simon', *Forum* 56, no. 3 (2014): 541–66.

Martin, J., 'Telling stories about comprehensive education: Hidden histories of politics, policy and practice in post-war England', *British Journal of Educational Studies* 68, no. 5 (2020): 649–69.

Matthews, S., '"Say not the struggle naught availeth": *Scrutiny* (1932–53)', in *The Oxford Critical and Cultural History of Modernist Magazines*, vol. 1, Britain and Ireland 1880–1955, ed. P. Brooker & A. Thacker (Oxford: Oxford University Press, 2009, 833–56).

Maud, J., 'The twentieth-century administrator', in *Pioneers of English Education*, ed. A. V. Judges (London: Faber and Faber, 1952), 227–47.

May, H., Nawrotski, K. & Prochner, L. (eds), *Kindergarten Narratives on Froebelian Education: Transnational investigations* (London: Bloomsbury, 2017).

McCulloch, G., *The Politics of the Popular Front, 1935–45* (Unpublished PhD thesis, University of Cambridge, 1980).

McCulloch, G., '"Teachers and missionaries": The Left Book Club as an educational agency', *History of Education* 14, no. 2 (1985): 137–53.

McCulloch, G., 'Policy, politics and education: The technical and vocational education initiative', *Journal of Education Policy* 1, no. 1 (1986): 35–52.

McCulloch, G., *Educational Reconstruction: The 1944 Education Act and the 21st Century* (London: Routledge, 1994).

McCulloch, G., *Failing the Ordinary Child? The theory and practice of working-class secondary education* (London: Open University Press, 1998).

McCulloch, G., 'Local Education Authorities and the organisation of secondary education, 1943–1950', *Oxford Review of Education* 28, no. 2–3 (2002): 235–46.

McCulloch, G., 'Education, history and social change: The legacy of Brian Simon' (inaugural address of Brian Simon Chair of the History of Education, 21 October 2004) (London: UCL Press, 2004).

McCulloch, G., 'A people's history of education: Brian Simon, the British Communist Party and studies in the history of education, 1780–1870', *History of Education* 39, no. 4 (2010): 437–57.

McCulloch, G., *The Struggle for the History of Education* (London: Routledge, 2011).

McCulloch, G., 'British Labour Party education policy and comprehensive education: from Learning to Live to Circular 10/65', *History of Education* 45, no. 2 (2016): 234–37.

McCulloch, G., 'Educational research: Which way now?', *British Educational Research Journal* 44, no. 2 (2018): 175–90.

McCulloch, G., 'History of education in Britain since 1960', in *Histoire de l'education* 2, no. 154 (2020):119–41.

McCulloch, G., & Cowan, S., *A Social History of Educational Studies and Research* (London: Routledge, 2018).

McCulloch, G., Cowan, S. & Woodin, T., 'The British Conservative government and the raising of the school leaving age, 1959–1964', *Journal of Education Policy* 27, no. 4 (2012): 509–27.

McCulloch, G. & Woodin, T., 'Learning and liberal education: The case of the Simon family, 1912–1939', *Oxford Review of Education* 36, no. 2 (2010): 187–201.

Miliband, D., *Markets, Politics and Education: Beyond the Education Reform Act* (London: Institute for Public Policy Research, 1991).

Mitchell, F. W., *Sir Fred Clarke, Master Teacher, 1880–1952* (London: Longman, 1967).

Morgan, K. O., *Britain since 1945: The people's peace* (Oxford: Oxford University Press, 2001).

Morris, M., *The People's Schools* (London: Gollancz, 1939).

Morris, P., 'The English tradition of education', in *Pioneers of English Education*, ed. A.V. Judges (London: Faber and Faber, 1952), 42–63.

Muller, D., Ringer, F., & Simon, B. (eds), *The Rise of the Modern Educational System: Structural change and social reproduction, 1870–1920* (Cambridge: CUP, 1987).

Niven, B., 'Proposals for the arts', *Marxism Today*, April, 4 (4): 1960, 117–22.

Olssen, E., 'Truby King and the Plunket Society: An analysis of a prescriptive ideology', *New Zealand Journal of History* 15, no. 1 (1981): 3–23.

Orwell, G., *Homage to Catalonia* (London: Penguin, 1938/1977).

Pala, G., *Cultura Clandestina: Los Intelectuales del PSUC Bajo el Franquismo* (Granada: Comares, 2016).

Peden, G. C., *British Economic and Social Policy: Lloyd George to Margaret Thatcher* (London: Philip Allan, 1991).

Pelling, H., *The British Communist Party: A historical profile* (London: A&C Black, 1958).

Penrose, B. & Freeman, S., *Conspiracy of Silence: The secret life of Anthony Blunt* (New York, NY: Farrar Straus and Giroux, 1987).

Pimlott, B., *Labour and the Left in the 1930s* (Cambridge: CUP, 1977).

Rattansi, A. & Reeder, D. (eds), *Rethinking Radical Education* (London: Lawrence & Wishart, London, 1993).

Rubinstein, D. & Simon B., *The Evolution of the Comprehensive School, 1926–1972* (2nd edition) (London: Routledge & Kegan Paul, 1973).

Samuel, R. (ed.), *People's History and Socialist Theory* (London: Routledge and Kegan Paul, 1981).

Schwartz, B., '"The people" in history: The Communist Party's Historians' Group, 1946–56', in *Making Histories: Studies in history-writing and politics* (London: Centre for Contemporary Cultural Studies & Hutchinson, 1982), 44–92.

Simon, B., *A Student's View of the Universities* (London: Longman, 1943).

Simon, B., 'Science and pseudo-science in psychology,' *Educational Bulletin,* October 1949, 12.

Simon, B., *Intelligence Testing and the Comprehensive School* (London: Lawrence & Wishart, 1953).

Simon, B., *Education in the New Poland* (London: Lawrence & Wishart, 1954).

Simon, B., 'Leicestershire Schools 1625–40', *British Journal of Educational Studies* 3, no. 1 (1954): 42–58.

Simon, B., 'Polytechnic education in Soviet schools', *The Vocational Aspect of Secondary and Further Education* 6, no. 12 (1954): 3–13.

Simon, B., *The Common Secondary School* (London: Lawrence & Wishart, 1955).

Simon, B., 'Polytechnic Education in the USSR', *The Vocational Aspect of Education* 7, no. 15 (1955): 135–41.

Simon, B., *Freedom* (London: Communist Party, 1960).

Simon, B., *Studies in the History of Education, 1780–1870* (later retitled *The Two Nations and the Educational Structure, 1780–1870*) (London: Lawrence & Wishart, 1960).

Simon, B., *Non-streaming in the Junior School,* ed. B. Simon (Leicester: PSW Educational Publications, 1964), 7–28.

Simon, B., *Education and the Labour Movement, 1870–1920* (London: Lawrence & Wishart, 1965).

Simon, B., 'The history of education', in J. W. Tibble (ed.), *The Study of Education* (London: Routledge, 1966), 91–131.

Simon, B., *Education: The New Perspective* (Leicester: Leicester University Press, 1967).

Simon, B., 'Streaming and unstreaming in the secondary school', in *Education for Democracy*, ed. D. Rubinstein & C. Stoneman (Harmondsworth: Penguin Books, 1972), 142–50.

Simon, B., *The Politics of Educational Reform, 1920–1940* (London: Lawrence & Wishart, 1974).

Simon, B., 'Educational research – which way?', *Research Intelligence* 4, no. 1 (1978): 2–7.

Simon, B., *Intelligence, Psychology and Education: A Marxist critique* (London: Lawrence & Wishart, 1978).

Simon, B., 'Education: The new perspective', in *The Study of Education: Inaugural lectures* (volume 2, The Last Decade), ed. P. Gordon (London: Woburn Press, 1980), 71–94.

Simon, B., 'Why no pedagogy in England', in *Education in the Eighties: The central issues*, ed. B. Simon and W. Taylor (London: Batsford, 1981), 124–45.

Simon, B., 'Popular, local and democratic: Karl Marx's formula', *Education* 11 (March 1983): 186–7.

Simon, B., 'Comprehensive ideals', *Comprehensive Education* 50 (1985): 15–16.

Simon, B., *Does Education Matter?* (London: Lawrence & Wishart, 1985).

Simon, B., *Defend Comprehensive Schools* (London: Communist Party, 1986).

Simon, B., 'Systematisation and segmentation in education: The case of England', in *The Rise of the Modern Educational System: Structural change and social reproduction, 1870–1920*, ed. D. Muller, F. Ringer & B. Simon (Cambridge: CUP, 1987), 88–108.

Simon, B., *Bending the Rules: The Baker 'reform' of education* (London: Lawrence & Wishart, 1988).

Simon, B., *Education and the Social Order, 1940–1990* (London: Lawrence & Wishart, 1991).

Simon, B., 'The politics of comprehensive reorganization: A retrospective analysis', *History of Education* 21, no. 4 (1992): 355–62.

Simon, B., *What Future for Education?* (London: Lawrence & Wishart, 1992).

Simon, B., *A Life in Education* (London: Lawrence & Wishart, 1997).

Simon, B., *In Search of a Grandfather: Henry Simon of Manchester, 1835–1899* (Leicester: Pendene Press, 1997).

Simon, B. & Simon, J. (eds). *Psychology in the Soviet Union* (London: Routledge and Kegan Paul, 1957).

Simon, B. & Simon, J. (eds). *Educational Psychology in the USSR* (London: Routledge and Kegan Paul, 1963).

Simon, J., 'Educational policies and programmes', *Modern Quarterly* 4, no. 2 (1949): 154–68.

Simon, J., 'A.F. Leach on the Reformation: I', *British Journal of Educational Studies* 3, no. 2 (1955): 128–43.

Simon, J., 'A. F. Leach on the Reformation: II', *British Journal of Educational Studies* 4, no. 1 (1955): 32–48.

Simon, J., *Education and Society in Tudor England* (Cambridge: CUP, 1966).

Simon, J., *Indictment of Margaret Thatcher, Secretary of State for Education 1970–3* (Leicester: PSW Educational Publications, 1973).

Simon, J., *Shena Simon: Feminist and educationist* (Leicester: privately printed, 1986).

Simon, J., 'Promoting educational reform on the Home Front: The *TES* and *The Times* 1940–1944', *History of Education* 18, no. 2 (1989):195–211.

Simon, J., 'The state and schooling at the Reformation and after: From pious causes to charitable uses', *History of Education* 23, no. 2 (1994): 157–69.

Simon, J., 'An "energetic and controversial" historian of education yesterday and today: A. F. Leach (1851–1915)', *History of Education* 36, no. 3 (2007): 367–89.

Skidelsky, R., *Politicians and the Slump: The Labour government of 1929–1931* (London: Macmillan, 1967).

Smart, K. F., 'The polytechnic principle', in *Communist Education*, ed. E. King (London: Methuen, 1963), 153–76.

Soler, A. M., 'Los intelectuales y la política cultural del Partido Comunista de España (1939–1956)', in *Nosotros los comunistas: Memoria, identidad e historia social*, ed. M. B. Lluch & Sergio Gálvez Biesca (Madrid: Fundación de Investigaciones Marxistas, 2009), 367–87.

Spender, S., *World within World: The autobiography of Stephen Spender* (London: Hamish Hamilton, 1951).

Steele, T., 'Hey Jimmy! The legacy of Gramsci in British cultural politics', in *New Left, New Right and Beyond: Taking the Sixties seriously*, ed. G. Andrews, R. Cockett, A. Hooper & M. Williams (London: Palgrave Macmillan, 1999), 26–41.

Stocks, M., *Ernest Simon of Manchester* (Manchester: Manchester University Press, 1963).

Thom, D., 'Politics and the people: Brian Simon and the campaign against intelligence tests in British schools', *History of Education* 33, no. 5 (2004): 515–29.

Thomas, H., *The Spanish Civil War* (3rd edition) (London: Penguin, 1961/1977).

Tibble, J. W. (ed.), *The Study of Education* (London: Routledge and Kegan Paul, 1966).

Tomlinson, S., 'Phrenology, education and the politics of human nature: The thought and influence of George Combe', *History of Education* 26, no. 1 (1997): 1–22.

UNESCO Institute for Statistics, *Government Expenditure on Education, Total (% of GDP) – United Kingdom*. Accessed 30 January 2023. https://data.worldbank.org/indicator/SE.XPD.TOTL.GD.ZS?end=2017&locations=GB&start=1971&view=chart.

Vittoria, A., *Togliatti e Gli Intellettuali: Storia dell'Istituto Gramsci negli anni cinquanta e sessanta* (Roma: Editori Riuniti, 1992).

Vygotsky, L., *Thought and Language* (Cambridge, MA: MIT Press, 1986).

Waite, M., 'Sex 'n' drugs 'n' rock 'n' roll (and communism) in the 1960s', in *Opening the Books: Essays on the social and cultural history of the British Communist Party*, ed. G. Andrews, N. Fishman & K. Morgan (London: Pluto, 1995), 210–24.

Wasmuth, H., *Froebel's pedagogy of kindergarten play: Modifications in Germany and the United States* (London: Routledge, 2020).

Watts, R., 'Obituary: Joan Simon (1915–2005)', *History of Education* 35, no. 1 (2006): 5–9.

Wright, P., *The Spycatcher's Encyclopedia of Espionage* (Australia: Random House, 1991).

Yasnitsky, A., 'Vygotsky circle as a personal network of scholars: Restoring connections between people and ideas', *Integrative Psychological and Behavioral Science* 45, no. 4 (2011): 422–57.

Yasnitsky, A., 'The archetype of Soviet psychology: From the Stalinism of the 1930s to the "Stalinist science" of our time', in *Revisionist Revolution in Vygotsky Studies*, ed. A. Yasnitsky & R. van der Veer (London: Routledge, 2016), 3–26.

Yasnitsky, A., (ed.), *A History of Marxist Psychology: The golden age of Soviet science* (New York, NY: Routledge, 2020).

Index

Page numbers for illustrations are in *italics*. Brian Simon is BS throughout.

Aaronovitch, Sam 93, 98
Abbott Street School, Manchester 39–40, *147*
Adonis, Andrew 176
Agathangelou, Tony 110
Alexander, Maj. W.A. 35–6
Althusser, Louis 106
Andrews, Geoff 106, 113–14
anti-war movement 17
Army Bureau of Current Affairs (ABCA) 36
Assisted Places Scheme 154, 166
Association for Education in Citizenship 9
Astbury, Peter 35
Attlee, Clement 37, 75
Auden, W.H. 12, 21–2
Ayer, A.J. 100

'backwardness' 39, 41, 127
Baker, Kenneth 158–65, 166
Ball, Stephen 156, 159, 165
Bandinelli, Ranuccio Bianchi 96
Bantock, Geoffrey 74
Barker, Ernest 18, 38
Barnard, H.C. 82–3
Beloe Report (1960) 125, 134, 139
Beloff, Lord (Mark) 155
Benn, Caroline
    BS and 135, 151, 174, 176
    CSC and 127
    Hillcole Group 165
    Half Way There 130, 131–2, 133
Berger, John 99–100, 101
Bernal, John Desmond 98
Black Papers 66, 134, 139
Bloomsfield, John 114
Blum, Léon 16
Blunt, Anthony 17
Bode, Boyd H. 65
Bond, Ralph 97
Bourdieu, Pierre 173, 174
bourgeoisie 43, 76, 78, 79, 84
Boyle, Edward 125
Boyson, Rhodes 152–5
Brehony, Kevin J. 66
British Educational Management and
    Administration Society (BEMAS) 164
British Educational Research Association
    (BERA) 2, 122, 138, 161, 174
British Student Congress (BSC) 34–5

Broom Croft (family home) 7–8
Buchanan-Smith, Brig. A.D. 37
Burke, Peter 175
Burt, Cyril 134, 139, 141n.13
Bush, Alan 92, 94

Callaghan, James, 'Ruskin Speech' 136–7,
    140, 153
Cambridge, University of 15
Campbell, Alastair 176
capitalism 42, 58, 61, 77, 94, 105, 155
Carlisle, Mark 154, 159
Carr, E.H. 98
Carritt, Bill 94, 97
Carstairs, Morris 100
Carter, Miranda 3
Central Advisory Council for Education 123
Centre 42 Movement 97
Centre d'Études et de Recherches Marxistes
    (CERM) 96, 109
Centre for the Study of the Comprehensive
    School 158
Certificate of Pre-Vocational Education
    (CPVE) 155
Certificate of Secondary Education
    (CSE) 125, 134, 156
Chartist movement 79
Chitty, Clyde 159, 161, 165, 176
Churchill, Winston 75
City Technology College (CTC) 159, 161, 162,
    164, 165, 166
Clarke, Fred 20–1, 34, 44, 74, 84
classes, social 42–3, 44, 53, 64, 76, 78–82, 84,
    128, 153
clerical work, teaching and 41
Cohen, Jack 92, 108
Cold War 51, 71
Comintern 16
    Communist Party of Great Britain (CPGB)
    Committee of Arts and Entertainment 115
    congresses 85, 91, 93
    Department of Organization 97
    Economic Committee 111, 115
    Education Advisory Committee 121, 157,
    158
    Executive Committee 72, 83, 93, 97, 104,
    107, 110–11, 116
    Historians' Group 77

League of Women Communists 93
National Cultural Committee 88, 91–116, 121
Policy for Leisure (EC) 96
Political Committee 91, 104, 107, 109, 115, 116, 118n.49
Second World War 33
Simon family funding 72–3
Spanish Civil War 23
Theory and Ideology Committee 115, 116
Trinity College members 15–16, 17
Weeks of Marxist Debate 98–9, 109, 114
Young Communist League 31, 97
'Battle for Educational Opportunity' 134
'The British Road to Socialism' 140n.4
Daily Worker 73
Defend Comprehensive Schools 158
The Educational Bulletin 63, 76
Marxism Today 92, 96, 101, 106, 108, 110, 111, 153
Questions of Ideology and Culture 104–7, 114
Communist Party of the Soviet Union (CPSU) 16, 54, 63
Communist University of London (CUL) 113–15
comprehensive schools 42, 51, 52, 65, 67, 81
campaign for 121–40
defending education in 151–67
Comprehensive Schools Committee (CSC) 127–8, 139
conscience, concept of 55, 56, 57, 58, 63
Conservative Party
conferences 131, 132–3, 159
CP and 16, 23
governments 13, 75, 122–7, 130–5, 139, 151, 152–67
market philosophy 140
monetarist policy 153
neoconservatives 152, 165
neoliberals 140, 152, 165
Better Schools 157
Education: A Framework for Expansion 132
Secondary Education for All: A New Drive 124–5
Cornford, John 17, 21, 80, 81, 98
Cornforth, Maurice 77, 85, 92, 107, 108
Costello, Mick 110
Crosland, Anthony 127, 129
Crowther Report (1959) 125, 139
culture, ideology and 103–7
Cunningham, Peter 2
Czechoslovakia 109, 111

Dale, Roger 164
Devine, Pat 111
Dewey, John 64
Di Maggio, Marco 109, 110
Direct Grant Grammar Schools Regulations 136, 139
direct-grant schools 123, 130, 131, 136
Dobb, Maurice 18, 20, 38, 77, 98, 99
Donnison, David 130
Drake, Barbara 24
Dubček, Alexander 111
Dunn, Robert 157

Eccles, Sir David 75, 123
Eccles, J.R. 12–13, 15
Economic Affairs, Institute of (IEA) 152
Eden, Anthony 75
Education Acts
1902 79
1944 37, 40, 43, 53, 84, 128–9, 132
1968 132
1976 136, 139, 154
1980 154
Education and Science, Department of (DES), Assessment of Performance Unit (APU) 138
Circular 4/74 135
Circular 10/65 127–8, 130, 131, 139
Circular 10/66 128, 130
Circular 10/70 131, 132, 135
A New Choice of School 159
School Education in England: Problems and Initiatives 136
Education, Ministry of 37, 44
Education Reform Act (1988) 151, 158–65, 175
education, Soviet 52, 124
Ehrenburg, Ilya 98
elementary education 79
Elementary Education Act (1870) 43, 78, 80
eleven-plus examination 38, 39, 53, 81, 127
eugenics 57
Evans, Alan 132
Eysenck, Hans 134, 139

Feltrinelli, Giangiacomo 101
Ferri, Franco 96
First World War 8
Flanders, Mary 54
Ford, Boris 52
Forgacs, David 107, 113
formal education 10–11, 59, 66
France 16, 33, 100, 173
Franco, Gen Francisco 16, 21
Freeland, G.C. 127
French Communist Party (PCF) 95–6, 103–4, 106–7, 109
Froebel, Friedrich 11
Fukuyama, Francis 176

Gaitskell, Hugh 75, 126
Gale, Margot 92
Garaudy, Roger 96, 98
General Certificate Examination (GCE) 123, 125–6, 134, 156
General Certificate of Secondary Education (GCSE) 157
General Strike (1926) 16, 21
Germany 16, 33, 173
Godden, Charles 136
Gollan, John 72, 93, 99, 107
Gordon, Hugh 16
Gordonstoun, Scotland 14
grammar schools 37, 42, 52, 122, 123–4, 128, 131, 132
Gramsci, Gramsci, Antonio 96, 103, 107–11, 113–15, 175
grant-maintained schools 129, 160, 161, 162, 163
Great Debate (1974–79) 135–8

Great Education Reform Bill (GERBIL) 151, 161–4
Gregory, Joan 158
Gresham's school, Holt, Norfolk 10, 11–13, 14, 15, 17, 21, 25, 35
Gurrey, D. 38–9

Hahn, Kurt 14
Haldane, John 93
Hamley, H.R. 38–9
Hawthorn, Jeremy 111
Heinemann, Margot 94
'hereditary' intelligence 57, 133, 139, 157
higher education 84, 126
Hill, Christopher 74, 98
Hillcole Group, *Changing the Future: Redprint for education* 165
History of Education, International Standing Conference for the (ISCHE) 173
History of Education Society, UK (HES) 1, 173–4
Hitler, Adolf 13, 14, 16
Hoare, Quintin 111
Hobsbawm, Eric 3, 16, 17, 21, 24, 72, 98, 112
Horsbrugh, Florence 122–3
Howson, George 12
Hungary 23, 71–2, 83, 91, 92, 95, 121
Hunt, Alan 110

ideology, and culture 103–7
independent schools 79, 81, 123, 131, 161, 162
'innate' intelligence 41, 57, 58, 59
Institute of Education, London (IOE) 7, 19–20, 23–4, 38, 43, 87, 176
intelligence tests 10, 51, 53–9, 73, 122, 134, 139
International Standing Conference for History of Education (ISCHE) 1, 173
Istituto Gramsci, Italy 96, 109
Italian Communist Party (PCI) 95–6, 109
Italy 13, 100

Jacques, Martin 110, 111, 113, 115, 116
Japan 133
Jeffrey, Nora 93, 94, 108
Jensen, Arthur 133–4
Johnson, Richard 164–5
Johnstone, Monty 110, 116
Jones, Ken 165
Joseph, Keith 152, 154–9, 166
Journal of Education 34
Judges, A.V. 75–6
Judt, Tony 109, 119n.76

Kammari, Mikhail 58
Kell, Col Sir Vernon 31
Kettle, Arnold 92, 94, 98, 101–3, 106
Klugmann, James
  advice to BS 78, 80–2, 85
  BS and 17, 32, 108
  CP Cultural Committee 94
  Marxism Today 92, 110
Krupskaya, Nadezhda Konstantinovna 60, 63
Kuhn, Thomas S. 104

Labour Party 16, 23, 24, 75, 115
  governments 13, 37, 86, 122, 127–30, 135–9, 153, 176
  Education in Schools: A Consultative Document 137
  Learning to Live 126
Lakatos, Imre 57
Lamarckism 56
Lavery, Kevin P. 31
Lawrence & Wishart 52, 72–3, 80, 83, 92, 98, 108
Lawton, Denis 161
Leach, A.F. 75, 86
Leavis, F.R. 15
Left Book Club 16
Leicester, University of 72, 74, 86, 122, 173
Lenin, Vladimir 60, 62, 65
Leontiev, A.N. 55, 56
Lewis, John 92, 106, 107
Liberal Party, National 13
Linfield, Eric 127
Lloyd, Bert 97
Lloyd George, David 13
Local Education Authorities (LEAs) 24, 37–8, 123, 126, 127–9, 132, 135, 139
Lower Achieving Pupils Project (LAPP) 156, 157
Luria, Alexander Romanovich 55
Lysenko, Trofim Denisovich 56, 93, 102

McColl, Ewan 97
Maclean, Donald 15
Macmillan, Harold 75
Makarenko, Anton 59, 63
Manpower Services Commission (MSC) 155–6, 157
manual–intellectual division 59, 62
Martin, Jane 2
Marxism 2–3, 99–100, 102–4, 109–10, 114–15
  articulating 94, 106
  'The education campaign' 42
  psychology and pedagogy 51–67
  Simons' commitment to 18–19, 21, 30, 32, 73
Marx, Karl 62, 63, 66, 85, 106, 124, 137, 155
materialism, dialectical 17–18, 56
Matthews, Betty 92, 108, 110
Matthews, George 92
Maud, Sir John 76
meals, school 40
Menchinskaya, Natalia Alexandrovna 55
Mensheviks 105
MI5 3, 16, 30, 31, 35–6, 71, 83, 175–6
middle class 43, 78–9, 80, 81, 82, 128, 153
mixed-ability groups 66
Montessori education 9, 30
Moor Allerton School, Manchester 11
Morgan, Kenneth O. 152
Morris, Max 43, 83
Morris, Sir Philip 76
Morton, Arthur 77, 80, 82
Muller, Detlef 176
Munby, Lionel 102–3, 106
Mussolini, Benito 13

INDEX **189**

National Union of Students (NUS) 20, 33–5, 92, 98
National Union of Teachers (NUT) 131, 156
Nazi Party 11, 13, 14
New Education 20, 42, 53, 63–6
New Left 91, 92, 102, 114
New Right 151, 152, 153, 166, 167
Newsom Reports (1963/68) 125, 129, 139
Niven, Barbara 94, 96
No Turning Back Group 157
Nowell-Smith, Geoffrey 111

Oakdene School, Manchester 11–12
Oakeshott, Michael 18
O'Brien, Edna 100
Orwell, George 22
Owen, Robert 82

parental choice, informed 151, 152–3, 154, 162, 165, 166
Pasternak, Boris 101
Patten, Chris 157
Pavlov, Ivan 55
pedagogy, Marxism, psychology and 51–67
Pedley, Robin 124, 126
Petrie, Sir David 31
phrenology 9
Pinsent, Lt.Col. J.R. 35
Plowden Report (1967) 66, 127, 139
Poland 33, 62, 124
Policy Studies, Centre for 152
polytechnic education 51, 59–63, 124
popular front 32–3
Prentice, Reg 135
primary education 123, 126–7, 139, 165
progressive education 9, 53, 64–5, 136
psychology and pedagogy, Marxism 51–67
psychology, educational 44
psychometrics 51, 53
Public Policy Research, Institute for (IPPR) 165
public schools 44, 79, 80, 123, 126, 129, 131
Public Schools Commission 129–30, 139

'Rassemblement Mondiale des Étudiants' (RME) 32
Reid, Betty 115
Rhodes James, Robert 155
Ringer, Fritz 174
Robbins Report (1963) 126, 139
ruling class 42–3, 44, 79
Russell, Bertrand 98

Salem school, Germany 11, 14
Salford Grammar School 40, 44, *148–9*
Samuel, Raphael 76–7
school-leaving age 79, 123, 125, 135
Schools Council for Curriculum and Examinations 134–5, 155
Schwartz, Bill 77
science education 56–7, 62–3
secondary education 24, 35, 37–8, 53, 79, 84
secondary modern schools 37, 42, 122, 125
Secondary Schools Examinations Council (SSEC) 125
Second World War 32–7, 151

security services, British see MI5
Seldon, Arthur 157
Sexton, Stuart 155
Shapiro, Monte 54
Shelton, William 155
Shields-Collins, Elizabeth 31
Short, Edward 129, 139
Simm, E.G. 40
Simon, Antonia 9, 10
Simon, Brian (BS)
  becomes professor 83–8
  British Educational Research Association president 122
  campaign for comprehensive education 121–40
  'changing man' ideal 25
  CP Executive Committee 72, 91, 121, 124
  CP membership 42–4
  death 176
  defending comprehensive education 151–67
  education 10–19, 44
  Education Advisory Committee 121
  family background 7–10, 72
  father's death 72–3
  Forum articles 122, 124–9, 132, 135–6, 137, 159
  funding CP 72–3
  History of Education Society role 173–4
  history of education volumes 173, 174
  on Joan 83
  joins CP 17–19, 23–4, 91
  Labour Party's education advisory committee 24
  MI5 and 3, 30, 31, 71
  National Cultural Committee chairman 91–116, 121
  NUS roles 20, 33–5
  portraits *47–8*
  press and 72
  public figure 71–88
  published articles and conference presentations 51–67, 93–5, 124, 137, 156, 161, 163
  schoolteacher 37–44
  soldier 29, 32–7
  Spanish Civil War and 21, 22–3
  teacher training 19–23, 24
  teaching career 29, 122, *147–9*
  visits Poland 124
  visits USA *150*
  visits USSR 18, 52, 124, *147*, *150–1*
  Bending the Rules 163
  The Common Secondary School 123
  Does Education Matter? 2
  Educational Psychology in the USSR 55
  'Education and the Right Offensive 153
  'The education campaign' 42–3
  Half Way There 130, 131, 134, 176
  'Intellectual and Professional People' 93–4
  Intelligence, Psychology and Education: A Marxist Critique 134
  'Marxism and education' 83

Psychology in the Soviet Union (ed.) 55
A Student's View of the Universities 34–5
Studies in the History of Education,
  1780–1870 73–83, 163–4
The Study of Education 86–7
Simon, Emily, (née Stoehr) 8
Simon, Ernest
  BS and 7, 11, 13–15, 17, 18–19, 24, 32
  death 72–3
  family background 8–10
Simon, Henry 8, 32
Simon, Joan (née Peel) 29–31
  BS and 4, 25, 32, 176
  CP Historians' Group secretary 77, 83
  death 176
  English Reformation education studies 74,
    75
  Marxism Today and 92
  MI5 and 36, 37, 71, 83
  portraits *49*
  press and 72
  TES journalist 31, 37
  visit to Leningrad 31
  Educational Psychology in the U.S.S.R. 55
  Education and Society in Tudor England 86
  'Indictment of Margaret Thatcher' 132–3
Simon, Roger
  army service 29, 36–7
  CP and 22, 72–3
  death 176
  education 7, 11, 12, 14
  family background 9, 10
  father's death 72–3
  Gramsci and 111
Simon, Shena 7, 8–9, 18, 52, 80, 131, 138
Smirnov, A.A. 55
Smith, Adam 79
Snow, C.P. 98
social conditions 57–9
Social-Revolutionaries 105
Society for Cultural Relations (SCR) 54
Solzhenitsyn, Aleksandr 112–13
Soviet Academy of Educational Sciences 55
Soviet psychology 44, 51–5, 57
Soviet Union see USSR
Spain 16, 100
Spanish Civil War 7, 21–2, 29–33
Spender, Stephen 12
Spens report (1938) 24
Stakhanov, Alexei 61
Stalinism 52, 55, 56
Stevenson, W.T. 39
Stewart, Michael 126
Stock, Mary 8
Straight, Whitney 16–17
Stratton Park, Great Brickhill 11
Straw, Jack 161
Sweden 133, 153

Tawney, R.H. 35
teacher, role of the 59, 65
Technical and Vocational Education Initiative
  (TVEI) 155–6, 157
technical schools 37, 42, 122
technology education 62–3
Thatcher, Margaret 130–5, 152–8
Thomas, Hugh 23
Thom, Deborah 53
Thompson, Denys 15
Thomson, George 98
Tibble, J.W. 86, 87
Times Literary Supplement (*TES*) 31, 37
trade unions 85, 97, 131, 155
Trent, Peter 71–2
Trinity College, Cambridge 15–19
tripartite system (tripartism) 37, 53, 122, 126,
  128, 134, 141n.13
Tynan, Kenneth 100
Tyndale affair (1974) 136, 145n.192

United States 13, 66, 133, 153
Unity Theatre, London 97
universities 78, 173
upper-middle class 79
USSR (Soviet Union) 16, 33, 105, 109,
  112–13, 173
  education in 51, 52, 133, 153
  invade Hungary 23, 71–2, 91
  special schools 54
utilitarianism 78–9

Vatican Council, Second 105
vocationalism 60, 62–3, 122, 124, 155–6
voluntary-aided schools 129, 131, 135, 136,
  139
Vygotsky, Lev 55, 57

Wainwright, Bill 93
Walton, Jack 124
Warren, Bill 111
Watkinson, Ray 94
Watts, Ruth 30
Whewell's Court, Trinity College 16, 17
Williams, Raymond 95, 98, 100, 101–2
Wilson, Harold 86, 130, 136
Workers' Educational Association (WEA) 74,
  87
working class 43, 53, 64, 76, 78–82, 84,
  128
World Youth Congress Movement (WYCM) 31
Wright, Peter 175–6

Yew Tree Central School, Manchester 39, 40
youth movements 31–2

Zinchenko, Peter 68n.25
Zinoviev, Grigory 16

INDEX   **191**

Milton Keynes UK
Ingram Content Group UK Ltd.
UKHW021416270524
443328UK00046B/1432